Hands-On RESTful Web Services with Go

Second Edition

Develop elegant RESTful APIs with Golang for microservices and the cloud

Naren Yellavula

BIRMINGHAM - MUMBAI

Hands-On RESTful Web Services with Go
Second Edition

Copyright © 2020 Packt Publishing

Commissioning Editor: Richa Tripathi
Acquisition Editor: Denim Pinto
Content Development Editor: Divya Vijayan
Senior Editor: Mohammed Yusuf Imaratwale
Technical Editor: Praveen Gaurav
Copy Editor: Safis Editing
Project Coordinator: Kinjal Bari
Proofreader: Safis Editing
Indexer: Pratik Shirodkar
Production Designer: Jyoti Chauhan

First published: December 2017
Second edition: February 2020

Production reference: 1280220

Published by Packt Publishing Ltd.
Livery Place
35 Livery Street
Birmingham
B3 2PB, UK.

ISBN 978-1-83864-357-7

www.packt.com

*I dedicate this book to my lovely grandmother, **Tayamma**, for raising me to be helpful to others in every possible way.*

She is my role model.

Packt.com

Subscribe to our online digital library for full access to over 7,000 books and videos, as well as industry leading tools to help you plan your personal development and advance your career. For more information, please visit our website.

Why subscribe?

- Spend less time learning and more time coding with practical eBooks and Videos from over 4,000 industry professionals

- Improve your learning with Skill Plans built especially for you

- Get a free eBook or video every month

- Fully searchable for easy access to vital information

- Copy and paste, print, and bookmark content

Did you know that Packt offers eBook versions of every book published, with PDF and ePub files available? You can upgrade to the eBook version at www.packt.com and as a print book customer, you are entitled to a discount on the eBook copy. Get in touch with us at customercare@packtpub.com for more details.

At www.packt.com, you can also read a collection of free technical articles, sign up for a range of free newsletters, and receive exclusive discounts and offers on Packt books and eBooks.

Contributors

About the author

Naren Yellavula, known in the developer community as Naren Arya, started his programming career in a somewhat surprising manner. He ditched mechanical engineering in favor of computer science after watching *The Matrix* for the first time. With domain expertise in cloud telephony and e-commerce, Naren has a total of 6 years' professional experience and 10 years of programming experience. His articles on open source have been read over a million times worldwide.

Naren has spoken at the PyCon India conference on two occasions. He currently works as a software engineer, building microservices for *Tradebyte Software GmbH* (a Zalando enterprise). In his spare time, he travels to new places. He also loves reading – nonfiction most of the time, and Victorian and Russian fiction on occasion.

For me, writing this book was not simple. With daily commitments, vacation plans, and relocating to a new country, it proved to be a tough transition period with lots of emotional moments and experiences. However, all my efforts spent compiling this book were worthwhile knowing that this book will help you, the reader.

*On this occasion, I would like to thank my parents and my younger brother, **Saikiran Yellavula**, who was very patient with me all the time spent writing this book. I am also happy to have a wonderful friend in the shape of **Zahra Zaredar**, who has earnestly wished me success throughout my life. Lots of love to you guys!*

*I am greatly indebted to my mentor, **Chandrashekar Munibudha**, Senior Solutions Architect at Amazon Web Services, for his encouragement and guidance throughout my career.*

This book would not have been possible without the help of Denim Pinto, Acquisition Editor at Packt, and a good friend of mine. He was the one who approached me for both editions of my book. I would also like to thank Divya Vijayan, my content editor, who was very patient throughout the book's timeline and monitored its progress closely. I also want to thank Vincent Smith for reviewing the chapters and providing insightful feedback. If you were anticipating this book much sooner, forgive me, but I am responsible. There were a few awkward moments when I annoyed the editorial team owing to poor communication. Ultimately, I am human too, but the Packt team always supported me with the necessary tools and resources. Kudos!

About the reviewer

Vincent Smith has been a software engineer for 10 years, having worked in various fields from health and IT to machine learning and large-scale web scrapers. He has worked for both large Fortune 500 companies and start-ups alike and has honed his skills by taking the best of both worlds. While obtaining a degree in electrical engineering, he learned the foundations of writing good code through his Java courses. These basics helped spur his career in software development early in his professional life in order to provide support for his team. He fell in love with the process of teaching computers how to behave, which set him on the path he still walks today.

Packt is searching for authors like you

If you're interested in becoming an author for Packt, please visit authors.packtpub.com and apply today. We have worked with thousands of developers and tech professionals, just like you, to help them share their insight with the global tech community. You can make a general application, apply for a specific hot topic that we are recruiting an author for, or submit your own idea.

Table of Contents

Preface

My association with this book has been a memorable journey. Three years back, when Packt contacted me to write a book for them, I was not sure that would be something I would be able to achieve in the first place. But, with support from my family, friends, and a few great mentors at work, I have successfully made it. I always have a habit of explaining things, and I wanted to turn that into a more significant form – a book. That desire ended up evolving into a book called *Building RESTful Web Services with Go* in 2017. Looking back, it was not a bad idea at all.

I am an open source blogger apart from my full-time software development job. What I write about is what I learn at work. Every month, I work on many features, fix many bugs, and review many merge requests. I convert all that experience into articles. This book is a valuable collection of many of those experiences. You could ask me what provoked me to write this book? It is the burning desire to share things I know. Software engineering is a hard skill, and it has always been a practical discipline, unlike academic studies. That drove me to write *Hands-On RESTful Web Services with Go*, which is a supercharged sequel to my first book.

In this age of information technology, products talk with each other using **Application Programming Interfaces (APIs)**. In the last decade, the rise of a new generation of web languages, such as Python, JavaScript (Node.js), and Go, has shown a different approach to web development compared to traditional ones, such as ASP.NET and Java's Spring. In particular, the Go programming language hits the sweet spot of the enterprise versus prototype landscape. We can compare Go simultaneously to what "*Python is to prototyping*" and what "*Java is to the enterprise.*" Some of the best open source tools, such as Docker, Terraform, and Kubernetes, are written in Go. Google uses it heavily for its internal services. You can see a list of Go-using companies at `https://github.com/golang/go/wiki/GoUsers`.

With less verbose code, strict type checking, and support for concurrency, Go is a better language to write modern web servers. An intermediate Go developer can benefit a lot by knowing how to create RESTful services using Go. This book is an attempt to make the reader comfortable with web services development. Remember, it is a hands-on guide.

Industry experts are suggesting that, shortly, Python may move further into the data science domain, which could create a vacuum in the web development domain. Go has all the qualifications to fill that space. The paradigm shift from monoliths to microservices, and the need for robust API interfaces, may place Go high above interpreted languages.

Even though this book is not a cookbook, it offers many tips and tricks throughout your journey as a reader. This book is for software developers and web developers who want to develop RESTful web services and APIs using Go. It will also assist Python and Node.js developers who are interested in learning web development with Go.

I hope you enjoy this book, and that it helps take your career to the next level!

Who this book is for

This book is for any Go developers who are comfortable with the language and seeking to learn REST API development. Even senior engineers will enjoy this book, as it discusses many cutting-edge concepts, such as building microservices, developing APIs with GraphQL, using protocol buffers, asynchronous API design, and infrastructure as code.

Developers who are already familiar with REST concepts and stepping into the Go world from other platforms, such as Python and Ruby, will also benefit a lot from reading this book.

What this book covers

Chapter 1, *Getting Started with REST API Development*, discusses the fundamentals of REST architecture and verbs.

Chapter 2, *Handling Routing for our REST Services*, describes how to define basic routes and handler functions for a REST API.

Chapter 3, *Working with Middleware and RPC*, covers working with middleware handlers and basic RPC.

Chapter 4, *Simplifying RESTful Services with Popular Go Frameworks*, presents quick prototyping of a REST API with a few open source frameworks.

Chapter 5, *Working with MongoDB and Go to Create a REST API*, explains how to use MongoDB as a storage backend for a REST API.

Chapter 6, *Working with Protocol Buffers and gRPC*, shows how to use protocol buffers and gRPC over HTTP/JSON to obtain a performance boost.

Chapter 7, *Working with PostgreSQL, JSON, and Go*, explains how to use PostgreSQL as a storage backend and leverage JSON stores to create REST APIs.

Chapter 8, *Building a REST API Client in Go*, presents techniques for building client software and API testing tools.

Chapter 9, *Asynchronous API Design*, presents techniques for scaling APIs by leveraging asynchronous design patterns.

Chapter 10, *GraphQL and Go*, discusses a different API query language in contrast to REST.

Chapter 11, *Scaling our REST API Using Microservices*, covers building microservices using Go Micro.

Chapter 12, *Containerizing REST Services for Deployment*, shows how to prepare a containerized ecosystem for API deployment.

Chapter 13, *Deploying REST Services on Amazon Web Services*, shows how to deploy a containerized ecosystem to AWS Cloud using infrastructure as code.

Chapter 14, *Handling Authentication for our REST Services,* discusses securing an API with simple authentication and **JSON Web Tokens (JWT)**.

To get the most out of this book

For this book, you need a laptop/PC with Linux (Ubuntu 18.04), macOS X >=10.13, or Windows installed. We will use Go 1.13.x as the version of our compiler and will install many third-party packages, so a working internet connection is required.

We will also use Docker in the final chapters to explain the concepts of API Gateway. Docker's latest stable version is recommended. If Windows users have problems with the native Go installation or using CURL for any examples, use Docker Desktop for Windows and run an Ubuntu container to test your code samples; refer to https://www.docker.com/docker-windows for more details.

Before diving into the book, refresh your language basics at https://tour.golang.org/welcome/1.

Even though these are the basic requirements, we will guide you through the installations whenever required.

Download the example code files

You can download the example code files for this book from your account at www.packt.com. If you purchased this book elsewhere, you can visit www.packtpub.com/support and register to have the files emailed directly to you.

You can download the code files by following these steps:

1. Log in or register at www.packt.com.
2. Select the **Support** tab.
3. Click on **Code Downloads**.
4. Enter the name of the book in the **Search** box and follow the onscreen instructions.

Once the file is downloaded, please make sure that you unzip or extract the folder using the latest version of:

- WinRAR/7-Zip for Windows
- Zipeg/iZip/UnRarX for Mac
- 7-Zip/PeaZip for Linux

The code bundle for the book is also hosted on GitHub at https://github.com/PacktPublishing/Hands-On-Restful-Web-services-with-Go. In case there's an update to the code, it will be updated on the existing GitHub repository.

We also have other code bundles from our rich catalog of books and videos available at https://github.com/PacktPublishing/. Check them out!

Download the color images

We also provide a PDF file that has color images of the screenshots/diagrams used in this book. You can download it here: https://static.packt-cdn.com/downloads/9781838643577_ColorImages.pdf.

Conventions used

There are a number of text conventions used throughout this book.

CodeInText: Indicates code words in text, database table names, folder names, filenames, file extensions, pathnames, dummy URLs, user input, and Twitter handles. Here is an example: "Name the preceding program basicHandler.go."

A block of code is set as follows:

```
{
  "ID": 1,
  "DriverName": "Menaka",
}
```

When we wish to draw your attention to a particular part of a code block, the relevant lines or items are set in bold:

```
{
  "ID": 1,
  "DriverName": "Menaka",
}
```

Any command-line input or output is written as follows:

```
> go run customMux.go
```

Bold: Indicates a new term, an important word, or words that you see onscreen. For example, words in menus or dialog boxes appear in the text like this. Here is an example: "It returns a message saying **Logged In successfully**."

Warnings or important notes appear like this.

Tips and tricks appear like this.

Get in touch

Feedback from our readers is always welcome.

General feedback: If you have questions about any aspect of this book, mention the book title in the subject of your message and email us at customercare@packtpub.com.

Errata: Although we have taken every care to ensure the accuracy of our content, mistakes do happen. If you have found a mistake in this book, we would be grateful if you would report this to us. Please visit www.packtpub.com/support/errata, selecting your book, clicking on the Errata Submission Form link, and entering the details.

Piracy: If you come across any illegal copies of our works in any form on the Internet, we would be grateful if you would provide us with the location address or website name. Please contact us at copyright@packt.com with a link to the material.

If you are interested in becoming an author: If there is a topic that you have expertise in and you are interested in either writing or contributing to a book, please visit authors.packtpub.com.

Reviews

Please leave a review. Once you have read and used this book, why not leave a review on the site that you purchased it from? Potential readers can then see and use your unbiased opinion to make purchase decisions, we at Packt can understand what you think about our products, and our authors can see your feedback on their book. Thank you!

For more information about Packt, please visit packt.com.

Getting Started with REST API Development

1

A web service is a communication mechanism defined between various computer systems. Without web services, custom peer-to-peer communication becomes cumbersome and platform-specific. The web needs to understand and interpret a hundred different things in the form of protocols. If computer systems can align with the protocols that the web can understand easily, it is a great help.

A web service is a software system designed to support interoperable machine-to-machine interaction over a network, as defined by the **World Wide Web Consortium (W3C)** at `https://www.w3.org/TR/ws-arch/`.

Now, in simple words, a web service is a road between two endpoints where messages are transferred smoothly. The message transfer is usually one way. Two individual programmable entities can also communicate with each other through their own APIs. Two people communicate through language, two applications communicate through an **Application Programming Interface (API)**.

The reader might be wondering; what is the importance of the API in the current digital world? The rise of the **Internet of Things (IoT)** made API usage heavier than before. Awareness of APIs is growing day by day, and there are hundreds of APIs that are being developed and documented all over the world every day. Notable major businesses are seeing the future in the **API as a Service (AaS)**. A bright example in recent times is **Amazon Web Services (AWS)**. AWS is a huge success in the cloud world. Developers write their own applications using the **Representational State Transfer (REST)** API provided by AWS and access it via **Command-Line Interface (CLI)**.

A few more hidden use cases are from travel sites such as `http://Booking.com` and `https://www.expedia.com/`, which fetch real-time prices by calling the APIs of third-party gateways and data vendors. Web service usage is often charged these days by the amount of data requests.

In this chapter, we will focus on the following topics:

- The different web services available
- REST architecture in detail
- The rise of **Single-page applications (SPAs)** with REST
- Setting up a Go project and running a development server
- Building our first service for finding the fastest mirror site from a list of Debian servers hosted worldwide
- The Open API specification and Swagger documentation

Technical requirements

The following are the pieces of software that should be pre-installed for running the code samples in this chapter:

- OS: Linux (Ubuntu 18.04)/ Windows 10/Mac OS X >=10.13
- Software: Docker >= 18 (Docker Desktop for Windows and Mac OS X)
- The latest version of the Go compiler == 1.13.5

We use Docker in this book to run a few sandbox environments. Docker is a virtualization platform that imitates an OS in a sandbox. Using it, we can cleanly run an application or service without affecting the host system.

You can find the code used in this chapter on the book's GitHub repository at `https://github.com/PacktPublishing/Hands-On-Restful-Web-services-with-Go/tree/master/chapter1`.

Types of web services

There are many types of web services that have evolved over time. Some of the more prominent ones are as follows:

- **Simple Object Access Protocol (SOAP)**
- **Universal Description, Discovery, and Integration (UDDI)**

- **Web Services Description Language (WSDL)**
- **Representational State Transfer (REST)**

Out of these, SOAP became popular in the early 2000s, when XML riding on a high wave. The XML data format is used by various distributed systems to communicate with each other.

A SOAP request usually consists of these three basic components:

- The envelope
- The header
- The body

Just to perform an HTTP request and response cycle, we have to attach a lot of additional data in SOAP. A sample SOAP request to a fictional book server, www.example.org, looks like this:

```
POST /Books HTTP/1.1
Host: www.example.org
Content-Type: application/soap+xml; charset=utf-8
Content-Length: 299
SOAPAction: "https://www.w3.org/2003/05/soap-envelope"

<?xml version="1.0"?>
<soap:Envelope xmlns:soap="http://www.w3.org/2003/05/soap-envelope"
xmlns:m="https://www.example.org">
  <soap:Header>
  </soap:Header>
  <soap:Body>
    <m:GetBook>
      <m:BookName>Alice in the wonderland</m:BookName>
    </m:GetBook>
  </soap:Body>
</soap:Envelope>
```

This is a standard example of a SOAP request for getting book data. If we observe carefully, it is in XML format, with special tags specifying the envelope and body. Since XML works by defining a lot of namespaces, the response gets bulky.

The main drawback of SOAP is that it is too complex for implementing web services and is a heavyweight framework. A SOAP HTTP request can get very bulky and can cause bandwidth wastage. The experts looked for a simple alternative, and in came REST. In the next section, we will briefly discuss REST.

The REST API

The name **Representational state transfer (REST)** was coined by Roy Fielding from the University of California. It is a very simplified and lightweight web service compared to SOAP. Performance, scalability, simplicity, portability, and flexibility are the main principles behind the REST design.

The REST API allows different systems to communicate and send/receive data in a very simple way. Each and every REST API call has a relation between an HTTP verb and the URL. The resources in the database in an application can be mapped with an API endpoint in the REST architecture.

When you are using a mobile app on your phone, your phone might be talking to many cloud services to retrieve, update, or delete your data. REST services have a huge impact on our daily lives.

REST is a stateless, cacheable, and simple architecture that is not a protocol, but a pattern. This pattern allows different endpoints to communicate with each other over HTTP.

Characteristics of REST services

These are the main properties that make REST simple and unique compared to its predecessors:

- **Client-server based architecture**: This architecture is most essential for the modern web to communicate over HTTP. A single client-server may look naive initially, but many hybrid architectures are evolving. We will discuss more of these shortly.
- **Stateless**: This is the most important characteristic of a REST service. A REST HTTP request consists of all the data needed by the server to understand and return the response. Once a request is served, the server doesn't remember whether the request arrived after a while. So, the operation will be a stateless one.
- **Cacheable**: In order to scale an application well, we need to cache certain responses. REST services can be cached for better throughput.
- **Representation of resources**: The REST API provides the uniform interface to talk to. It uses a **Uniform Resource Identifier (URI)** to map the resources (data). It also has the advantage of requesting a specific data

- **Implementation freedom**: REST is just a mechanism to define your web services. It is an architectural style that can be implemented in multiple ways. Because of this flexibility, you can create REST services in the way you wish to. As long as it follows the principles of REST, you have the freedom to choose the platform or technology for your server.

Thoughtful caching is essential for REST services to scale.

We have seen the types of web services and understood what is REST API. We also looked at the characteristics that make REST services unique. In the next section, we will take a look at REST verbs and status code and cover a few examples of path parameters.

REST verbs and status codes

REST verbs specify an action to be performed on a specific resource or a collection of resources. When a request is made by the client, it should send the following information in the HTTP request:

- The REST verb
- Header information
- The body (optional)

As we mentioned previously, REST uses the URI to decode the resource to be handled. There are quite a few REST verbs available, but six of them are used particularly frequently. They are presented, along with their expected actions, in the following table:

REST Verb	Action
GET	Fetches a record or set of resources from the server
OPTIONS	Fetches all available REST operations
POST	Creates a resource or a new set of resources
PUT	Updates or replaces the given record
PATCH	Modifies the given record
DELETE	Deletes the given resource

The status of these operations can be known from HTTP status codes. Whenever a client initiates a REST operation, since REST is stateless, the client should know a way to find out whether the operation was successful or not. For that reason, HTTP responses have a status code. REST defines a few standard status code types for a given operation. This means a REST API should strictly follow the following rules to achieve stable results in client-server communication. There are three important ranges available based on the types of error. See the following table for error ranges:

Status Code Type	Number Range	Action
Success	200 - 226	The 2xx family is used for successful responses.
Error	400 - 499 (client), 500 - 599 (server)	The 4xx family is used for indicating client errors. The 5xx is for server failures to process the request.
Redirect	300 - 308	The 3xx family is for URL redirection.

The detail of what each status code does is very precisely defined, and the overall count of codes increases every year. We mention the important ones in the upcoming section.

All requests to REST services have the following format. It consists of the host and the API endpoint. The API endpoint is the URL path that is predefined by the server. It can also include optional query parameters.

A trivial REST API URI looks like the following: `http://HostName/APIEndpoint/?key=value(optional)`

Let's look at all the verbs in more detail. The REST API design starts with the defining of operations and API endpoints. Before implementing the API, the design document should list all the endpoints for the given resources.

In the following section, we carefully observe the REST API endpoints using PayPal's REST API as a use case.

GET

A `GET` method fetches the given resource from the server. To specify a resource, `GET` uses a few types of URI queries:

- Query parameters
- Path-based parameters

In case you didn't know, most of your browsing of the web is done by performing a `GET` request to the server. For example, if you type `www.google.com`, you are actually making a `GET` request to fetch the search page. Here, your browser is the client and Google's web server is the backend implementer of web services. A successful `GET` operation returns a `200` status code.

Examples of path parameters

Everyone knows **PayPal**. PayPal creates billing agreements with companies. If you register with PayPal for a payment system, they provide you with a REST API for all your billing needs. The sample `GET` request for getting the information of a billing agreement looks like this: `/v1/payments/billing-agreements/agreement_id`.

Here, the resource query is with the path parameter. When the server sees this line, it interprets it as *I got an HTTP request with a need for* `agreement_id` *from the billing agreements.* Then it searches through the database, goes to the `billing-agreements` table, and finds an agreement with the given `agreement_id`. If that resource exists, it sends back a copy of the details in response (`200 OK`), or else it sends a response saying, "resource not found" (`404`).

Using `GET`, you can also query a list of resources, instead of a single one as in the preceding example. PayPal's API for getting billing transactions related to an agreement can be fetched with `/v1/payments/billing-agreements/transactions`. This line fetches all transactions that occurred on that billing agreement. In both instances, the data is retrieved in the form of a JSON response. The response format should be designed beforehand so that the client can consume it in the agreement.

Examples of query parameters are as follows:

- Query parameters are intended to add detailed information to identify a resource from the server. For example, imagine a sample fictitious API. Let's assume this API is created for fetching, creating, and updating the details of the book. A query parameter based `GET` request will be in this format:

  /v1/books/?category=fiction&publish_date=2017

- The preceding URI has a couple of query parameters. The URI is requesting a book from the `books` resource that satisfies the following conditions:
  - It should be a fiction book
  - The book should have been published in the year 2017

Get all the fiction books that are released in the year 2017 is the question the client is posing to the server.

`Path` vs `Query` parameters—When to use them? It is a common rule of thumb that `Query` parameters are used to fetch multiple resources based on the `Query` parameters. If a client needs a single resource with exact URI information, it can use `Path` parameters to specify the resource. For example, a user dashboard can be requested with `Path` parameters, and fetch data on filtering can be modeled with `Query` parameters.

 Use `Path` parameters for a single resource and `Query` parameters for multiple resources in a `GET` request.

POST, PUT, and PATCH

The `POST` method is used to create a resource on the server. In the previous `books` API, this operation creates a new book with the given details. A successful `POST` operation returns a 2xx status code. The `POST` request can update multiple resources: `/v1/books`.

The `POST` request can have a JSON body like the following:

```
{"name" : "Lord of the rings", "year": 1954, "author" : "J. R. R. Tolkien"}
```

This actually creates a new book in the database. An ID is assigned to this record so that when we `GET` the resource, the URL is created. So, `POST` should be done only once, in the beginning. In fact, *Lord of the Rings* was published in *1955*. So, we entered the published date incorrectly. In order to update the resource, let's use the `PUT` request.

The `PUT` method is similar to `POST`. It is used to replace the resource that already exists. The main difference is that `PUT` is an idempotent operation. A `POST` call creates two instances with the same data. But `PUT` updates a single resource that already exists:

```
/v1/books/1256
```

`PUT` does this using a body containing JSON syntax, as follows:

```
{"name" : "Lord of the rings", "year": 1955, "author" : "J. R. R. Tolkien"}
```

1256 is the ID of the book. It updates the preceding book with `year:1955`. Did you observe the drawback of `PUT`? It actually replaced the entire old record with the new one. We needed to change a single column. But `PUT` replaced the whole record. That is bad. For this reason, the `PATCH` request was introduced.

The `PATCH` method is similar to `PUT`, except it won't replace the whole record. `PATCH`, as the name suggests, patches the column that is being modified. Let's update the book 1256 with a new column called `ISBN`:

```
/v1/books/1256
```

Let's use put the following JSON in the body:

```
{"isbn" : "0618640150"}
```

It tells the server, "*search for the book with ID* 1256. *Then add/modify this column with the given value.*"

`PUT` and `PATCH` both return a 2xx status for success and 404 for not found.

DELETE and OPTIONS

The `DELETE` API method is used to delete a resource from the database. It is similar to `PUT` but without a body. It just needs an ID of the resource to be deleted. Once a resource gets deleted, subsequent `GET` requests return a 404 not found status.

Responses to this method are *not cacheable* (should caching be implemented) because the `DELETE` method is idempotent.

The `OPTIONS` API method is the most underrated in API development. Given the resource, this method tries to find all possible methods (`GET`, `POST`, and so on) defined on the server. It is like looking at the menu card at a restaurant and then ordering an item that is available (whereas if you randomly order a dish, the waiter will tell you it is not available). It is best practice to implement the `OPTIONS` method on the server. From the client, make sure `OPTIONS` is called first, and if the method is available, then proceed with it.

Cross-Origin Resource Sharing (CORS)

The most important application of this OPTIONS method is **Cross-Origin Resource Sharing** (**CORS**). Initially, browser security prevented the client from making cross-origin requests. It means a site loaded with the www.foo.com URL can only make API calls to that host. If the client code needs to request files or data from www.bar.com, then the second server, bar.com, should have a mechanism to recognize foo.com to get its resources.

The following is the diagram depicting the CORS process:

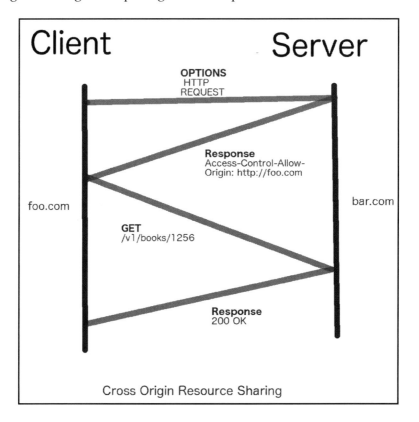

Cross Origin Resource Sharing

Let's examine the steps followed in the preceding CORS diagram:

1. foo.com requests the OPTIONS method on bar.com
2. bar.com sends a header like Access-Control-Allow-Origin: http://foo.com in response to the client
3. Next, foo.com can access the resources on bar.com without any restrictions that call any REST method

If `bar.com` feels like supplying resources to any host after one initial request, it can set the access control to `*`.

In the next section, we see why the REST API plays such a major role in the next generation of web services. SPAs made it possible to leverage APIs for all purposes, including the UI, clients, and so on.

The rise of the REST API with SPAs

Let's try to understand why SPAs are already standards of today's web. Instead of building a UI in the traditional way (that is, requesting rendered web pages), SPA designs allow developers to write code in a totally different way. There are many **Model-View-Controller** (**MVC**) frameworks, including Angular, React, Vue.js, and so on, for developing web UIs rapidly, but the essence of each of them is pretty simple. All MVC frameworks help us to implement one design pattern. That design pattern is *no requesting of web pages, only REST API usage.*

Modern frontend web development has advanced a lot in the last decade (2010-2020). In order to exploit the features of the MVC architecture, we have to consider the frontend as a separate entity that talks to the backend only using the REST API (preferably using JSON data).

Old and new methods of data flow in SPA

In the traditional flow of serving requests, the order looks like this:

1. The client requests a web page from the server
2. The server authenticates and returns a rendered response
3. Every rendered response is in HTML with embedded data

With SPAs, however, the flow is quite different:

1. Request the HTML templates with the browser in one single go
2. Then, query the JSON REST API to fill a model (the data object)
3. Adjust the UI according to the data in the model (in JSON)
4. From the browser, push back the changes to the server via an API call

In this way, communication happens only in the form of the REST API. The client takes care of logically representing the data. This causes systems to move from **Response-Oriented Architecture (ROA)** to **Service-Oriented Architecture (SOA)**. Take a look at the following diagram:

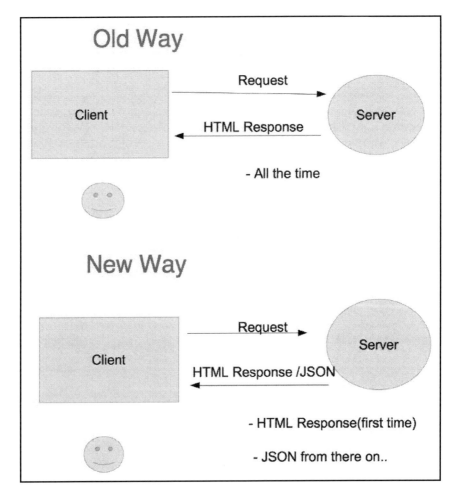

SPAs reduce bandwidth usage and improve site performance. SPAs are a major boost for API-centric server development because now a server can satisfy requirements for both browser and API clients.

Why use Go for REST API development?

REST services are trivial in the modern web. SOA (which we discuss in more detail later) created an activity space for REST services to take web development to the next level. **Go** is a programming language from the house of Google for solving the bigger problems they have. It has been over ten years since its first appearance. It matured along the way with the developer community jumping in and creating huge-scale systems in it.

 Go is the darling of the web. It solves bigger problems in an easy way.

We could choose Python or JavaScript (*Node.js*) for our REST API development, but the main advantage of Go lies in its speed and compile-time error detection. Go has been proven to be faster than dynamic programming languages in terms of computational performance according to various benchmarks. These are the three reasons why a company should write their next API in Go:

- To scale your API for a wider audience
- To enable your developers to build robust systems
- To start simple and go big

As we progress through this book, we learn how to build efficient REST services in Go.

Setting up the project and running the development server

This is a building series book. It assumes you already know the basics of Go. If not, no worries. You can get a jump-start and learn the basics quickly from Go's official site at `https://golang.org/`. Writing a simple standalone program with Go is straightforward. But for big projects, we have to set up a clean project layout. For that reason, as a Go developer, you should know how Go projects are laid out and the best practices to keep your code clean.

Make sure you have done the following things before proceeding:

- Install the Go compiler on your machine
- Set the `GOROOT` and `GOPATH` environment variables

There are many online references from which you can get to know the preceding details. Depending on your machine type (Windows, Linux, or Mac OS X), set up a working Go compiler. We will see more details about GOPATH in the following section.

Demystifying GOPATH

GOPATH is nothing but the current appointed workspace on your machine. It is an environment variable that tells the Go compiler where your source code, binaries, and packages are placed.

The programmers coming from a Python background may be familiar with the Virtualenv tool for creating multiple projects (with different Python interpreter versions) at the same time. But at a given time, you can activate the environment for the project that you wish to work on and develop your project. Similarly, you can have any number of Go projects on your machine. While developing, set the GOPATH to one of your projects. The Go compiler now activates that project.

It is a common practice to create a project under the home directory and set the GOPATH environment variable as follows:

```
mkdir /home/user/workspace
export GOPATH=/home/user/workspace
```

Now, we install external packages like this:

```
go get -u -v github.com/gorilla/mux
```

Go copies a project called mux from GitHub into the currently activated project workspace.

For go get, use the -u flag to install the updated dependencies of the external package, and -v to see the verbose details of the installation.

A typical Go project, hello, should reside in the src directory in GOPATH, as mentioned on the official Go website:

```
bin/
    hello                   # command executable
pkg/
    linux_amd64/            # this will reflect your OS and architecture
        github.com/user/
            stringutil.a  # package object
src/
    github.com/user/
        hello/
            hello.go        # command source
        stringutil/
            reverse.go    # package source
```

Let's understand this structure before digging further:

- `bin`: Stores the binary of our project; a shippable binary that can be run directly
- `pkg`: Contains the package objects; a compiled program that supplies package methods
- `src`: The place for your project source code, tests, and user packages

In Go, all the packages imported into the main program have an identical structure, `github.com/user/project`. But who creates all these directories? Should the developer do that? Yes. It is the developer's responsibility to create directories for their project. It means they only create the `src/github.com/user/hello` directory.

When a developer runs the `install` command, the `bin` and `package` directories are created if they did not exist before. `.bin` consists of the binary of our project source code and `.pkg` consists of all internal and external packages we use in our Go programs:

```
go install github.com/user/project
```

Let's build a small service to brush up on our Go language skills. Operating systems such as Debian and Ubuntu host their release images on multiple FTP servers. These are called mirrors. Mirrors are helpful in serving an OS image from the closest point to a client. Let's build a service that finds the fastest mirror from a list of mirrors.

Building our first service – finding the fastest mirror site from a list

With the concepts we have built up to now, let's write our first REST service. Many mirror sites exist for hosting operating system images including Ubuntu and Debian. The mirror sites here are nothing but websites on which OS images are hosted to be geographically close to the downloading machines.

Let's look at how we can create our first service:

Problem:

Build a REST service that returns the information of the fastest mirror to download a given OS from a huge list of mirrors. Let's take the Debian OS mirror list for this service. You can find the list at https://www.debian.org/mirror/list.

We use that list as input when implementing our service.

Design:

Our REST API should return the URL of the fastest mirror.

The block of the API design document may look like this:

HTTP Verb	PATH	Action	Resource
GET	/fastest-mirror	fetch	URL: string

Implementation:

Now we are going to implement the preceding API step by step:

 The code for this project is available at https://github.com/ PacktPublishing/Hands-On-Restful-Web-services-with-Go in the chapter1 subdirectory.

1. As we previously discussed, you should set the GOPATH variable first. Let's assume the GOPATH variable is /home/user/workspace. Create a directory called mirrorFinder in the following path. git-user should be replaced with your GitHub username under which this project resides:

   ```
   mkdir -p $GOPATH/src/github.com/git-user/chapter1/mirrorFinder
   ```

2. Our project is ready. We don't have any data store configured yet. Create an empty file called main.go:

   ```
   touch $GOPATH/src/github.com/git-user/chapter1/mirrorFinder/main.go
   ```

3. Our main logic for the API server goes into this file. For now, we can create a data file that works as a data service for our main program. Create one more directory for packaging the mirror list data:

   ```
   mkdir $GOPATH/src/github.com/git-user/chapter1/mirrors
   ```

4. Now, create an empty file called `data.go` in the `mirrors` directory. The `src` directory structure so far looks like this:

```
github.com \
-- git-user \
   -- chapter1
      -- mirrorFinder \
         -- main.go
      -- mirrors \
         -- data.go
```

5. Let's start adding code to the files. Create an input data file called `data.go` for our API to use:

```go
package mirrors

// MirrorList is list of Debian mirror sites
var MirrorList = [...]string{
    "http://ftp.am.debian.org/debian/",
    "http://ftp.au.debian.org/debian/",
    "http://ftp.at.debian.org/debian/",
    "http://ftp.by.debian.org/debian/",
    "http://ftp.be.debian.org/debian/",
    "http://ftp.br.debian.org/debian/",
    "http://ftp.bg.debian.org/debian/",
    "http://ftp.ca.debian.org/debian/",
    "http://ftp.cl.debian.org/debian/",
    "http://ftp2.cn.debian.org/debian/",
    "http://ftp.cn.debian.org/debian/",
    "http://ftp.hr.debian.org/debian/",
    "http://ftp.cz.debian.org/debian/",
    "http://ftp.dk.debian.org/debian/",
    "http://ftp.sv.debian.org/debian/",
    "http://ftp.ee.debian.org/debian/",
    "http://ftp.fr.debian.org/debian/",
    "http://ftp2.de.debian.org/debian/",
    "http://ftp.de.debian.org/debian/",
    "http://ftp.gr.debian.org/debian/",
    "http://ftp.hk.debian.org/debian/",
    "http://ftp.hu.debian.org/debian/",
    "http://ftp.is.debian.org/debian/",
    "http://ftp.it.debian.org/debian/",
    "http://ftp.jp.debian.org/debian/",
    "http://ftp.kr.debian.org/debian/",
    "http://ftp.lt.debian.org/debian/",
    "http://ftp.mx.debian.org/debian/",
    "http://ftp.md.debian.org/debian/",
    "http://ftp.nl.debian.org/debian/",
```

```
      "http://ftp.nc.debian.org/debian/",
    "http://ftp.nz.debian.org/debian/",
      "http://ftp.no.debian.org/debian/",
    "http://ftp.pl.debian.org/debian/",
      "http://ftp.pt.debian.org/debian/",
    "http://ftp.ro.debian.org/debian/",
      "http://ftp.ru.debian.org/debian/",
    "http://ftp.sg.debian.org/debian/",
      "http://ftp.sk.debian.org/debian/",
    "http://ftp.si.debian.org/debian/",
      "http://ftp.es.debian.org/debian/",
    "http://ftp.fi.debian.org/debian/",
      "http://ftp.se.debian.org/debian/",
    "http://ftp.ch.debian.org/debian/",
      "http://ftp.tw.debian.org/debian/",
    "http://ftp.tr.debian.org/debian/",
      "http://ftp.uk.debian.org/debian/",
    "http://ftp.us.debian.org/debian/",
    }
```

We create a map of strings called `MirrorList`. This map holds information on the URL to reach the mirror site. We are going to import this information into our main program to serve the request from the client.

6. Open `main.go` and add the following code:

```go
import (
  "encoding/json"
  "fmt"
  "log"
  "net/http"
  "time"

  "github.com/git-user/chapter1/mirrors"
)


type response struct {
  FastestURL string `json:"fastest_url"`
  Latency time.Duration `json:"latency"`
}


func main() {
  http.HandleFunc("/fastest-mirror", func(w http.ResponseWriter,
  r *http.Request) {
    response := findFastest(mirrors.MirrorList)
    respJSON, _ := json.Marshal(response)
```

```
    w.Header().Set("Content-Type", "application/json")
    w.Write(respJSON)
  })
  port := ":8000"
  server := &http.Server{
    Addr: port,
    ReadTimeout: 10 * time.Second,
    WriteTimeout: 10 * time.Second,
    MaxHeaderBytes: 1 << 20,
  }
  fmt.Printf("Starting server on port %sn", port)
  log.Fatal(server.ListenAndServe())
}
```

We created the main function that runs an HTTP server. Go provides the `net/http` package for that purpose. The response of our API is a struct with two fields:

- `fastest_url`: The fastest mirror site
- `latency`: The time it takes to download the README from the Debian OS repository

7. We will code a function called `findFastest` to make requests to all the mirrors and calculate the fastest of all. To do this, instead of making sequential API calls to each and every URL one after the other, we use Go routines to parallelly request the URLs and once a goroutine returns, we stop there and return that data back.:

```
func findFastest(urls []string) response {
  urlChan := make(chan string)
  latencyChan := make(chan time.Duration)

  for _, url := range urls {
    mirrorURL := url
    go func() {
      start := time.Now()
      _, err := http.Get(mirrorURL + "/README")
      latency := time.Now().Sub(start) / time.Millisecond
      if err == nil {
        urlChan <- mirrorURL
        latencyChan <- latency
      }
    }()
  }
  return response{<-urlChan, <-latencyChan}
}
```

The `findFastest` function is taking a list of URLs and returning the response struct. The function creates a goroutine per mirror site URL. It also creates two channels, `urlChan` and `latencyChan`, which are passed to the goroutines. In the goroutines, we calculate the latency (time taken for the request).

The smart logic here is, whenever a goroutine receives a response, it writes data into two channels with the URL and latency information respectively. Upon receiving data, the two channels make the response struct and return from the `findFastest` function. When that function is returned, all goroutines spawned from that are stopped from whatever they are doing. So, we will have the shortest URL in `urlChan` and the smallest latency in `latencyChan`.

8. Now if you add this function to the main file (`main.go`), our code is complete for the task:

Always use the Go `fmt` tool to format your Go code. Some example usage of `fmt` looks like the following: `go fmt github.com/narenaryan/romanserver`

9. Now, install this project with the Go command, `install`:

```
go install github.com/git-user/chapter1/mirrorFinder
```

This step does two things:

- Compiles the package `mirrors` and places a copy in the `$GOPATH/pkg` directory
- Places a binary in the `$GOPATH/bin`

10. We can run the preceding API server like this:

```
$GOPATH/bin/mirrorFinder
```

The server is up and running on `http://localhost:8000`. Now we can make a GET request to the API using a client such as a browser or a curl command. Let's fire a `curl` command with a proper API GET request.

Request one is as follows:

```
curl -i -X GET "http://localhost:8000/fastest-mirror" # Valid
request
```

The response is as follows:

```
HTTP/1.1 200 OK
Content-Type: application/json
Date: Wed, 27 Mar 2019 23:13:42 GMT
Content-Length: 64

{"fastest_url":"http://ftp.sk.debian.org/debian/","latency":230}
```

Our fastest-mirror-finding API is working great. The right status code is being returned. The output may change with each API call, but it fetches the lowest-latency link at any given moment. This example also shows where goroutines and channels shine.

In the next section, we'll look at an API specification called Open API. An API specification is for documenting the REST API. To visualize the specification, we will use the Swagger UI tool.

Open API and Swagger

Because APIs are very common, the Open API Specification is a community-driven open specification within the OpenAPI Initiative, a Linux Foundation Collaborative Project.

The **OpenAPI Specification (OAS)**, formerly called the Swagger Specification, is an API description format for REST APIs. An Open API file allows you to describe your entire API, including the following:

- Available endpoints
- Endpoint operations (GET, PUT, DELETE, and so on)
- Parameter input and output for each operation
- Authentication methods
- Contact information, license, terms of use, and other information.

Open API has many versions and is rapidly developing. The current stable version is 3.0.

There are two formats, **JSON** and **YAML**, that are supported by OAS. Swagger and Open API both are different. Swagger has many products, including the following:

- Swagger UI (for validating Open API files and interactive docs)
- Swagger Codegen (for generating server stubs)

Whenever we develop a REST API, it is a better practice to create an Open API/Swagger file that captures all the necessary details and descriptions of the API. The file can then be used in Swagger UI to create interactive documentation.

Installing Swagger UI

Swagger UI can be installed/downloaded on various operating systems, but the best way could be using Docker. A Swagger UI Docker image is available on the Docker Hub. Then we can pass our Open API/Swagger file to the Docker container we run out of the image. Before that, we need to create a JSON file. The Swagger JSON file has few sections:

- `info`
- `servers`
- `paths`

Let's create a Swagger file with the preceding sections for the first service we built. Let's name it `openapi.json`:

```json
{
  "openapi": "3.0.0",
  "info": {
    "title": "Mirror Finder Service",
    "description": "API service for finding the fastest mirror from the
     list of given mirror sites",
    "version": "0.1.1"
  },
  "servers": [
    {
      "url": "http://localhost:8000",
      "description": "Development server[Staging/Production are different
       from this]"
    }
  ],
  "paths": {
    "/fastest-mirror": {
      "get": {
        "summary": "Returns a fastest mirror site.",
        "description": "This call returns data of fastest reachable mirror
         site",
        "responses": {
          "200": {
            "description": "A JSON object of details",
            "content": {
              "application/json": {
```

```
              "schema": {
                "type": "object",
                "properties": {
                  "fastest_mirror": {
                    "type": "string"
                  },
                  "latency": {
                    "type": "integer"
                  }
                }
              }
            }
          }
        }
      }
    }
  }
}
```

Please notice how we defined the info, servers, and paths sections.

The openapi tag specifies the version of the API document we are using.

The info section has a service-related description. The servers section has the URL of the server where the application/server is running. We used localhost:8000 as we are running it locally. The paths section has information about all the API endpoints a service provides. It also has information about the request body, response type, and body structure. Even the possible error codes can be encapsulated into paths.

Now let's install Swagger UI and make use of our Swagger file:

1. To install Swagger UI via Docker, run this command from your shell:

   ```
   docker pull swaggerapi/swagger-ui
   ```

   If you are on Windows 10/Mac OS X , make sure Docker Desktop is running. On Linux, Docker is available all the time once installed.

2. This pulls the image from the Docker Hub to your local machine. Now we can run a container that can take an openapi.json file and launch Swagger UI. Assuming that you have this file in the chapter1 directory, let's use the following command:

   ```
   docker run --rm -p 80:8080 -e SWAGGER_JSON=/app/openapi.json -v
   $GOPATH/github.com/git-user/chapter1:/app swaggerapi/swagger-ui
   ```

This command tells Docker to do the following things:

- Run a container using the `swaggerapi/swagger-ui` image
- Mount `chapter1` (where `openapi.json` resides) to the `/app` directory in the container
- Expose host port `80` to container port `8080`
- Set the `SWAGGER_JSON` environment variable to `/app/openapi.json`

When the container starts, launch `http://locahost` in the browser. You will see nice documentation for your API:

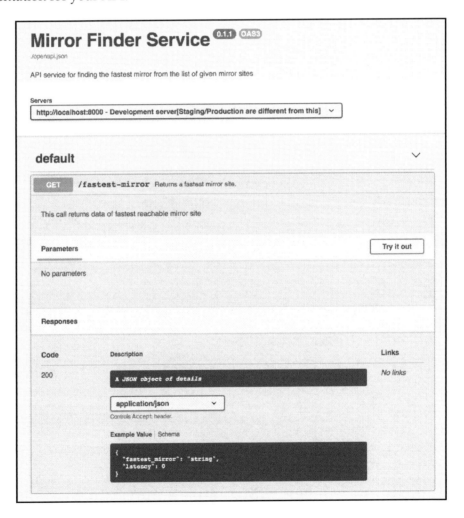

In this way, without any cost, we can create instant documentation of our REST API using Swagger UI and Open API 3.0.

 For testing an API within Swagger UI, the REST API server needs to be accessible to the Docker container (for example, via a network bridge).

From now on, in all chapters, we will try to create Swagger files to document our API design. It is a wise decision to start API development by creating API specifications first and then jumping into implementation. I hope this chapter helped you to brush up on the basics of REST API fundamentals. In the following chapters, we will go deeply into many diverse topics.

Summary

In this chapter, we gave an introduction to the REST API. We saw that REST is not a protocol, but an architectural pattern. HTTP is the actual protocol on which we can implement our REST service. We jumped into the fundamentals of the REST API to be clear about what they actually are. Then we explored types of web services. Before REST, we had something called SOAP, which used XML as its data format. REST operates on JSON as its primary format. REST has verbs and status codes. We saw what these status codes refer to.

We designed and implemented a simple service that finds the fastest mirror site to download OS images from all Debian mirror sites hosted worldwide. In this process, we also saw how to package a Go project into a binary. We understood the GOPATH environment variable, which is a workspace definition in Go. We now know that all packages and projects reside on that path.

Next, we jumped into the world of OpenAPI specification by introducing Swagger UI and Swagger files. The structure of these files and how to run Swagger UI with the help of Docker were discussed briefly. We also saw why a developer should start API development by writing down the specifications in the form of a Swagger file.

In the next chapter, we will dig deeper into URL routing. Starting from the built-in router, we will explore Gorilla Mux, a powerful URL routing library.

Handling Routing for our REST Services

2

In this chapter, we will discuss routing for a REST application. To create an API, the first step is to define routes. To define routes, we have to figure out the available system packages in Go. We'll begin this chapter by exploring the basic internal routing mechanism in Go. We then see how to create a custom multiplexer, an entity that matches a given URL to a registered pattern. A multiplexer basically allows a developer to create a route to listen to client requests and attaches handlers that hold the business logic of the application. The `ServeMux` package is the basic multiplexer provided by Go. We'll then explore a few other frameworks as `ServeMux` capabilities are very limited.

This chapter also includes the likes of third-party libraries such as `httprouter` and `gorilla/mux`. Then, we'll discuss topics such as SQL injection. The crux of this chapter is to teach you how to create elegant HTTP routers in Go using `gorilla/mux`. We'll also briefly discuss designing a URL shortening service.

We will cover the following topics:

- Understanding Go's `net/http` package
- `ServeMux`—a basic router in Go
- Understanding `httprouter`—a lightweight HTTP router
- Introducing `gorilla/mux`—a powerful HTTP router
- Reader's challenge: an API for URL shortening

Technical requirements

The following are the software that should be pre-installed for running code samples:

- OS: Linux (Ubuntu 18.04)/Windows 10/Mac OS X >=10.13
- Go latest version compiler >= 1.13.5

You can download the code for this chapter from `https://github.com/PacktPublishing/`
`Hands-On-Restful-Web-services-with-Go/tree/master/chapter2`. Clone the code and use
the code samples in the `chapter2` directory.

Understanding Go's net/http package

Accepting HTTP requests is the primary goal of a web server. In Go, there is a `system-level` package that helps developers create HTTP servers and clients. The name of the
package is `net/http`. We can understand the functionality of the `net/http` package by
creating a small example. The example accepts an incoming request and returns the
timestamp of the server. Let us see the steps for creating such a server:

1. Create the program file as follows:

   ```
   touch -p $GOPATH/src/github.com/git-
   user/chapter2/healthCheck/main.go
   ```

   Now, we have a file where we can develop a server with a Health Check API that
   returns a date/time string.

2. Import the `net/http` package and create a function handler called
   `HealthCheck`. The `http.HandleFunc` is a method that takes a route and a
   function handler as its arguments. This function handler has to return
   an `http.ResponseWriter` object:

   ```go
   package main

   import (
     "io"
     "log"
     "net/http"
     "time"
   )

   // HealthCheck API returns date time to client
   func HealthCheck(w http.ResponseWriter, req *http.Request) {
   ```

```
    currentTime := time.Now()
    io.WriteString(w, currentTime.String())
}

func main() {
  http.HandleFunc("/health", HealthCheck)
  log.Fatal(http.ListenAndServe(":8000", nil))
}
```

The preceding code creates a `HealthCheck` function and attaches it to an HTTP route. `HandleFunc` is used to attach a route pattern to a handler function. `ListenAndServe` starts a new HTTP server. It returns an error if the server launch is unsuccessful. It takes `address:port` as the first argument and the second argument is `nil`, which says use the default multiplexer. We will see multiplexers in detail in the upcoming sections.

 Use the `log` function to debug potential errors. The `ListenAndServe` function returns an error if there is one.

3. Now, we can start the web server using this command:

   go run $GOPATH/src/github.com/git-user/chapter2/healthCheck/main.go

   Run the `healthCheck.go` file from a shell.

4. Now, fire up a shell or browser to see the server in action. Here, we use the `curl` request:

   curl -X GET http://localhost:8000/health

   The response is as follows:

   2019-04-10 17:54:05.450783 +0200 CEST m=+6.612810181

Go has a different concept for handling request and response. We used the `io` library to write to the response. For web development, we can use a template to automatically fill in the details. Go's internal URL handlers use a ServeMux multiplexer. In the next section, we will discuss more on ServeMux, a built-in URL router in Go.

ServeMux – a basic router in Go

ServeMux is an HTTP request multiplexer. The `HandleFunc` we used in the preceding section is actually a method of ServeMux. By using ServeMux, we can handle multiple routes. We can also create our own multiplexer. A multiplexer handles the logic of separating routes with a function called `ServeHTTP`. So, if we create a Go struct with the `ServeHTTP` method, it can do the job as the in-built multiplexer.

Consider a route as a key in a Go dictionary (map) and a multiplexer as its value. Go finds the multiplexer from the route and tries to execute the `ServeHTTP` function. In the following section, we will see the usage of ServeMux by creating an API that generates UUID strings.

Developing a UUID generation API using ServeMux

A UUID is a unique identifier for a resource or a transaction. UUIDs are widely used for identifying an HTTP request. Let us develop an API for generating a UUID. Please follow these steps:

1. Create the program file as follows:

   ```
   touch -p $GOPATH/src/github.com/git-
   user/chapter2/uuidGenerator/main.go
   ```

2. Any Go struct with a few dedicated HTTP methods is qualified to be a ServeMux. For example, we can create a custom `UUID struct` and implement the `ServeHTTP` function in order to make it a `ServeMux` object. Following is the implementation for the `uuidGenerator.go` module:

   ```
   import (
     "crypto/rand"
     "fmt"
   )

   // UUID is a custom multiplexer
   type UUID struct {
   }

   func (p *UUID) ServeHTTP(w http.ResponseWriter, r *http.Request) {
     if r.URL.Path == "/" {
       giveRandomUUID(w, r)
   ```

```
      return
  }
  http.NotFound(w, r)
  return
}

func giveRandomUUID(w http.ResponseWriter, r *http.Request) {
 c := 10
  b := make([]byte, c)
  _, err := rand.Read(b)
  if err != nil {
    panic(err)
  }
  fmt.Fprintf(w, fmt.Sprintf("%x", b))
}
```

It consists of the UUID struct that acts as a ServeMux object. We can access the URL path in the handler function and use that information to manually route the requests to different response generators.

giveRandomUUID is a response generator function that sets a random UUID string to response. Go's crypto package has a Read function that fills random characters into a byte array.

3. Now add a main function to the module using the ServeMux object. We should pass our ServeMux to the http.ListenAndServe function to get our content served. We are serving our content on port 8000:

```
package main

import (
  "net/http"
)

func main() {
  mux := &UUID{}
  http.ListenAndServe(":8000", mux)
}
```

We use UUID as a multiplexer in the ListenAndServe function, which starts an HTTP server. The server executes the ServeHTTP method that is defined preceding on the mux object.

4. Run the following command from your shell/Terminal:

```
go run $GOPATH/src/github.com/git-
user/chapter2/uuidGenerator/main.go
```

5. We can make a `curl` request like this to make a request to the web server that is listening on port 8000:

```
curl -X GET http://localhost:8000/
```

The response that is returned will be a random string:

```
544f5519592ac25bb2c0
```

Use *Ctrl + C* or *Cmd + C* to stop your Go server. If you are running it as a background process, use `sudo kill` `sudo lsof -t -i:8000` to kill a process running on port 8000.

Until now, we have worked with a single handler. Let us see how we can add multiple handlers to route to different function handlers using ServeMux.

Adding multiple handlers using ServeMux

Let us say we have an API requirement that generates random numbers of different types such as int, float, and so on. The custom **multiplexer (mux)** we developed can be cumbersome when there are multiple endpoints with different functionalities. To add that logic, we need to add multiple `if/else` conditions to manually check the URL route. To overcome that complex code structure, we can instantiate a new in-built `ServeMux` object and define many handlers. Let's look at the code with `ServeMux`:

```
newMux := http.NewServeMux()

newMux.HandleFunc("/randomFloat", func(w http.ResponseWriter,
r *http.Request) {
 fmt.Fprintln(w, rand.Float64())
})

newMux.HandleFunc("/randomInt", func(w http.ResponseWriter,
r *http.Request) {
 fmt.Fprintln(w, rand.Int(100))
})
```

This code snippet shows how to create a `ServeMux` and attach multiple handlers to it.

randomFloat and randomInt are the two routes we create for returning a random float and random int, respectively. Now, we pass that to the ListenAndServe function. Int(100) returns a random integer number from the range 0-100.

 For more details on random functions, visit the Go random package page at: http://golang.org.

Let us see a complete example:

1. Create a file to hold our program and call it multipleHandlers.go in the following path:

   touch -p $GOPATH/src/github.com/git-user/chapter2/multipleHandlers/main.go

2. Now create a main function and add the code for creating the ServeMux object and function handlers.

3. Finally, run the server with the http.ListenAndServe method:

```
package main

import (
    "fmt"
    "math/rand"
    "net/http"
)

func main() {
    newMux := http.NewServeMux()
    newMux.HandleFunc("/randomFloat", func(w http.ResponseWriter,
    r *http.Request) {
        fmt.Fprintln(w, rand.Float64())
    })
    newMux.HandleFunc("/randomInt", func(w http.ResponseWriter,
    r *http.Request) {
        fmt.Fprintln(w, rand.Intn(100))
    })
    http.ListenAndServe(":8000", newMux)
}
```

4. We can run the program directly using the run command:

   go run $GOPATH/src/github.com/git-user/chapter2/multipleHandlers/main.go

5. Now, let us fire two `curl` commands and see the output:

```
curl -X GET http://localhost:8000/randomFloat
curl -X GET http://localhost:8000/randomInt
```

The responses will be:

```
0.6046602879796196
87
```

We saw how we can create a URL router with basic Go constructs. Let us have a look at a few popular URL routing frameworks that are widely used by the Go community for their API servers.

Understanding httprouter – a lightweight HTTP router

`httprouter`, as the name suggests, routes the HTTP requests to particular handlers. `httprouter` is a well-known package in Go for creating simple routers with an elegant API. The developers coming from the Python/Django community are very familiar with a full-blown URL dispatcher in the Django framework. `httprouter` provides similar features:

- Allows variables in the route paths
- Matches the REST methods (`GET`, `POST`, `PUT`, and so on)
- No compromise of performance

We are going to discuss these qualities in more detail in the following section. Before that, there are a few noteworthy points that make `httprouter` an even better URL router:

- `httprouter` plays well with the in-built `http.Handler`
- `httprouter` explicitly says that a request can only match to one route or no route
- The router's design encourages building sensible, hierarchical RESTful APIs
- You can build simple and efficient static file servers

In the next section, we see the installation of `httprouter` and its basic usage.

Installing httprouter

httprouter is an open source Go package and can be installed using the go get command. Let us see the installation and basic usage in the steps given as follows:

1. Install httprouter using this command:

    ```
    go get github.com/julienschmidt/httprouter
    ```

    We can import the library in our source code, like this:

    ```
    import "github.com/julienschmidt/httprouter"
    ```

2. The basic usage of httprouter can be understood through an example. Let us write a REST service in Go that provides two things:

    *   Gets the Go compiler version
    *   Gets the content of a given file

    We need to use a system package called os/exec to fetch the preceding details.

3. The os/exec package has a Command function, using which we can make any system call and the function signature is this:

    ```
    // arguments... means an array of strings unpacked as arguments
    // in Go
    cmd := exec.Command(command, arguments...)
    ```

4. The exec.Command function takes the command and an additional argument's array. Additional arguments are the options or input for the command. It can then be executed by calling the Output function, like this:

    ```
    out, err := cmd.Output()
    ```

5. This program uses httprouter to create the service. Let us create it at the following path:

    ```
    touch -p $GOPATH/src/github.com/git-
    user/chapter2/httprouterExample/main.go
    ```

The program's main function creates two routes and two function handlers. The responsibilities of function handlers are:

- To get the current Go compiler version
- To get the contents of a file

The program is trying to implement a REST service using `httprouter`. We are defining two routes here:

- `/api/v1/go-version`
- `/api/v1/show-file/:name`

```
package main

import (
  "fmt"
  "io"
  "log"
  "net/http"
  "os/exec"

  "github.com/julienschmidt/httprouter"
)


func main() {
  router := httprouter.New()
  router.GET("/api/v1/go-version", goVersion)
  router.GET("/api/v1/show-file/:name", getFileContent)
  log.Fatal(http.ListenAndServe(":8000", router))
}
```

`:name` is a path parameter. The basic Go router cannot define these special parameters. By using `httprouter`, we can match the REST methods. In the main block, we are matching `GET` requests to their respective routes.

Now we are coming to the implementation of three handler functions:

```
func getCommandOutput(command string, arguments ...string) string {
  out, _ := exec.Command(command, arguments...).Output()
  return string(out)
}

func goVersion(w http.ResponseWriter, r *http.Request, params
httprouter.Params) {
  response := getCommandOutput("/usr/local/go/bin/go", "version")
```

```
    io.WriteString(w, response)
    return
}

func getFileContent(w http.ResponseWriter, r *http.Request, params
httprouter.Params) {
  fmt.Fprintf(w, getCommandOutput("/bin/cat", params.ByName("name")))
}
```

`exec.Command` takes the `bash` command and respective options as its arguments and returns an object. That object has an `Output` method that returns the output result of command execution. We are utilizing this utility `getCommandOutput` function in both `goVersion` and `getFileContent` handlers. We use shell command formats such as `go --version` and `cat file_name` in handlers.

 If you observe the code, we used `/usr/local/go/bin/go` as the Go executable location because it is the Go compiler location in Mac OS X. While executing `exec.Command`, you should give the absolute path of the executable. So, if you are working on an Ubuntu machine or Windows, use the path to your installed Go executable. On Linux machines, you can easily find that out by using the `$ which go` command.

Now create two new files in the same directory. These files will be served by our file server program. You can create any custom files in this directory for testing:

`Latin.txt`:

```
Lorem ipsum dolor sit amet, consectetuer adipiscing elit. Aenean commodo
ligula eget dolor. Aenean massa. Cum sociis natoque penatibus et magnis dis
parturient montes, nascetur ridiculus mus. Donec quam felis, ultricies nec,
pellentesque eu, pretium quis, sem. Nulla consequat massa quis enim. Donec
pede justo, fringilla vel, aliquet nec, vulputate eget, arcu.
```

`Greek.txt`:

Οἱ δὲ Φοίνικες οὗτοι οἱ σὺν Κάδμῳ ἀπικόμενοι.. ἐσήγαγον διδασκάλια ἐς τοὺς Ἕλληνας καὶ δὴ καὶ γράμματα, οὐκ ἐόντα πρὶν Ἕλλησι ὡς ἐμοὶ δοκέειν, πρῶτα μὲν τοῖσι καὶ ἅπαντες χρέωνται Φοίνικες· μετὰ δὲ χρόνου προβαίνοντος ἅμα τῇ φωνῇ μετέβαλον καὶ τὸν ῥυθμὸν τῶν γραμμάτων. Περιοίκεον δέ σφεας τὰ πολλὰ τῶν χώρων τοῦτον τὸν χρόνον Ἑλλήνων Ἴωνες· οἳ παραλαβόντες διδαχῇ παρὰ τῶν Φοινίκων τὰ γράμματα, μεταρρυθμίσαντές σφεων ὀλίγα ἐχρέωντο, χρεώμενοι δὲ ἐφάτισαν, ὥσπερ καὶ τὸ δίκαιον ἔφερε ἐσαγαγόντων Φοινίκων ἐς τὴν Ἑλλάδα, φοινικήια κεκλῆσθαι.

Now run the program with this command. This time, instead of firing a `curl` command, let us use the browser as our output for `GET`. Windows users may not have curl as the first-hand application. They can use API testing software such as the Postman client while developing the REST API. Take a look at the following command:

```
go run $GOPATH/src/github.com/git-user/chapter2/httprouterExample/main.go
```

The output for the first `GET` request looks like this:

```
curl -X GET http://localhost:8000/api/v1/go-version
```

The result will be this:

```
go version go1.13.5 darwin/amd64
```

The second `GET` request requesting `Greek.txt` is:

```
curl -X GET http://localhost:8000/api/v1/show-file/greek.txt
```

Now, we will see the file output in Greek:

Οἱ δὲ Φοίνικες οὗτοι οἱ σὺν Κάδμῳ ἀπικόμενοι.. ἐσήγαγον διδασκάλια ἐς τοὺς Ἕλληνας καὶ δὴ καὶ γράμματα, οὐκ ἐόντα πρὶν Ἕλλησι ὡς ἐμοὶ δοκέειν, πρῶτα μὲν τοῖσι καὶ ἅπαντες χρέωνται Φοίνικες· μετὰ δὲ χρόνου προβαίνοντος ἅμα τῇ φωνῇ μετέβαλον καὶ τὸν ῥυθμὸν τῶν γραμμάτων. Περιοίκεον δέ σφεας τὰ πολλὰ τῶν χώρων τοῦτον τὸν χρόνον Ἑλλήνων Ἴωνες· οἳ παραλαβόντες διδαχῇ παρὰ τῶν Φοινίκων τὰ γράμματα, μεταρρυθμίσαντές σφεων ὀλίγα ἐχρέωντο, χρεώμενοι δὲ ἐφάτισαν, ὥσπερ καὶ τὸ δίκαιον ἔφερε ἐσαγαγόντων Φοινίκων ἐς τὴν Ἑλλάδα, φοινικήια κεκλῆσθαι.

 Never give the user the power to execute system commands over the REST API. In the `exec` example, we made handlers use a `getCommandOutput` helper function to execute system commands.

The endpoint `/api/v1/show-file/` we defined in the `exec` example is not so efficient. Using `httprouter`, we can build advanced and performance-optimized file servers. In the next section, we'll learn how to do that.

Building a simple static file server in minutes

Sometimes, an API can serve files. The other application of `httprouter`, apart from routing, is building an efficient file server. It means that we can build a content delivery platform of our own. Some clients need static files from the server. Traditionally, we use Apache2 or Nginx for that purpose. If one has to create something similar purely in Go, they can leverage `httprouter`.

Let us build one. From the Go server, in order to serve the static files, we need to route them through a universal route, like this:

```
/static/*
```

The plan is to use `http` package's `Dir` method to load the filesystem, and pass filesystem handler it returns to `httprouter`. We can use the `ServeFiles` function of the `httprouter` instance to attach a router to the filesystem handler. It should serve all the files in the given public directory. Usually, static files are kept in the `/var/public/www` folder on a Linux machine. Create a folder called `static` in your home directory:

```
mkdir -p /users/git-user/static
```

Now, copy the `Latin.txt` and `Greek.txt` files, which we created for the previous example, to the preceding static directory. After doing that, let us write the program for the file server using the following steps. You will be amazed at the simplicity of `httprouter`:

1. Create a program at the following path:

   ```
   touch -p $GOPATH/src/github.com/git-
   user/chapter2/fileServer/main.go
   ```

2. Update the code like the following. You have to add a route that links a static file path route to a filesystem handler:

   ```
   package main

   import (
     "log"
     "net/http"

     "github.com/julienschmidt/httprouter"
   )

   func main() {
     router := httprouter.New()
   ```

```
        // Mapping to methods is possible with HttpRouter
        router.ServeFiles("/static/*filepath",
         http.Dir("/Users/git-user/static"))
        log.Fatal(http.ListenAndServe(":8000", router))
    }
```

3. Now run the server and see the output:

   go run $GOPATH/src/github.com/git-user/chapter2/fileServer/main.go

4. Open another Terminal and fire this `curl` request:

   http://localhost:8000/static/latin.txt

5. Now, the output will be a static file content server from our file server:

   Lorem ipsum dolor sit amet, consectetuer adipiscing elit. Aenean commodo ligula eget dolor. Aenean massa. Cum sociis natoque penatibus et magnis dis parturient montes, nascetur ridiculus mus. Donec quam felis, ultricies nec, pellentesque eu, pretium quis, sem. Nulla consequat massa quis enim. Donec pede justo, fringilla vel, aliquet nec, vulputate eget, arcu.

In the next section, we discuss about a widely used HTTP router called `gorilla/mux`.

Introducing gorilla/mux – a powerful HTTP router

The word `Mux` stands for the multiplexer. `gorilla/mux` is a multiplexer designed to multiplex HTTP routes (URLs) to different handlers. Handlers are the functions that can handle the given requests. `gorilla/mux` is a wonderful package for writing beautiful routes for our API servers.

`gorilla/mux` provides tons of options to control how routing is done to your web application. It allows a lot of features, such as:

- Path-based matching
- Query-based matching
- Domain-based matching

- Sub-domain-based matching
- Reverse URL generation

Which type of routing to use depends on the types of clients requesting the server. We first see the installation and then a basic example to understand the gorilla/mux package.

Installing gorilla/mux

Follow these steps to install the mux package:

1. You need to run this command in the Terminal (Mac OS X and Linux):

   go get -u github.com/gorilla/mux

2. If you get any errors saying package github.com/gorilla/mux: cannot download, $GOPATH not set. For more details see--go help gopath, set the $GOPATH environment variable using the following command:

   export GOPATH=~/go

3. As we discussed in Chapter 1, *Getting Started with REST API Development*, all the packages and programs go into GOPATH. It has three folders: bin, pkg, and src. Now, add GOPATH to the PATH variable to use the installed bin files as system utilities that have no ./executable style. Refer to the following command:

   PATH="$GOPATH/bin:$PATH"

4. These settings stay until you turn off your machine. So, to make it a permanent change, add the preceding line to your bash/zsh profile file:

   vi ~/.profile
   (or)
   vi ~/.zshrc

We can import gorilla/mux in our programs, like this:

import "github.com/gorilla/mux"

Now, we are ready to go. Assuming gorilla/mux is installed, we can now explore its basics.

Fundamentals of gorilla/mux

The `gorilla/mux` package primarily helps to create routers, similar to `httprouter`. The difference between both is the attachment of a handler function to a given URL. If we observe, the `gorilla/mux` way of attaching a handler is similar to that of basic ServeMux. Unlike `httprouter`, `gorilla/mux` wraps all the information of an HTTP request into a single request object.

The three important tools provided in the `gorilla/mux` API are:

- The `mux.NewRouter` method
- The `*http.Request` object
- The `*http.ResponseWriter` object

The `NewRouter` method creates a `new router` object. That object basically maps a route to a function handler. `gorilla/mux` passes a modified `*http.Request` and `*http.ResponseWriter` object to the function handler. These special objects have lots of additional information about headers, path parameters, request body, and query parameters. Let us explain how to define and use different routers in `gorilla/mux` with two common types:

- Path-based matching
- Query-based matching

Path-based matching

A path parameter in the URL of an HTTP GET request looks like this:

```
https://example.org/articles/books/123
```

Since it is passed after the base URL and API endpoint, in this case `https://example.org/articles/`, they are called path parameters. In the preceding URL, `books` and `123` are path parameters. Let us see an example of how to create routes that can consume data supplied as path parameters. Follow these steps:

1. Create a new file for our program at the following path:

   ```
   touch -p $GOPATH/src/github.com/git-user/chapter2/muxRouter/main.go
   ```

2. The idea is to create a new router, `mux.NewRouter`, and use it as a handler with in-built `http.Server`. We can attach URL endpoints to handler functions on this router object. The URL endpoints attached can also be regular expressions. The simple program to collect path parameters from a client HTTP request and return back the same looks like this:

```go
package main

import (
  "fmt"
  "log"
  "net/http"
  "time"

  "github.com/gorilla/mux"
)

func ArticleHandler(w http.ResponseWriter, r *http.Request) {
  vars := mux.Vars(r)
  w.WriteHeader(http.StatusOK)
  fmt.Fprintf(w, "Category is: %v\n", vars["category"])
  fmt.Fprintf(w, "ID is: %v\n", vars["id"])
}

func main() {
  r := mux.NewRouter()
  r.HandleFunc("/articles/{category}/{id:[0-9]+}", ArticleHandler)
  srv := &http.Server{
    Handler: r,
    Addr: "127.0.0.1:8000",
    WriteTimeout: 15 * time.Second,
    ReadTimeout: 15 * time.Second,
  }
  log.Fatal(srv.ListenAndServe())
}
```

3. Now run the server using the following command in a shell:

```
go run $GOPATH/src/github.com/git-user/chapter2/muxRouter/main.go
```

4. Make a `curl` request from another shell and we can get the output as follows:

```
curl http://localhost:8000/articles/books/123

Category is: books ID is: 123
```

This example shows how to match and parse path parameters. There is one more popular way to collect variable information from an HTTP request and that is with query parameters. In the next section, we see how to create routes that match HTTP requests with query parameters.

Query-based matching

Query parameters are variables that get passed along with the URL in an HTTP request. This is what we commonly see in a REST GET request. The gorilla/mux route can match and collect query parameters. See this following URL, for example:

```
http://localhost:8000/articles?id=123&category=books
```

It has id and category as query parameters. All query parameters begin after the ? character.

Let us modify our copy of our previous example into a new one with the name queryParameters/main.go. Modify the route object to point to a new handler called QueryHandler, like this:

```
// Add this in your main program
r := mux.NewRouter()
r.HandleFunc("/articles", QueryHandler)
```

In QueryHandler, we can use request.URL.Query() to obtain query parameters from the HTTP request. QueryHandler looks like this:

```
// QueryHandler handles the given query parameters
func QueryHandler(w http.ResponseWriter, r *http.Request) {
  queryParams := r.URL.Query()
  w.WriteHeader(http.StatusOK)
  fmt.Fprintf(w, "Got parameter id:%s!\n", queryParams["id"][0])
  fmt.Fprintf(w, "Got parameter category:%s!", queryParams["category"][0])
}
```

This program is similar to the previous example, but processes query parameters instead of path parameters.

Run the new program:

```
go run $GOPATH/src/github.com/git-user/chapter2/queryParameters/main.go
```

Fire a `curl` request in this format in a Terminal:

```
curl -X GET http://localhost:8000/articles\?id\=1345\&category\=birds
```

We need to escape special characters in the shell. If it is in the browser, there is no problem of escaping. The output looks like this:

```
Got parameter id:1345!
Got parameter category:birds!
```

The `r.URL.Query()` function returns a map with all the parameter and value pairs. They are basically strings and, in order to use them in our program logic, we need to convert the number strings to integers. We can use Go's `strconv` package to convert a string to an integer, and vice versa.

> We have used `http.StatusOK` to write a successful HTTP response. Similarly, use appropriate status codes for different REST operations. For example, 404 – Not found, 500 – Server error, and so on.

Other notable features of gorilla/mux

We have seen two basic examples. What next? The `gorilla/mux` package provides many handy features that makes an API developer's life easy. It gives a lot of flexibility while creating routes. In this section, we try to discuss a few important features. The first feature of interest is generating a dynamic URL with the **reverse mapping** technique.

In simple words, reverse mapping a URL is getting the complete API route for an API resource. Reverse mapping is quite useful when we share links to our web application or API. However, in order to create a URL from data, we should associate a `Name` with the `gorilla/mux` route. You can name a multiplexer route, like this:

```
r.HandlerFunc("/articles/{category}/{id:[0-9]+}", ArticleHandler).
  Name("articleRoute")
```

Now, we can get a dynamically generated API route by using the `url` method:

```
url, err := r.Get("articleRoute").URL("category", "books", "id", "123")
fmt.Printf(url.Path) // prints /articles/books/123
```

If a route consists of the additional path parameters defined, we should pass that data as arguments to the `URL` method.

The next important feature of a URL router is **path prefix**. A path prefix is a wildcard route for matching all possible paths. It matches all the routes to the API server, post a root word. The general use case of path prefixes is a static file server. Then, when we serve files from a static folder, the API paths should match to filesystem paths to successfully return file content.

For example, if we define `/static/` as a path prefix, every API route that has this root word as a prefix is routed to the handler attached.

These paths are matched:

- `http://localhost:8000/static/js/jquery.min.js`
- `http://localhost:8000/static/index.html`
- `http://localhost:8000/static/some_file.extension`

Using gorilla/mux's `PathPrefix` and `StripPefix` methods, we can write a static file server, like this:

```
r.PathPrefix("/static/").Handler(http.StripPrefix("/static/",
http.FileServer(http.Dir("/tmp/static"))))
```

The next important feature is **strict slash**. A strict slash activated on a `gorilla/mux` router allows a URL to redirect to the same URL with / appended at the end and vice versa.

For example, let us say we have an `/articles/` route that is attached to an `ArticleHandler` handler:

```
r.StrictSlash(true)
r.Path("/articles/").Handler(ArticleHandler)
```

In the preceding case, strict slash is set to `true`. The router then redirects even `/articles` (without '/' at the end) to the `ArticleHandler`. If it is set to `false`, the router treats both `/articles/` and `/articles` as different paths.

The next important feature of a URL router is to match encoded path parameters. The `gorilla/mux` `UseEncodedPath` method can be called on a router to match encoded path parameters.

A server can receive encoded paths from a few clients. We can match the encoded path parameter, we can even match the encoded URL route and forward it to the given handler:

```
r.UseEncodedPath()
r.NewRoute().Path("/category/id")
```

This can match the following URL:

```
http://localhost:8000/books/2
```

As well as this:

```
http://localhost:8000/books%2F2
```

Where `%2F2` stands for `/2` in encoded form.

 Its pattern-matching features and simplicity push `gorilla/mux` as a popular choice for an HTTP router in projects. Many successful projects worldwide are already using mux for their routing needs.

We are free to define routes for our application. Since routes are entry points to any API, developers should be careful about how they process the data received from a client. Clients can be attackers too, who can inject malicious scripts into the path or query parameters. That situation is called a **security vulnerability**. APIs are prone to a common application vulnerability called SQL injection. In the next section, we introduce it briefly and see possible countermeasure steps.

SQL injection in URLs and ways to avoid them

SQL injection is a process of attacking a database with malicious scripts. If one is not careful when defining URL routes, there may be an opportunity for SQL injection. These attacks can happen for all kinds of REST operations. For example, if we are allowing the client to pass parameters to the server, then there is a chance for an attacker to append an ill-formed string to those parameters. If we are using those variables/parameters directly into an SQL query executing on our database, it could lead to a potential vulnerability.

Look at the following Go code snippet that inserts `username` and `password` details into the database. It collects values from an HTTP `POST` request and appends raw values to the SQL query:

```
username := r.Form.Get("id")
password := r.Form.Get("category")
sql := "SELECT * FROM article WHERE id='" + username + "' AND category='" +
password + "'"
Db.Exec(sql)
```

In the snippet, we are executing a database SQL query, but since we are appending the values directly, we may include malicious SQL statements such as `--` comments and `ORDER BY n` range clauses in the query:

```
?category=books&id=10 ORDER BY 10--
```

If the application returns the database response directly to the client, it can leak information about the columns the table has. An attacker can change the `ORDER BY` to another number and extract sensitive information:

```
Unknown column '10' in 'order clause'
```

We will see more about this in our upcoming chapters where we build fully-fledged REST services with other methods, such as `POST`, `PUT`, and so on:

Now, how to avoid these injections. There are several precautions:

- Set the user level permissions to various tables in the database
- Log the requests and find the suspicious ones
- Use the `HTMLEscapeString` function from Go's `text/template` package to escape special characters in the API parameters, such as `body` and `path`
- Use a driver program instead of executing raw SQL queries
- Stop relaying database debug messages back to the client
- Use security tools such as `sqlmap` to find out vulnerabilities

With the basics of routing and security covered, in the next section we present an interesting challenge for the reader. It is to create a URL shortening service. We provide all the background details briefly in the next section.

Reader's challenge – an API for URL shortening

With all the basics you have learned up to now, try to implement a URL shortening service. A URL shortener takes a very long URL and returns a shortened, crisp, and memorable URL back to the user. At first sight, it looks like magic, but it is a simple math trick.

In a single statement, URL shortening services are built upon two things:

- A string mapping algorithm to map long strings to short strings (Base 62)
- A simple web server that redirects a short URL to the original URL

There are a few obvious advantages of URL shortening:

- Users can remember the URL; easy to maintain
- Users can use the links where there are restrictions on text length, for example, Twitter
- Predictable shortened URL length

Take a look at the following diagram:

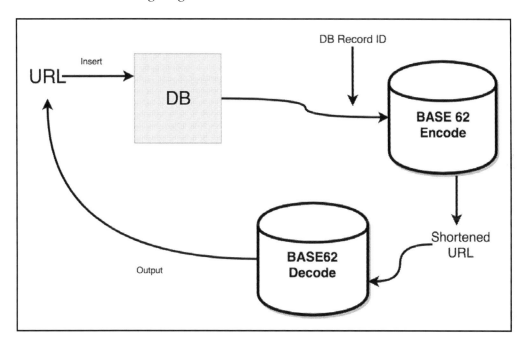

Under the hood, the following things happen in a URL shortening service:

1. Take the original **URL**
2. Apply **BASE62** encoding on it; it generates a **Shortened URL**
3. Store that URL in the database. Map it to the original URL ([shortened_url: original_url])
4. Whenever a request comes to the shortened URL, just do an HTTP redirect to the original URL

We will implement a full example in upcoming chapters when we integrate databases to our API server, but before that, though, we should specify the API design documentation.

Take a look at the following table:

URL	REST Verb	Action	Success	Failure
/api/v1/new	POST	Create a shortened URL	200	500, 404
/api/v1/:url	GET	Redirect to original URL	301	404

 You can use a dummy JSON file/Go map to store the URL for now instead of a database.

Summary

In this chapter, we first introduced the HTTP router. We tried to create HTTP routes using Go's net/http package. Then, we briefly discussed ServeMux with an example. We saw how to add multiple handler functions to multiple routes. Then, we introduced a lightweight router package called httprouter, which allows developers to create elegant routes, with the option of parsing parameters passed in the URL path.

We can also serve files over the HTTP using httprouter. We built a small service to get the Go version and file contents (read-only). That example can be extended to fetch any system information or run a system command.

Next, we introduced the popular Go routing library, gorilla/mux. We discussed how it is different from httprouter and explored its functionality by implementing two examples. We explained how Vars can be used to get path parameters and r.URL.Query to parse query parameters.

As part of securing API routes, we discussed SQL injection and how it can happen in our applications. We have also seen the counter measures. By the end of this chapter, one can define routes and handler functions to accept HTTP API requests.

In the next chapter, we will look at Middleware functions, which act as tamperers for HTTP requests and responses. That phenomenon helps us to modify the API response on the fly. The next chapter also features **Remote Procedure Call (RPC)**.

Working with Middleware and RPC

3

In this chapter, we are going to look at two new concepts. First, we will learn about middleware, and how can we build one from scratch. Then, we will move to a better middleware solution written by the community, called **Gorilla handlers**. We will then see the use cases where middleware is helpful. After that, we will learn about developing **Remote Procedure Call** (**RPC**) services with Go's internal RPC and JSON-RPC. Then, we will move to an advanced RPC framework called Gorilla HTTP RPC.

The topics we cover in this chapter are as follows:

- What is middleware?
- Multiple middleware and chaining
- Painless middleware chaining with `alice`
- Using Gorilla handlers middleware for logging
- What is RPC?
- JSON-RPC using Gorilla RPC

Technical requirements

The following software should be pre-installed for running code samples:

- OS: Linux (Ubuntu 18.04)/Windows 10/Mac OS X >= 10.13
- Software: Docker >= 18 (Docker Desktop for Windows and Mac OS X)
- Go latest version compiler >= 1.13.5

You can download the code for this chapter from `https://github.com/PacktPublishing/Hands-On-Restful-Web-services-with-Go/tree/master/chapter3`. Clone the code and use the code samples in the `chapter3` directory.

What is middleware?

Middleware is an entity that hooks into a server's request/response life cycle. The middleware can be defined in many components. Each component has a specific function to perform. Whenever we define handlers for URL patterns (as in `Chapter 2`, *Handling Routing for our REST Services*), a handler executes some business logic for every incoming request. But middleware, as the name specifies, sits between a request and the handler, or between a handler and a response. So, virtually every middleware can perform these functions:

- Process the request before reaching the handler (function)
- Pass the modified request to the handler function (execute some business logic)
- Process the response coming from the handler
- Pass the modified response to the client

We can see the previous points in the form of a visual illustration, as shown in the following diagram:

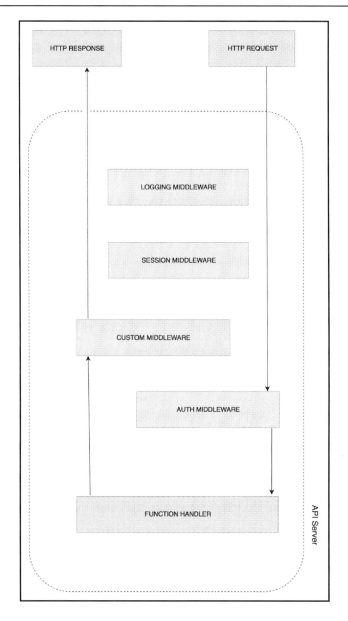

If we observe the diagram carefully, the journey of a request starts from the client. The request first reaches a middleware called **AUTH MIDDLEWARE** and is then forwarded to a **FUNCTION HANDLER**. Once a response is generated from a handler, it is then forwarded to another middleware called **CUSTOM MIDDLEWARE** that can modify the response.

In an application with no middleware, a request reaches the API server and gets handled by a function handler directly. The response is immediately sent back from the server, and the client receives it. But in applications with middleware configured to a function handler, it can pass through a set of stages, such as logging, authentication, session validation, and so on, and then proceeds to the business logic. This is to filter the requests from interacting with the business logic. The most common use cases are as follows:

- Use a logger to log each and every request for a REST API
- Validate the session of the user and keep the communication alive
- Authenticate the user, if not identified
- Attach properties to responses while serving the client

With the help of middleware, we can do any housekeeping work, such as authentication, in its proper place. Let's create a basic middleware and tamper an HTTP request in Go.

Middleware functions can be handy when many function handlers have the same business logic to execute.

Creating a basic middleware

Building middleware functions is simple and straightforward. Let's build a program based on the knowledge gained from Chapter 2, *Handling Routing for our REST Services*. If you are not familiar with closure functions, a closure function returns another function. This principle helps us write middleware. A middleware should return another function, which can be either a middleware or a function handler. It is similar to JavaScript chain methods, whereby one function returns a new function as a return value. Let's create a closure function in Go, by doing the following:

1. Create a program file, like so:

```
touch -p $GOPATH/src/github.com/git-user/chapter3/closureExample/main.go
```

We use this file to add our code.

2. A closure function returns another function. Let's create a closure function that generates positive integers, using the following code:

```
// This function returns another function
func generator() func() int { // Outer function
    var i = 0
    return func() int { // Inner function
        i++
```

```
        return i
    }
}
```

The function is a generator that returns a sequence of integers. A generator pattern generates a new item each time, based on given conditions. The inner function is returning an anonymous function with no arguments and one return type of integer. The i variable that is defined inside the outer function is available to the anonymous function, making it remember the state between upcoming function calls.

3. Now, we can use the previous generator in our main program, like this:

```
package main

import (
    "fmt"
)

...
func main() {
    numGenerator := generator()
    for i := 0; i < 5; i++ {
        fmt.Print(numGenerator(), "\t")
    }
}
```

4. We can run the previous code as a standalone program, as follows:

go run $GOPATH/src/github.com/git-user/chapter3/closureExample/main.go

The following numbers will be generated and printed using *Tab* spaces:

1 2 3 4 5

In Go, the function signature of the outer function should exactly match the anonymous function's signature. In the previous example, func() int is the signature for both the outer and inner functions. The only exception is that the outer function can have an interface as a return type, and the inner function can implement that interface. We will see how in the next few lines.

Now, coming to how closures help to build a middleware: any generator function that can return another function that satisfies the `http.Handler` interface can be a middleware. Let's validate this statement with an example, as follows:

1. Create a file for our program, like this:

```
touch -p $GOPATH/src/github.com/git-
user/chapter3/customMiddleware/main.go
```

2. The middleware takes a normal HTTP handler function as its argument and returns another handler function. The function looks like this:

```
func middleware(originalHandler http.Handler) http.Handler {
    return http.HandlerFunc(func(w http.ResponseWriter,
    r *http.Request) {
        fmt.Println("Executing middleware before request phase!")
        // Pass control back to the handler
        originalHandler.ServeHTTP(w, r)
        fmt.Println("Executing middleware after response phase!")
    })
}
```

If you notice the preceding middleware function, it is taking `originalHandler`, an HTTP handler, as its argument, and is returning another HTTP handler. The inner function is using the original handler to execute the logic. Before and after that handler is where the middleware operates on request and response objects. This makes all the requests coming to the main handler pass through the middleware logic.

3. Now, Let's define the main logic that uses the middleware function we have created, as follows:

```
package main
import (
    "fmt"
    "net/http"
)

func handle(w http.ResponseWriter, r *http.Request) {
    // Business logic goes here
    fmt.Println("Executing mainHandler...")
    w.Write([]byte("OK"))
}
func main() {
    // HandlerFunc returns a HTTP Handler
    originalHandler := http.HandlerFunc(handle)
    http.Handle("/", middleware(originalHandler))
```

```
        http.ListenAndServe(":8000", nil)
}
```

4. Run the code, as follows:

   ```
   go run $GOPATH/src/github.com/git-
   user/chapter3/customMiddleware/main.go
   ```

5. If you do a `curl` request to—or visit— http://localhost:8000 in your
   browser, the console will receive this message:

   ```
   Executing middleware before request phase!
   Executing mainHandler...
   Executing middleware after response phase!
   ```

This program is denoted by the rectangle block to the right in the preceding diagram, with
the label **CUSTOM MIDDLEWARE**. If you observe the middleware visual illustration
provided previously, the request phase direction is to the right, and the response direction
is to the left.

Go web frameworks such as Martini and Gin provide middleware by default. We will see
more about them in `Chapter 4`, *Simplifying RESTful Services with Popular Go Frameworks*. It is
good for a developer to understand the low-level details of middleware.

The following diagram can help you understand how the logic flow happens in the
middleware. This diagram explains how a handler is converted into a wrapper handler:

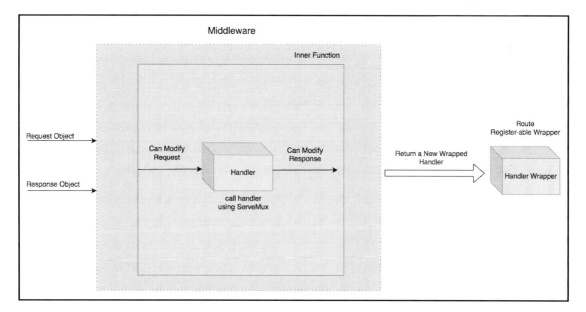

We have seen the creation of a simple middleware, but in a real scenario, multiple middleware are required to log requests, authenticate, and so on. In the next section, we will see how to chain multiple middleware.

Multiple middleware and chaining

In the previous section, we built a single middleware to perform an action before or after a request hits the handler. It is also possible to chain a group of middleware. In order to do that, we should follow the same closure logic as in the preceding section. Let's create a `cityAPI` program for saving city details. For simplicity's sake, the API will have one POST method, and the body will consist of two fields: city name and city area.

Let's us think about a scenario where a client is only allowed to send a JSON `Content-Type` request to an API. The main function of the API is to send a response to the client with a UTC timestamp cookie attached to it. We can add that content check in the middleware.

The functions of the two middleware are as follows:

- In the first middleware, check whether the content type is JSON. If not, don't allow the request to proceed.
- In the second middleware, add a timestamp called Server-Time (UTC) to the response cookie.

Before adding the middleware, Let's create a POST API that collects the name and area of a city and returns a message with a status code of 201, to show it has been successfully created. This can be done in the following way:

1. Create a file for our program, like this:

```
touch -p $GOPATH/src/github.com/git-user/chapter3/cityAPI/main.go
```

2. Now, write the function that handles the POST request from the client. It decodes the body and reads the name and area, and fills them into a struct called `city`, like this:

```
type city struct {
  Name string
  Area uint64
}

func postHandler(w http.ResponseWriter, r *http.Request) {
  if r.Method == "POST" {
```

```
    var tempCity city
    decoder := json.NewDecoder(r.Body)
    err := decoder.Decode(&tempCity)
    if err != nil {
      panic(err)
    }
    defer r.Body.Close()
    fmt.Printf("Got %s city with area of %d sq miles!\n",
     tempCity.Name, tempCity.Area)
    w.WriteHeader(http.StatusOK)
    w.Write([]byte("201 - Created"))
  } else {
    w.WriteHeader(http.StatusMethodNotAllowed)
    w.Write([]byte("405 - Method Not Allowed"))
  }
}
```

postHandler is handling a client request in this snippet. It returns a status code of 405 - Method Not Allowed if a client tries to perform a GET request. json.NewDecoder is used to read the body from a request. Decode maps the body parameters to a struct, of the city type.

3. Now comes the main logic, as shown here:

```
package main

import (
  "encoding/json"
  "fmt"
  "net/http"
)

func main() {
  http.HandleFunc("/city", postHandler)
  http.ListenAndServe(":8000", nil)
}
```

4. We can start the API server by using the following code:

```
go run $GOPATH/src/github.com/git-user/chapter3/cityAPI/main.go
```

5. Then, fire a couple of curl requests, like so:

```
curl -H "Content-Type: application/json" -X POST
http://localhost:8000/city -d '{"name":"New York", "area":304}'

curl -H "Content-Type: application/json" -X POST
http://localhost:8000/city -d '{"name":"Boston", "area":89}'
```

6. The server logs this output:

```
Got New York city with area of 304 sq miles!
Got Boston city with area of 89 sq miles!
```

The `curl` responses are as follows:

```
201 - Created
201 - Created
```

7. Now comes the content checks. In order to chain middleware functions, we have to pass the handler between multiple middleware. Only one handler is involved in the preceding example. But now, for the upcoming task, the idea is to pass the main handler to multiple middleware handlers. We can modify the `cityAPI` program to a new file, like this:

```
touch -p $GOPATH/src/github.com/git-
user/chapter3/multipleMiddleware/main.go
```

8. Let's first create the content-check middleware. Let's call it `filterContentType`. This middleware checks the MIME header from the request and, if it is not JSON, returns a response of status code `415- Unsupported Media Type`, as shown in the following code block:

```
func filterContentType(handler http.Handler) http.Handler {
 return http.HandlerFunc(func(w http.ResponseWriter,
  r *http.Request) {
 log.Println("Currently in the check content type middleware")
 // Filtering requests by MIME type
 if r.Header.Get("Content-type") != "application/json" {
 w.WriteHeader(http.StatusUnsupportedMediaType)
 w.Write([]byte("415 - Unsupported Media Type. Please send JSON"))
 return
 }
 handler.ServeHTTP(w, r)
 })
}
```

9. Now, Let's define a second middleware called `setServerTimeCookie`. After receiving a proper content type while sending a response back to the client, this middleware adds a cookie called `Server-Time(UTC)` with the server UTC timestamp as the value, as shown in the following code block:

```
func setServerTimeCookie(handler http.Handler) http.Handler {
 return http.HandlerFunc(func(w http.ResponseWriter,
  r *http.Request) {
```

```
    handler.ServeHTTP(w, r)
    // Setting cookie to every API response
    cookie := http.Cookie{Name: "Server-Time(UTC)",
     Value: strconv.FormatInt(time.Now().Unix(), 10)}
    http.SetCookie(w, &cookie)
    log.Println("Currently in the set server time middleware")
  })
}
```

10. The main function has a slight variation in the mapping of a route to the handler. It uses nested function calls for chaining middleware, as can be seen here:

```
func main() {
  originalHandler := http.HandlerFunc(handle)
  http.Handle("/city",
    filterContentType(setServerTimeCookie(originalHandler)))
  http.ListenAndServe(":8000", nil)
}
```

We chain the middleware by using `filterContentType(setServerTimeCookie(originalHandler))`. Please carefully observe the order of chaining.

11. Now, run the updated server, as follows:

```
go run $GOPATH/src/github.com/git-
user/chapter3/multipleMiddleware/main.go
```

Then, fire a `curl` request, like this:

```
curl -i -H "Content-Type: application/json" -X POST
http://localhost:8000/city -d '{"name":"Boston", "area":89}'
```

The response output is the following:

```
HTTP/1.1 200 OK
Date: Sat, 27 May 2017 14:35:46 GMT
Content-Length: 13
Content-Type: text/plain; charset=utf-8

201 - Created
```

12. But if we remove `Content-Type: application/json` from the `curl` request, the middleware blocks us from executing the main handler, as shown in the following code block:

```
curl -i -X POST http://localhost:8000/city -d '{"name":"New York",
"area":304}'
```

```
Result:
HTTP/1.1 415 Unsupported Media Type
Date: Sat, 27 May 2017 15:36:58 GMT
Content-Length: 46
Content-Type: text/plain; charset=utf-8

415 - Unsupported Media Type. Please send JSON
```

This is the simplest way of chaining middleware in Go API servers.

If an API server wishes a request to go through many middleware, then how can we make that chaining simple and readable? There is a very good library called `alice` to solve this problem. It allows you to semantically order and attach your middleware to the main handler. We will see it briefly in the next section.

Painless middleware chaining with Alice

The `alice` library reduces the complexity of chaining the middleware when the list of middleware is big. It provides us with a clean API to pass the handler to the middleware. It is a lightweight solution, unlike other middleware chaining Go packages.

Install `alice` via the `go get` command, like this:

```
go get github.com/justinas/alice
```

Now, we can import the `alice` package in our program and use it straight away. We can modify the sections of the previous program to bring the same functionality, with improved chaining. Let's call the program directory `multipleMiddlewareWithAlice`, and create a main program in this location:

```
touch -p $GOPATH/src/github.com/git-
user/chapter3/multipleMiddlewareWithAlice/main.go
```

In the `import` section, add `github.com/justinas/alice`, as shown in the following code snippet:

```
import (
    "encoding/json"
    "github.com/justinas/alice"
    "log"
    "net/http"
    "strconv"
    "time"
)
```

Now, in the `main` function, we can modify the handler part, like this:

```
func main() {
    originalHandler := http.HandlerFunc(handle)
    chain := alice.New(filterContentType,
      setServerTimeCookie).Then(originalHandler)
    http.Handle("/city", chain)
    http.ListenAndServe(":8000", nil)
}
```

The output of this program is similar to the previous one. With the knowledge of the preceding concepts, Let's build a logging middleware with a library from the Gorilla toolkit called **handlers**.

Using Gorilla handlers middleware for logging

The Gorilla handlers package provides various pre-written middleware for common tasks. The most important ones in the list are:

- `LoggingHandler`: For logging in Apache **Common Log Format (CLF)**
- `CompressionHandler`: For zipping the responses
- `RecoveryHandler`: For recovering from unexpected panics

Here, we use the `LoggingHandler` middleware to perform API-wide logging. First, install this library using `go get`, like this:

```
go get "github.com/gorilla/handlers"
```

This logging server enables us to create a server-like a log with time and options. For example, when you see `apache.log`, you find the log in a standard format, as shown in the following code block:

```
192.168.2.20 - - [28/Jul/2006:10:27:10 -0300] "GET /cgi-bin/try/ HTTP/1.0"
200 3395
127.0.0.1 - - [28/Jul/2006:10:22:04 -0300] "GET / HTTP/1.0" 200 2216
```

The format is this: IP-Date-Method:Endpoint-ResponseStatus. Writing our own middleware that mimics Apache-style logging takes some effort, but Gorilla Handlers already implemented one for us. Let's update the previous program in a few ways by creating a new program, like this:

```
touch -p $GOPATH/src/github.com/git-user/chapter3/loggingMiddleware/main.go
```

Now, Let's write the program, using the following steps:

1. First, we create a Gorilla router and attach it to the LoggingHandler.

2. The LoggingHandler registers a standard output (Let's say, in our case, os.Stdout) and returns a new router. We use that new router to register with the HTTP server, as shown in the following code block:

```go
package main
import (
    "github.com/gorilla/handlers"
    "github.com/gorilla/mux"
    "log"
    "os"
    "net/http"
)
func handle(w http.ResponseWriter, r *http.Request) {
    log.Println("Processing request!")
    w.Write([]byte("OK"))
    log.Println("Finished processing request")
}
func main() {
    r := mux.NewRouter()
    r.HandleFunc("/", handle)
    loggedRouter := handlers.LoggingHandler(os.Stdout, r)
    http.ListenAndServe(":8000", loggedRouter)
}
```

3. Start the server by running the following code:

```
go run $GOPATH/src/github.com/git-
user/chapter3/loggingMiddleware/main.go
```

4. Now, open `http://127.0.0.1:8000` in the browser, or fire a `curl` request, and you will see the following output:

```
2017/05/28 10:51:44 Processing request!
2017/05/28 10:51:44 Finished processing request
127.0.0.1 - - [28/May/2017:10:51:44 +0530] "GET / HTTP/1.1" 200 2
127.0.0.1 - - [28/May/2017:10:51:44 +0530] "GET /favicon.ico
HTTP/1.1" 404 19
```

If you observe, the last two logs are generated by the middleware. Gorilla `LoggingMiddleware` writes them at response time.

In the previous example, we always checked the API on the localhost. In this example, we explicitly specified replacing the localhost with `127.0.0.1` because the former will show as an empty IP in the logs.

Coming to the program, we are importing the `gorilla/mux` router and `gorilla/handlers`. Then, we are attaching a handler called `handle` to the router. Next, we are wrapping the router in the `handlers.LoggingHandler` middleware. It returns one more handler, which we can pass safely to `http.ListenAndServe`.

You can try other middleware from handlers, too. This section's goal is to introduce you to `gorilla/handlers`. There are many other external packages available for Go. There is one library worth mentioning for writing middleware directly on `net/http`. It is Negroni (`github.com/urfave/negroni`). It also provides the functionality of `alice`, the Gorilla `LoggingHandler`. So, please have a look at it.

We can easily build cookie-based authentication middleware, using a library called `go.uuid` (`github.com/satori/go.uuid`) and cookies.

Systems talk to each other using web services. A client API can be powered by multiple server instances. RPC is a mechanism to delegate work to a remote server in an understandable fashion. RPC is an important concept in Go because it can play a part in supporting a REST service served to a client. The Gorilla toolkit provides packages to support RPC. We will understand it in detail in the next section.

What is RPC?

RPC is an inter-process communication that exchanges information between various distributed systems. A computer called Alice can call functions (procedures) in another computer called Bob in protocol format and can get the computed result back. Without implementing the functionality locally, we can request things from a network that lies in another place or geographical region.

The entire process can be broken down into the following steps:

1. Clients prepare function name and arguments to send
2. Clients send them to an RPC server by dialing the connection
3. The server receives the function name and arguments
4. The server executes the remote process
5. The message will be sent back to the client
6. The client collects the data from the request and uses it appropriately

The server needs to expose its service for the client to connect and request a remote procedure. Take a look at the following diagram:

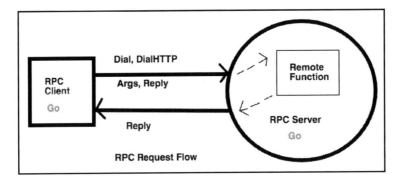

Go provides a library to implement both the **RPC Server** and **RPC Client**. In the preceding diagram, the **RPC Client** dials the connection with details such as the host and port. It sends two things along with the request. One is arguments, and the other is the reply pointer. Since it is a pointer, the server can modify it and send it back. Then, the client can use the data filled into the pointer. Go has two libraries, net/rpc and net/rpc/jsonrpc, for working with RPC. Let's write an RPC server that talks to the client and sends the server time.

Creating an RPC server

Let's create a simple RPC server that sends the UTC server time back to the RPC client. The RPC server and RPC client should agree upon two things:

- Arguments passed
- Value returned

The types of these two parameters should match exactly for both server and client. Let's look at the steps for creating an RPC server, as follows:

1. Let's create an RPC server program, like this:

   touch -p $GOPATH/src/github.com/git-user/chapter3/rpcServer/main.go

2. We should create an `Args struct` and a reply pointer to hold data for RPC calls.

3. Then, create a function for a remote client to execute, and name it `GiveServerTime`, as shown in the following code block:

   ```
   type Args struct{}

   type TimeServer int64

   func (t *TimeServer) GiveServerTime(args *Args, reply *int64) error
   {
     // Fill reply pointer to send the data back
     *reply = time.Now().Unix()
     return nil
   }
   ```

4. Now, we can activate `TimeServer` with a method called `rpc.Register`. The main logic looks like this:

   ```
   package main

   import (
     "log"
     "net"
     "net/http"
     "net/rpc"
     "time"
   )

   func main() {
     timeserver := new(TimeServer)
     rpc.Register(timeserver)
   ```

```
    rpc.HandleHTTP()
    // Listen for requests on port 1234
    l, e := net.Listen("tcp", ":1234")
    if e != nil {
      log.Fatal("listen error:", e)
    }
    http.Serve(l, nil)
}
```

There are a few points to note from the preceding example:

- `GiveServerTime` takes the `Args` object as the first argument and a reply pointer object
- It sets the reply pointer object but does not return anything except an error
- The `Args` struct here has no fields because this server is not expecting any arguments from clients

Before using this RPC server, Let's write the RPC client, too.

Creating an RPC client

A client also uses the same `net/rpc` package, but different methods to dial to the server and get the remote function executed. The only way to get data back is to pass the reply pointer object along with the request. Let's look at the steps for creating an RPC client, as follows:

1. Let's define that client program, like this:

    ```
    touch -p $GOPATH/src/github.com/git-user/chapter3/rpcClient/main.go
    ```

2. A client dials to an RPC server, using the `rpc.DialHTTP` method. It returns a `client` object. Once dial-in is successful, it can then execute a remote function using the `client.Call` method, as shown in the following code block:

    ```
    package main
    import (
        "log"
        "net/rpc"
    )
    type Args struct {
    }
    func main() {
        var reply int64
        args := Args{}
    ```

```
client, err := rpc.DialHTTP("tcp", "localhost"+":1234")
if err != nil {
    log.Fatal("dialing:", err)
}
err = client.Call("TimeServer.GiveServerTime",
 args, &reply)
if err != nil {
    log.Fatal("arith error:", err)
}
log.Printf("%d", reply)}
```

3. Now, we can run both the server and client to see them in action. This runs the server, like this:

   go run $GOPATH/src/github.com/git-user/chapter3/rpcServer/main.go

4. Now, open another shell tab and run this, like so:

   go run $GOPATH/src/github.com/git-user/chapter3/rpcClient/main.go

   Now, the server console will output the following Unix time string:

   2017/05/28 19:26:31 1495979791

Did you see the magic? The client is running as an independent program from the server. Here, both the programs can be on different machines, and computing can still be shared. This is the core concept of distributed systems. The tasks are divided and given to various RPC servers. Finally, the client collects the results and uses them to take further decisions.

 RPC should be secured because it is executing the remote functions. Authorization is a must while collecting requests from the client.

Custom RPC code is only useful when the client and server are both written in Go. So, in order to have the RPC server consumed by multiple services, we need to define the JSON-RPC over HTTP. Then, any other programming language can send a JSON string and get JSON as the result back.

JSON-RPC using Gorilla RPC

We saw that the Gorilla toolkit helps us by providing many useful libraries. It has libraries such as Mux for routing, Handlers for middleware, and now, the `gorilla/rpc` library. Using this, we can create RPC servers and clients that talk using JSON instead of a custom reply pointer. Let's convert the preceding example into a much more useful one.

Consider this scenario. We have a JSON file on the server that has details of books (name, ID, author). The client requests book information by making an HTTP request. When the RPC server receives the request, it reads the file from the filesystem and parses it. If the given ID matches any book, then the server sends the information back to the client in JSON format. Let's look at the steps here:

1. We can install Gorilla RPC with the `go get` command:

   ```
   go get github.com/gorilla/rpc
   ```

   This package derives from the standard `net/rpc` package but uses a single HTTP request per call instead of persistent connections. Other differences compared to `net/rpc` are explained in the next few lines. Multiple codecs can be registered on the same server. A codec is chosen based on the `Content-Type` header from the request. Service methods also receive the `http.Request` as a parameter.

2. Now, Let's write an RPC JSON server. Here, we are implementing the JSON 1.0 specification. For 2.0, you should use Gorilla JSON2. Let's define a dummy JSON file that has information on books, like this:

   ```
   touch -p $GOPATH/src/github.com/git-
   user/chapter3/jsonRPCServer/books.json
   ```

3. Let's us add a few books to the JSON file, like so:

   ```
   [
     {
       "id": "1234",
       "name": "In the sunburned country",
       "author": "Bill Bryson"
     },
     {
       "id":"2345",
       "name": "The picture of Dorian Gray",
       "author": "Oscar Wilde"
     }
   ]
   ```

4. Now, we have a book database file (JSON, in this case). Let's us write the RPC server similar to the previous example, by running the following code:

```
touch -p $GOPATH/src/github.com/git-
user/chapter3/jsonRPCServer/main.go
```

5. The process is to define a struct to hold types for a book. Then, create a JSONServer struct for registering with the RPC Server. It should have a method as an RPC action. Read the JSON file from the given file using the `filepath` built-in utility function. The `reply` argument of JSONServer is filled with the matched book information, as shown in the following code block:

```go
// Args holds arguments passed to JSON-RPC service
type Args struct {
  ID string
}

// Book struct holds Book JSON structure
type Book struct {
  ID string `json:"id,omitempty"`
  Name string `json:"name,omitempty"`
  Author string `json:"author,omitempty"`
}

type JSONServer struct{}

// GiveBookDetail is RPC implementation
func (t *JSONServer) GiveBookDetail(r *http.Request, args *Args,
reply *Book) error {
  var books []Book
  // Read JSON file and load data
  absPath, _ := filepath.Abs("chapter3/books.json")
  raw, readerr := ioutil.ReadFile(absPath)
  if readerr != nil {
    log.Println("error:", readerr)
    os.Exit(1)
  }
  // Unmarshal JSON raw data into books array
  marshalerr := jsonparse.Unmarshal(raw, &books)
  if marshalerr != nil {
    log.Println("error:", marshalerr)
    os.Exit(1)
  }
  // Iterate over each book to find the given book
  for _, book := range books {
    if book.ID == args.ID {
      // If book found, fill reply with it
```

```
            *reply = book
            break
        }
    }
    return nil
}
```

It looks similar to the last example, but a clear difference is that the server here expects an ID from the client. That ID is a key to fetch the book from JSON. In `GiveBookDetail`, we are using `ioutil.ReadFile` to read file content and unmarshal it into the `books` struct. We then iterate over a list of books to match the key and fill the `reply` pointer with the matched book.

6. Now, Let's us finish the `main` block, which registers the `JSONServer` defined previously as an RPC service, like this:

```
package main

import (
    jsonparse "encoding/json"
    "io/ioutil"
    "log"
    "net/http"
    "os"

    "path/filepath"

    "github.com/gorilla/mux"
    "github.com/gorilla/rpc"
    "github.com/gorilla/rpc/json"
)

func main() {
    // Create a new RPC server
    s := rpc.NewServer()
    // Register the type of data requested as JSON
    s.RegisterCodec(json.NewCodec(), "application/json")
    // Register the service by creating a new JSON server
    s.RegisterService(new(JSONServer), "")
    r := mux.NewRouter()
    r.Handle("/rpc", s)
    http.ListenAndServe(":1234", r)

}
```

A slight difference here is we have to register codec type using the `RegisterCodec` method. That is JSON codec in this case. Then, we can register the service using the `RegisterService` method and start a normal HTTP server. If you have noticed well, we used the alias `jsonparse` for the `encoding/json` package because it can conflict with another package, `github.com/gorilla/rpc/json`.

7. We can start this `jsonRPCServer`, as follows:

```
go run $GOPATH/src/github.com/git-
user/chapter3/jsonRPCServer/main.go
```

8. Now, do we have to develop a client? Not necessarily, because a client can be a `curl` program since the RPC server is serving requests over HTTP, we need to post JSON with a book ID to get the details. So, fire up another shell and execute this `curl` request:

```
curl -X POST \
    http://localhost:1234/rpc \
    -H 'cache-control: no-cache' \
    -H 'content-type: application/json' \
    -d '{
    "method": "JSONServer.GiveBookDetail",
    "params": [{
    "ID": "1234"
    }],
    "id": "1"
}'
```

9. The output will be nice JSON that is served directly from the JSON-RPC server, like this:

```
{"result":{"id":"1234","name":"In the sunburned
country","author":"Bill Bryson"},"error":null,"id":"1"}
```

Make JSON-RPC your preferred choice when multiple client technologies need to connect to your RPC service.

RPC is a very common way of defining typed services in programming languages. The Gorilla toolkit is a very useful package while working with Go. When a REST JSON API needs to be provided, you can go ahead and use JSON-RPC.

Summary

In this chapter, we first looked into what middleware is and how middleware processes a request and response. We then explored the middleware code, with a few practical examples. After that, we saw how to chain many middleware, one after the other. A package such as `alice` can be used for intuitive chaining. A package from the Gorilla toolkit, `gorilla/handlers`, provides various middleware for logging, compression, and **Cross-Origin Resource Sharing (CORS)**.

Next, we learned what an RPC is, and how an RPC server and client can be built. After that, we explained what a JSON-RPC is, and we saw how to create a JSON-RPC using the Gorilla toolkit. We introduced many third-party packages for middleware and RPC along the way.

In the next chapter, we are going to explore a few famous web frameworks that further simplify REST API creation.

4
Simplifying RESTful Services with Popular Go Frameworks

In this chapter, we are going to use different frameworks for simplifying the process of building REST services. First, we will take a quick look at `go-restful`, a REST API creation framework, and then move to a framework called Gin. We will build a Metro Rail API in this chapter. The frameworks that we will discuss are fully-fledged web frameworks that can also be used to create REST APIs in a short time. We will also talk a lot about resources and REST verbs in this chapter. We will then try to integrate a small database called SQLite3 with our API. Finally, we explore `revel.go` and see how to prototype our REST API with it.

In this chapter, we will cover the following topics:

- `go-restful` – a framework for REST API creation
- SQLite3 basics and CRUD operations
- Building a Metro Rail API with `go-restful`
- Building a RESTful API with the Gin framework
- Building a RESTful API with `revel.go`

Technical requirements

The following are the software that should be pre-installed for running code samples:

- OS: Linux (Ubuntu 18.04)/Windows 10/Mac OS X >=10.13
- Software: Docker >= 18 (Docker Desktop for Windows and Mac OS X)
- Go latest version compiler >= 1.13.5

You can download the code for this chapter from `https://github.com/PacktPublishing/Hands-On-Restful-Web-services-with-Go/tree/master/chapter4`. Clone the code and use the code samples in the `chapter4` directory.

Introducing go-restful – a REST API framework

`go-restful` is a package for building REST-style web services in Go. REST, as we discussed in `Chapter 1`, *Getting Started with REST API Development*, asks developers to follow a set of design protocols. There we also discussed how the REST verbs are defined and what they do to the resources.

Using `go-restful`, we can separate the logic for API handlers and attach REST verbs. The benefit is that it clearly shows what resources are manipulated by looking at the code. Before jumping into an example, we have to install a database called SQLite3 for our REST API with `go-restful`. The installation steps are as follows:

1. First, install the dependencies for the `go-restful` package. On Ubuntu, run this command:

    ```
    > apt-get install sqlite3 libsqlite3-dev
    ```

    On Mac OS X, you can use the `brew` command to install `sqlite3`:

    ```
    > brew install sqlite3
    ```

2. Now, install the `go-restful` package with the following `get` command:

    ```
    > go get github.com/emicklei/go-restful
    ```

On Windows OS, you can download the SQLite3 executable from `https:/` `/www.sqlite.org`.

We are now ready to go. First, let's write a simple program showing what `go-restful` can do in a few lines of code. It provides a `WebService` using which we can attach a route to a handler. The use case is to create a simple ping server that echoes the server time back to the client. The steps are as follows:

1. Let's create a `basicExample.go` program:

   touch -p $GOPATH/src/github.com/git-user/chapter4/basicExample/main.go

2. Now, create a function that writes the server time to the response. It takes `Request` and `Response` objects:

   ```
   func pingTime(req *restful.Request, resp *restful.Response) {
   // Write to the response
   io.WriteString(resp, fmt.Sprintf("%s", time.Now()))
   }
   ```

   The `pingTime` handler is straightforward and simply writes a server time to the response.

3. We have to create an instance of `restful.WebService` to attach a given route to a verb and a handler. See how we can do it in the following `main` block:

   ```
   package main
   import (
       "fmt"
       "github.com/emicklei/go-restful"
       "io"
       "net/http"
       "time"
   )
   func main() {
       // Create a web service
       webservice := new(restful.WebService)
       // Create a route and attach it to handler in the service
       webservice.Route(webservice.GET("/ping").To(pingTime))
       // Add the service to application
       restful.Add(webservice)
       http.ListenAndServe(":8000", nil)
   }
   ```

4. Now, run the program:

```
go run $GOPATH/src/github.com/git-
user/chapter4/basicExample/main.go
```

5. The server will be running on port 8000 of localhost. So, we can either make a `curl` request or use a browser to see the GET request output:

```
curl -X GET "http://localhost:8000/ping"
2020-01-01 07:37:26.238146296 +0530 CET
```

In the preceding program, we imported the `go-restful` library and created a new service using an instance of the `restful.WebService` struct.

6. Next, we will create a REST verb using the following statement:

```
webservice.GET("/ping")
```

7. We then attach a function handler to execute this verb; `pingTime` is one such function. These chained functions are passed to a `Route` function to create a router. Then comes the following important statement:

```
restful.Add(webservice)
```

This registers the newly created `webservice` with `go-restful`. If you observe, we are not passing any `ServeMux` objects to the `http.ListenServe` function; `go-restful` will take care of it.

The main concept here is to use the resource-based REST API creation in `go-restful`. Going from the basic example, let's build something practical.

Take a scenario where your city is getting a new Metro Rail project and you have to develop a REST API for other developers to create apps around it. We will create one such API in this chapter and use various frameworks to show the implementation. Before that, for **Create**, **Read**, **Update**, **Delete** (**CRUD**) operations, we should know how to query or insert data into a database with Go code. We pick the simplest one called SQLite3 and discuss it in the next section.

SQLite3 basics and CRUD operations

SQLite3 is a lightweight, file-based SQL database. It is very useful to quickly build persistence for API. It leverages the SQL language and a relational database. In this section, we see how to interact with SQLite3 from Go.

All SQLite3 operations are going to be done using the `go-sqlite3` library. We can install that package using the following command:

```
go get github.com/mattn/go-sqlite3
```

The special thing about this library is that it uses the internal `sql` package of Go. We usually import `database/sql` and use SQL to execute database queries on the database (here, SQLite3):

```
import "database/sql"
```

Now, we can use the following steps to create a database driver and then execute the SQL commands on it using the `Query` method:

1. Let's create a file in this path:

   ```
   touch -p $GOPATH/src/github.com/git-
   user/chapter4/sqliteExample/main.go
   ```

2. Let's define the main block that creates a table if none exists and calls another function for CRUD operations:

   ```go
   package main

   import (
     "database/sql"
     "log"

     _ "github.com/mattn/go-sqlite3"
   )

   // Book is a placeholder for book
   type Book struct {
     id int
     name string
     author string
   }

   func main() {
     db, err := sql.Open("sqlite3", "./books.db")
     if err != nil {
   ```

```
      log.Println(err)
    }
    // Create table
    statement, err := db.Prepare("CREATE TABLE IF NOT EXISTS books
      (id INTEGER PRIMARY KEY, isbn INTEGER, author VARCHAR(64),
      name VARCHAR(64) NULL)")
    if err != nil {
      log.Println("Error in creating table")
    } else {
      log.Println("Successfully created table books!")
    }
    statement.Exec()
    dbOperations(db)
}
```

We are creating a database called `books.db` and execute a SQL statement for creating a `books` table. We created a SQL statement with the `db.Prepare` method. Then we executed it using the statement's `Exec` method.

3. If you notice, we called the `dbOperations` function for performing CRUD operations. In that function, we create a book, read it, then update, and then delete it. Let's see the implementation:

```
func dbOperations(db *sql.DB) {
  // Create
  statement, _ := db.Prepare("INSERT INTO books (name, author,
   isbn) VALUES (?, ?, ?)")
  statement.Exec("A Tale of Two Cities", "Charles Dickens",
   140430547)
  log.Println("Inserted the book into database!")

  // Read
  rows, _ := db.Query("SELECT id, name, author FROM books")
  var tempBook Book
  for rows.Next() {
    rows.Scan(&tempBook.id, &tempBook.name, &tempBook.author)
    log.Printf("ID:%d, Book:%s, Author:%s\n", tempBook.id,
     tempBook.name, tempBook.author)
  }
  // Update
  statement, _ = db.Prepare("update books set name=? where id=?")
  statement.Exec("The Tale of Two Cities", 1)
  log.Println("Successfully updated the book in database!")

  //Delete
  statement, _ = db.Prepare("delete from books where id=?")
```

```
statement.Exec(1)
log.Println("Successfully deleted the book in database!")
}
```

In addition to the `Prepare` function, now we have another `Query` method. This is mainly used for reading data from a database. `Exec` is a common function for executing a prepared/queried statement on SQLite.

 A Prepare statement is for performing actions on a database that causes a change in the database, and Query is for read-only.

4. Let's run the `sqliteFunamentals` program:

    ```
    go run $GOPATH/src/github.com/git-
    user/chapter4/sqliteExample/main.go
    ```

The output looks like the following, printing all the log statements:

```
2017/06/10 08:04:31 Successfully created table books!
2017/06/10 08:04:31 Inserted the book into database!
2017/06/10 08:04:31 ID:1, Book:A Tale of Two Cities, Author:Charles
Dickens
2017/06/10 08:04:31 Successfully updated the book in database!
2017/06/10 08:04:31 Successfully deleted the book in database!
```

There is an important thing related to security while running queries. Take a statement from the preceding code:

```
statement, _ = db.Prepare("INSERT INTO books (name, author, isbn)
VALUES (?, ?, ?)")
statement.Exec("A Tale of Two Cities", "Charles Dickens",
140430547)
```

If you pass incorrect values, such as strings that cause SQL injection, the driver rejects the SQL operation instantly. This is to avoid any raw strings being executed by the database engine. It could be dangerous as SQL can do anything, even dropping a database. Always prepare the statement first and then pass the necessary details.

In the next section, we try to build an example API with `go-restful` and SQLite3.

Building a Metro Rail API with go-restful

Let's use the knowledge of `go-restful` and SQLite3 we have gained and create an API for the Metro Rail project we talked about in the preceding section. The road map is as follows:

1. Design a REST API document
2. Create models for a database
3. Implement the API logic

Let's understand each of them in detail.

Design specification

Before creating any API, we should know what the specifications of APIs are in the form of a document. We showed an example in `Chapter 2`, *Handling Routing for our REST Services*, where we showed the URL shortener API design document. Let's try to create one for this Metro Rail project. Take a look at the following table:

HTTP verb	Path	Action	Resource
POST	/v1/train (details as JSON body)	Create	Train
POST	/v1/station (details as JSON body)	Create	Station
GET	/v1/train/id	Read	Train
GET	/v1/station/id	Read	Station
POST	/v1/schedule (source and destination)	Create	Route

We can also include the UPDATE and DELETE methods. By implementing the preceding design, it will be obvious for users to implement them on their own.

Creating database models

Let's write a few SQL strings for creating the tables for the preceding `train`, `station`, and `route` resources. We are going to create a project layout for this API. Create two directories called `railAPI` and `dbutils` in `$GOPATH/src/github.com/git-user/chapter4`.

Here, `railAPI` is our project source, and `dbutils` is our own package for handling database initialization utility functions. Follow these steps:

1. Let's start with the `dbutils/models.go` file. Add three models each for `train`, `station`, and `schedule` in the `models.go` file:

```
package dbutils

const train = `
    CREATE TABLE IF NOT EXISTS train (
        ID INTEGER PRIMARY KEY AUTOINCREMENT,
        DRIVER_NAME VARCHAR(64) NULL,
        OPERATING_STATUS BOOLEAN
    )
`

const station = `
    CREATE TABLE IF NOT EXISTS station (
        ID INTEGER PRIMARY KEY AUTOINCREMENT,
        NAME VARCHAR(64) NULL,
        OPENING_TIME TIME NULL,
        CLOSING_TIME TIME NULL
    )
`

const schedule = `
    CREATE TABLE IF NOT EXISTS schedule (
        ID INTEGER PRIMARY KEY AUTOINCREMENT,
        TRAIN_ID INT,
        STATION_ID INT,
        ARRIVAL_TIME TIME,
        FOREIGN KEY (TRAIN_ID) REFERENCES train(ID),
        FOREIGN KEY (STATION_ID) REFERENCES station(ID)
    )
`
```

These are plain multi-line strings that are delimited by the back tick ` character. `schedule` holds the information of a train arriving at a particular station at a given time. Here, `train` and `station` are foreign keys to the `schedule` table. For `train`, the details related to it are columns. The package name is `dbutils`. When we use the package names, all the Go programs in that package can share variables and functions without an explicit import.

2. Now, let's add code to initialize the (create tables) database in the `init-tables.go` file:

```
package dbutils
import "log"
import "database/sql"

func Initialize(dbDriver *sql.DB) {
    statement, driverError := dbDriver.Prepare(train)
    if driverError != nil {
        log.Println(driverError)
    }
    // Create train table
    _, statementError := statement.Exec()
    if statementError != nil {
        log.Println("Table already exists!")
    }
    statement, _ = dbDriver.Prepare(station)
    statement.Exec()
    statement, _ = dbDriver.Prepare(schedule)
    statement.Exec()
    log.Println("All tables created/initialized successfully!")
}
```

We are importing `database/sql` to pass the type of argument in the function. All other statements in the function are similar to the SQLite3 example we gave in the preceding section. It is creating three tables in the SQLite3 database. Our main program should pass the database driver to this function. If you observe here, we are not importing `train`, `station`, and `schedule`. However, since this file is in the `dbutils` package, variables in `models.go` are accessible here.

3. Now, our initial package is finished. Build the object code for this package using the following command:

    go build $GOPATH/src/github.com/git-user/chapter4/dbutils

4. It is not useful until we create and run our main program. So, let's write a simple main program that imports the `Initialize` function from the `dbutils` package. Let's call the `main.go` file:

    touch -p $GOPATH/src/github.com/git-user/chapter4/railAPI/main.go

5. Now, in the main function, let's import the `dbutils` package and initialize the tables:

```
package main

import (
    "database/sql"
    "log"

    _ "github.com/mattn/go-sqlite3"
    "github.com/git-user/chapter4/dbutils"
)

func main() {
    // Connect to Database
    db, err := sql.Open("sqlite3", "./railapi.db")
    if err != nil {
        log.Println("Driver creation failed!")
    }
    // Create tables
    dbutils.Initialize(db)
}
```

6. Run the program from the `railAPI` directory using the following command:

```
go run $GOPATH/src/github.com/git-user/chapter4/railAPI/main.go
```

7. The output should be something like the following:

```
2020/01/10 14:05:36 All tables created/initialized successfully!
```

In the previous `railAPI` example, we delegated the table creation task to the `Initialize` function in the `dbutils` package. We can do that straight away in our main program, but it is good practice to decompose the logic into multiple packages.

 The `railapi.db` file from the preceding directory tree screenshot gets created once we run our main program. SQLite3 will take care of creating the database file if it doesn't exist. SQLite3 databases are simple files. You can enter into the SQLite shell using the `$ sqlite3 file_name` command.

Let's extend the main program from `railAPI`. Our goal is to create an API that was mentioned in the *Design specification* section. We will go step by step and understand how to build REST services using `go-restful` and SQLite3 in this example:

1. First, add the necessary imports to the program:

```
package main
import (
    "database/sql"
    "encoding/json"
    "log"
    "net/http"
    "time"
    "github.com/emicklei/go-restful"
    _ "github.com/mattn/go-sqlite3"
    "github.com/git-user/chapter4/dbutils"
)
```

We need two external packages, `go-restful` and `go-sqlite3`, for building the API logic. The first one is for handlers and the second package is for adding storage. `dbutils` stays as it is from the `railAPI` example. The `time` and `net/http` packages are for general purpose tasks.

2. Even though concrete names are given to the columns in the SQLite database's tables, in Go programming, we need a few struct types to handle data going in and out of the database. Take a look at the following code snippet that defines necessary structs to hold data:

```
// DB Driver visible to whole program
var DB *sql.DB

// TrainResource is the model for holding rail information
type TrainResource struct {
    ID int
    DriverName string
    OperatingStatus bool
}
// StationResource holds information about locations
type StationResource struct {
    ID int
    Name string
    OpeningTime time.Time
    ClosingTime time.Time
}
// ScheduleResource links both trains and stations
type ScheduleResource struct {
```

```
        ID int
        TrainID int
        StationID int
        ArrivalTime time.Time
}
```

The DB variable is allocated to hold the global database driver. All the preceding structs are exact representations of the database models in SQL. Go's time.Time struct type can actually hold the Time field from the database.

3. Now comes the actual go-restful implementation. We need to create a container for our API in go-restful. Then, we should register the web services to that container. What we have to do now is pick a resource and define a Register method on it. In our case, say TrainResource struct is a resource. The method argument will be a go-restful container where we can attach a service to a namespace, as shown in the following code snippet:

```
// Register adds paths and routes to a new service instance
func (t *TrainResource) Register(container *restful.Container) {
    ws := new(restful.WebService)
    ws.Path("/v1/trains").Consumes(restful.MIME_JSON).Produces
    (restful.MIME_JSON)
    ws.Route(ws.GET("/{train-id}").To(t.getTrain))
    ws.Route(ws.POST("").To(t.createTrain))
    ws.Route(ws.DELETE("/{train-id}").To(t.removeTrain))
    container.Add(ws)
}
```

We first created a service, then added path and routes to the resource. Finally, we attached the service to the container. A path is the URL endpoint, and routes are the path parameters or query parameters attached to the function handlers.

We attached three REST methods, namely GET, POST, and DELETE to three function handlers, getTrain, createTrain, and removeTrain, respectively. We haven't implemented those handlers yet, but we will soon.

If you look at this special statement:

```
ws.Path("/v1/trains").Consumes(restful.MIME_JSON).Produces(restful.
MIME_JSON)
```

It tells us that our API will only entertain Content-Type as application/JSON in the request. For all other types, it automatically returns a 415--Media Not Supported error.

The returned response is automatically converted to a pretty JSON. We can also have a list of formats such as XML, JSON, and so on. `go-restful` provides this feature out of the box.

4. Now, let's define the function handlers. The `getTrain` handler takes an HTTP request and accesses the `path` parameter, then creates a `DB` query statement to fetch the row from the database. `WriteEntity` is used to write a struct as JSON to a response:

```
// GET http://localhost:8000/v1/trains/1
func (t TrainResource) getTrain(request *restful.Request,
 response *restful.Response) {
    id := request.PathParameter("train-id")
    err := DB.QueryRow("select ID, DRIVER_NAME, OPERATING_STATUS
     FROM train where id=?", id).Scan(&t.ID, &t.DriverName,
     &t.OperatingStatus)
    if err != nil {
        log.Println(err)
        response.AddHeader("Content-Type", "text/plain")
        response.WriteErrorString(http.StatusNotFound, "Train could
         not be found.")
    } else {
        response.WriteEntity(t)
    }
}
```

5. Now comes the `POST` handler, `createTrain`. It is similar to `GET`, but instead of fetching information from path parameters, it decodes the body of the incoming request. Then it prepares a database query statement to insert body data. It returns the `ID` of the inserted record in response with the `201-created` status:

```
// POST http://localhost:8000/v1/trains
func (t TrainResource) createTrain(request *restful.Request,
response *restful.Response) {
    log.Println(request.Request.Body)
    decoder := json.NewDecoder(request.Request.Body)
    var b TrainResource
    err := decoder.Decode(&b)
    log.Println(b.DriverName, b.OperatingStatus)
    // Error handling is obvious here. So omitting...
    statement, _ := DB.Prepare("insert into train (DRIVER_NAME,
     OPERATING_STATUS) values (?, ?)")
    result, err := statement.Exec(b.DriverName, b.OperatingStatus)
    if err == nil {
        newID, _ := result.LastInsertId()
        b.ID = int(newID)
```

```
            response.WriteHeaderAndEntity(http.StatusCreated, b)
        } else {
            response.AddHeader("Content-Type", "text/plain")
            response.WriteErrorString(http.StatusInternalServerError,
            err.Error())
        }
    }
```

6. The DELETE function is quite obvious if you understand the previous two handlers. We are making a DELETE SQL command using DB.Prepare and returning a 201 Status created back, telling us the delete operation was successful. Otherwise, we are sending back the actual error as a server error:

```
// DELETE http://localhost:8000/v1/trains/1
func (t TrainResource) removeTrain(request *restful.Request,
response *restful.Response) {
    id := request.PathParameter("train-id")
    statement, _ := DB.Prepare("delete from train where id=?")
    _, err := statement.Exec(id)
    if err == nil {
        response.WriteHeader(http.StatusOK)
    } else {
        response.AddHeader("Content-Type", "text/plain")
        response.WriteErrorString(http.StatusInternalServerError,
        err.Error())
    }
}
```

7. Now, let's write the main function handler, which is an entry point for our program. It creates a go-restful container and registers TrainResource:

```
func main() {
    var err error
    DB, err = sql.Open("sqlite3", "./railapi.db")
    if err != nil {
        log.Println("Driver creation failed!")
    }
    dbutils.Initialize(DB)
    wsContainer := restful.NewContainer()
    wsContainer.Router(restful.CurlyRouter{})
    t := TrainResource{}
    t.Register(wsContainer)
    log.Printf("start listening on localhost:8000")
    server := &http.Server{Addr: ":8000", Handler: wsContainer}
    log.Fatal(server.ListenAndServe())
}
```

The first few lines are performing the database-related housekeeping. Then, we are creating a new container using `restful.NewContainer`. The `go-restful` package provides a router called `CurlyRouter` (which allows us to use {train_id} syntax in paths while setting routes) for our container, and there are other types too. We have chosen that router for incoming HTTP requests. Then, we created an instance of the `TrainResource` struct and passed this container to the `Register` method. That container can act as a wrapped HTTP handler, so we can directly pass it to `http.Server` easily.

8. Use `request.QueryParameter` to fetch the query parameters from an HTTP request in the `go-restful` handler.

9. Let's run the program:

```
go run $GOPATH/src/github.com/git-user/chapter4/railAPI/main.go
```

10. Now, make a `curl POST` request to create a train:

```
curl -X POST \
    http://localhost:8000/v1/trains \
    -H 'cache-control: no-cache' \
    -H 'content-type: application/json' \
    -d '{"driverName": "Veronica", "operatingStatus": true}'
```

This creates a new train with the driver and operation status details. The response is the newly created resource with the train `ID` allocated:

```
{
"ID": 1,
"DriverName": "Veronica",
"OperatingStatus": true
}
```

11. Now, let's make a `curl` request to check `GET`:

```
curl -X GET "http://localhost:8000/v1/trains/1"
```

You will see the JSON output, as follows:

```
{
"ID": 1,
"DriverName": "Veronica",
"OperatingStatus": true
}
```

We can use the same names for both posting data and JSON returned, but in order to show the difference between two operations, different variable names are used.

12. Now, delete the resource we created in the preceding code snippet with the `DELETE` API call:

```
curl -X DELETE "http://localhost:8000/v1/trains/1"
```

It won't return any response body; it returns Status `200 OK` if the operation was successful.

13. Now, if we try to do `GET` on the `ID 1` train, then it returns us this response:

```
Train could not be found.
```

To support more API operations such as `PUT` and `PATCH`, we need to add two more routes to the web service in the `Register` method and define respective handlers. Here, we created a web service for `TrainResource`. In a similar way, web services can be created for doing CRUD operations on the `Station` and `Schedule` tables. That task is left as an exercise for the readers.

`go-restful` is a lightweight library that is powerful in creating RESTful services in an elegant way. The main theme is to convert resources (models) into consumable APIs. Using other heavy frameworks may speed up the development, but the API can end up slower because of the wrapping of code. `go-restful` is a lean and low-level package for API creation.

`go-restful` also provides built-in support for documenting the REST API with swagger. It is a tool that runs and generates templates for documenting the REST API we build. By integrating it with our `go-restful`-based web services, we can generate documentation on the fly. For more information, visit `https://github.com/emicklei/go-restful-swagger12`.

Building RESTful API with the Gin framework

Gin-Gonic is a framework based on `httprouter`. We learned about `httprouter` in `Chapter 2`, *Handling Routing for our REST Services*. It is an HTTP multiplexer like `gorilla/mux`, but it is faster. Gin allows a high-level API to create REST services in a clean way.

Gin can be compared to another web framework in Go called Martini. All web frameworks allow us to do a lot more things such as templates and web server design, in addition to service creation.

One can install the Gin package using the following command:

```
go get gopkg.in/gin-gonic/gin.v1
```

Let's write a simple hello world program in Gin to get familiarized with the Gin constructs:

1. First, create a file that holds our program:

    ```
    touch -p $GOPATH/src/github.com/git-
    user/chapter4/ginExample/main.go
    ```

2. Gin provides a `Default` method to create HTTP route/verb/handler combinations. It also provides a context object inside the handler function to easily operate on HTTP request and response. See an API created with Gin to request `serverTime` UTC here:

    ```go
    package main

    import (
        "time"
        "github.com/gin-gonic/gin"
    )
    func main() {
        r := gin.Default()
        r.GET("/pingTime", func(c *gin.Context) {
            // JSON serializer is available on gin context
            c.JSON(200, gin.H{
                "serverTime": time.Now().UTC(),
            })
        })
        r.Run(":8000") // Listen and serve on 0.0.0.0:8080
    }
    ```

   This simple server tries to implement a service that serves UTC server time to the clients. If you look carefully, Gin allows you to do a lot of stuff with just a few lines of code; all the boilerplate details such as route are taken away.

   Coming to the program, we are creating a router with the `gin.Default` function. Then, we are attaching routes with REST verbs as we did in `go-restful`; a route to the function handler. Then, we are calling the `Run` function by passing the port to run. The default port will be `8080`.

`c` is a context variable that holds the information about the individual request. We can serialize data into JSON before sending it back to the client using the `context.JSON` function.

3. Now, if we run the `ginBasic` program:

```
go run $GOPATH/src/github.com/git-user/chapter4/ginExample/main.go
```

4. Make a `curl` request to see the response:

```
curl -X GET "http://localhost:8000/pingTime"
```

```
{"serverTime":"2020-02-27T19:08:05.470955Z"}
```

At the same time, the Gin server console captures beautiful logs about HTTP requests to the server:

```
Hands-On-Restful-Web-services-with-Go/chapter4 on □ develop [!]
) go run ginExample/main.go
[GIN-debug] [WARNING] Creating an Engine instance with the Logger and Recovery middleware already attached.

[GIN-debug] [WARNING] Running in "debug" mode. Switch to "release" mode in production.
 - using env:   export GIN_MODE=release
 - using code:  gin.SetMode(gin.ReleaseMode)

[GIN-debug] GET    /pingTime                 --> main.main.func1 (3 handlers)
[GIN-debug] Listening and serving HTTP on :8000
[GIN] 2020/02/27 - 20:08:05 | 200 |     152.716µs |           ::1 | GET      /pingTime
```

It is an Apache-style log showing `<the endpoint, the latency of the request, and the REST method>`.

In order to run Gin in production mode, set the `GIN_MODE=release` environment variable. Then the console output will be muted and log files can be used for monitoring the logs.

Now, let's write our Metro Rail API in Gin to show how to implement exactly the same API, but with a different framework. We use the same project layout, name the new project `railAPIGin`, and use the `dbutils` as it is. Let's look at the steps:

1. First, let's prepare the imports for our program:

```
package main
import (
    "database/sql"
    "log"
    "net/http"
    "github.com/gin-gonic/gin"
```

```
    _ "github.com/mattn/go-sqlite3"
    "github.com/git-user/chapter4/dbutils"
)
```

We imported `sqlite3` and `dbutils` for database-related actions. We imported `gin` for creating our API server. `net/http` is useful in providing the intuitive status codes to be sent along with the response.

2. let's define a struct to represent a station in program memory and a database driver:

```
// DB Driver visible to whole program
var DB *sql.DB
// StationResource holds information about locations
type StationResource struct {
    ID int `json:"id"`
    Name string `json:"name"`
    OpeningTime string `json:"opening_time"`
    ClosingTime string `json:"closing_time"`
}
```

`StationResource` is the placeholder for two kinds of data. First, for the POST body coming from an HTTP request, and second for data queried from the database. This is why it is slightly modified from the `railAPI` example of `go-restful`.

Now, let's write the handlers implementing the GET, POST, and DELETE methods for the station resource. We define CRUD handlers similar to the previous Metro Rail API `go-restful` example.

1. The first handler is a GET handler. In `GetStation`, we use `c.Param` to strip the `station_id` path parameter. We use that value as an ID while querying a database record from the SQLite3 station table:

```
// GetStation returns the station detail
func GetStation(c *gin.Context) {
    var station StationResource
    id := c.Param("station_id")
    err := DB.QueryRow("select ID, NAME, CAST(OPENING_TIME as
    CHAR), CAST(CLOSING_TIME as CHAR) from station where id=?",
    id).Scan(&station.ID, &station.Name, &station.OpeningTime,
    &station.ClosingTime)
    if err != nil {
        log.Println(err)
        c.JSON(500, gin.H{
            "error": err.Error(),
        })
```

```
      } else {
         c.JSON(200, gin.H{
            "result": station,
         })
      }
   }
```

If you observe carefully, the SQL query is a bit different. We are using the CAST method to retrieve the SQL TIME field as a string for Go to consume properly. If you remove the casting, a panic error will be raised because we are trying to load a TIME field into the Go string at run time. To give you an idea, the TIME field looks like 8:00:00, 17:31:12, and so on. We are returning back the result using the gin.H method if there is no error.

2. In the POST handler, CreateStation, we perform a database insertion. We need to use the c.BindJSON function in Gin to extract data from the request body. This function loads the data into the struct that is passed as the argument. The idea is to load the station struct with body details. That is why StationResource has the JSON inference strings to tell what key values are expected. See the function body:

```
// CreateStation handles the POST
func CreateStation(c *gin.Context) {
    var station StationResource
    // Parse the body into our resource
    if err := c.BindJSON(&station); err == nil {
        // Format Time to Go time format
        statement, _ := DB.Prepare("insert into station (NAME,
         OPENING_TIME, CLOSING_TIME) values (?, ?, ?)")
        result, _ := statement.Exec(station.Name,
         station.OpeningTime, station.ClosingTime)
        if err == nil {
            newID, _ := result.LastInsertId()
            station.ID = int(newID)
            c.JSON(http.StatusOK, gin.H{
                "result": station,
            })
        } else {
            c.String(http.StatusInternalServerError, err.Error())
        }
    } else {
        c.String(http.StatusInternalServerError, err.Error())
    }
}
```

After collecting the data from a POST request body, we are preparing a database insert statement and executing it. The result is the ID of the inserted record. We are using that ID to send station details back to the client.

3. In the HTTP DELETE function handler RemoveStation, we should use a DELETE SQL query. If the operation is successful, we return a 200 OK status back. Otherwise, we send the appropriate response back with a 500-Internal Server Error:

```
// RemoveStation handles the removing of resource
func RemoveStation(c *gin.Context) {
    id := c.Param("station-id")
    statement, _ := DB.Prepare("delete from station where id=?")
    _, err := statement.Exec(id)
    if err != nil {
        log.Println(err)
        c.JSON(500, gin.H{
            "error": err.Error(),
        })
    } else {
        c.String(http.StatusOK, "")
    }
}
```

Now comes the main program, which runs the database logic first to make sure tables are created. Then, it tries to create a Gin router and adds routes to it:

```
func main() {
    var err error
    DB, err = sql.Open("sqlite3", "./railapi.db")
    if err != nil {
        log.Println("Driver creation failed!")
    }
    dbutils.Initialize(DB)
    r := gin.Default()
    // Add routes to REST verbs
    r.GET("/v1/stations/:station_id", GetStation)
    r.POST("/v1/stations", CreateStation)
    r.DELETE("/v1/stations/:station_id", RemoveStation)
    r.Run(":8000") // Default listen and serve on 0.0.0.0:8080
}
```

We are registering the GET, POST, and DELETE routes with the Gin router. Then, we are passing routes and handlers to them. Finally, we are starting the server using the Run function of Gin with 8000 as the port. Run the preceding program, as follows:

```
go run $GOPATH/src/github.com/git-user/chapter4/railAPIGin/main.go
```

Now, we can create a new station by performing a `POST` request:

```
curl -X POST \
  http://localhost:8000/v1/stations \
 -H 'cache-control: no-cache' \
 -H 'content-type: application/json' \
 -d '{"name":"Brooklyn", "opening_time":"8:12:00",
"closing_time":"18:23:00"}'
```

It returns:

```
{"result":{"id":1,"name":"Brooklyn","opening_time":"8:12:00","closing_time"
:"18:23:00"}}
```

Now try to fetch the station details using `GET`:

```
CURL -X GET "http://localhost:8000/v1/stations/1"

Output
======
{"result":{"id":1,"name":"Brooklyn","opening_time":"8:12:00","closing_time"
:"18:23:00"}}
```

We can also delete the station record using the following command:

```
curl -X DELETE "http://localhost:8000/v1/stations/1"
```

It returns a `200 OK` status, confirming the resource was successfully deleted. As we already discussed, Gin provides intuitive debugging on the console, showing the attached handler, and highlighting the latency and REST verbs with colors:

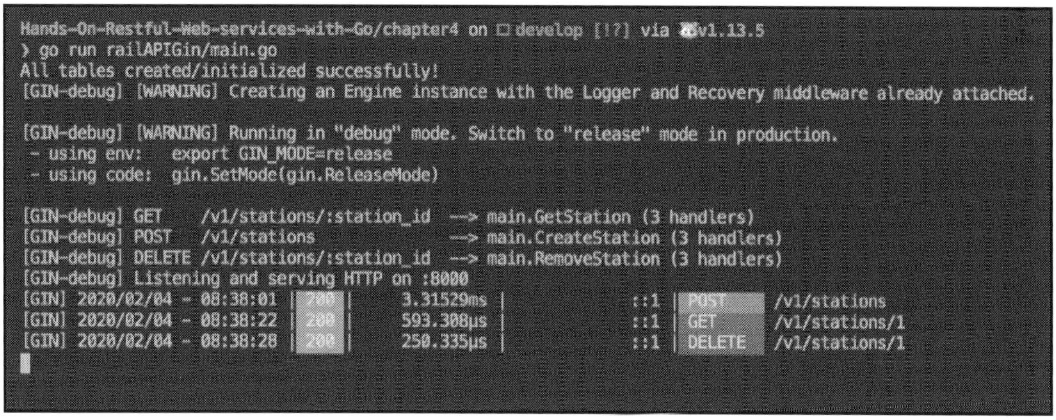

For example, a **200** is green, a **404** is yellow, **DELETE** is red, and so on. Gin provides many other features such as the categorization of routes, redirects, and middleware functions.

Use the Gin framework if you are quickly prototyping a REST web service. You can also use it for many other things such as static file serving, and so on. Remember that it is a fully-fledged web framework. For fetching the query parameters in Gin, use the following method on the Gin context object: `c.Query` (parameter).

Building a RESTful API with revel.go

`revel.go` is also a fully-fledged web framework like Python's Django. It is older than Gin and is termed as a highly productive web framework. It is an asynchronous, modular, and stateless framework. Unlike the `go-restful` and Gin frameworks where we created the project ourselves, Revel generates a scaffold for working directly:

1. Install `revel.go` using the following command:

   ```
   go get github.com/revel/revel
   ```

2. In order to run the scaffold tool, we should install one more supplementary package:

   ```
   go get github.com/revel/cmd/revel
   ```

   Make sure that `$GOPATH/bin` is in your PATH variable. Some external packages install the binary in the `$GOPATH/bin` directory. If it is in the path, we can access the executables system wide. Here, Revel installs a binary called `revel`.

3. On Ubuntu or Mac OS X, you can make sure to point Go binaries to the system path using this command:

   ```
   export PATH=$PATH:$GOPATH/bin
   ```

   Add this export statement to `~/.bashrc` to save the setting permanently. On Windows, you have to directly call the executable by its location. Now we are ready to go with Revel.

4. Let's create a new project called `railAPIRevel` in `github.com/git-user/chapter4`:

   ```
   revel new railAPIRevel
   ```

5. This creates a project scaffold without writing a single line of code. This is how web frameworks abstract things for quick prototyping. A Revel project layout tree looks like this:

```
conf/              Configuration directory
    app.conf       Main app configuration file
    routes         Routes definition file

app/               App sources
    init.go        Interceptor registration
    controllers/   App controllers go here
    views/         Templates directory

messages/          Message files

public/            Public static assets
    css/           CSS files
    js/            Javascript files
    images/        Image files

tests/             Test suites
```

Out of all those boilerplate directories, three things are important for creating an API. Those are:

- app/controllers
- conf/app.conf
- conf/routes

Controllers are the logic containers that execute the API logic. The app.conf file allows us to set the host, port, dev mode/production mode, and so on. routes defines the triple of the endpoint, REST verb, and function handler (here, controller's function). This is required for combining routes, verbs, and function handlers.

Let's use the same Rail API example we developed with go-restful and Gin. However, here, due to the redundancy, we drop the database logic. We will see shortly how to build GET, POST, and DELETE actions for the API using Revel:

1. Now, modify the routes file to this:

```
# Routes Config
#
# This file defines all application routes (Higher priority routes
  first)
#
```

```
module:testrunner
# module:jobs


GET /v1/trains/:train-id
App.GetTrain
POST /v1/trains
App.CreateTrain
DELETE /v1/trains/:train-id
App.RemoveTrain
```

The syntax may look a bit new. It is a configuration file where we simply define a route in this format:

```
VERB        END_POINT           HANDLER
```

VERB is a REST verb, END_POINT is the API endpoint, and HANDLER is the name of the function that processes requests.

We haven't defined handlers yet. In the endpoint, the path parameters are accessed using the :param notation. This means for a GET request to the server, train-id will be passed as the path parameter.

2. Now, navigate to the controllers folder and modify the existing controller in the app.go file.

3. We first create a struct that represents our application context. let's name it App. We should also define another struct for TrainResource that holds rail information:

```
type App struct {
    *revel.Controller
}
// TrainResource is the model for holding rail information
type TrainResource struct {
    ID int `json:"id"`
    DriverName string `json:"driver_name"`
    OperatingStatus bool `json:"operating_status"`
}
```

4. Now let's define CRUD handlers in Revel. First is `GetTrain`. Why a capital lettered name for a controller? Because Revel expects controllers to be exported out of the package. Go packages only export names starting with capital letters. The controller accesses the path parameter to get a train ID and uses it to query the database. Here we are mocking the database result for brevity:

```go
// GetTrain handles GET on train resource
func (c App) GetTrain() revel.Result {
    var train TrainResource
    // Getting the values from path parameters.
    id := c.Params.Route.Get("train-id")
    // use this ID to query from database and fill train table....
    train.ID, _ = strconv.Atoi(id)
    train.DriverName = "Logan" // Comes from DB
    train.OperatingStatus = true // Comes from DB
    c.Response.Status = http.StatusOK
    return c.RenderJSON(train)
}
```

5. In `CreateTrain`, we add the `POST` request logic. We should create an object of `TrainResource` struct and pass it to a function called `c.Params.BindJSON`. JSON tags(`'json:"id"`) gives us the flexibility of defining output fields. This is a good practice in Go while working with JSON. Then, we return an HTTP response with `201 created` status. We can use the `RenderJSON` method on context to marshal a struct to JSON on the fly:

```go
// CreateTrain handles POST on train resource
func (c App) CreateTrain() revel.Result {
    var train TrainResource
    c.Params.BindJSON(&train)
    // Use train.DriverName and train.OperatingStatus
    // to insert into train table....
    train.ID = 2
    c.Response.Status = http.StatusCreated
    return c.RenderJSON(train)
}
```

6. The `RemoveTrain` handler logic is similar to that of `GET`. A subtle difference is that nothing is sent in the body. As we previously mentioned, database CRUD logic is omitted from the preceding example. It is an exercise for readers to try adding SQLite3 logic by observing what we have done in the `go-restful` and Gin sections:

```
// RemoveTrain implements DELETE on train resource
func (c App) RemoveTrain() revel.Result {
    id := c.Params.Route.Get("train-id")
    // Use ID to delete record from train table....
    log.Println("Successfully deleted the resource:", id)
    c.Response.Status = http.StatusOK
    return c.RenderText("")
}
```

7. Finally, the default port on which the Revel server runs is `9000`. The configuration to change the port number is in the `conf/app.conf` file. Let's follow the tradition of running our app on `8000`. So, modify the HTTP port section of `app.conf` to the following. This tells the Revel server to run on a different port:

```
......
# The IP address on which to listen.
http.addr =

# The port on which to listen.
http.port = 8000 # Change from 9000 to 8000 or any port

# Whether to use SSL or not.
http.ssl = false
......
```

8. Now, we can run our Revel API server using this command:

```
revel run github.com/git-user/chapter4/railAPIRevel
```

9. Our app server starts at `http://localhost:8000`. Now, let's make a few API requests:

```
curl -X GET "http://localhost:8000/v1/trains/1"

Output
=======
{
  "id": 1,
  "driver_name": "Logan",
```

```
    "operating_status": true
}
```

POST request:

```
curl -X POST \
    http://localhost:8000/v1/trains \
    -H 'cache-control: no-cache' \
    -H 'content-type: application/json' \
    -d '{"driver_name":"Magneto", "operating_status": true}'

Output
======
{
  "id": 2,
  "driver_name": "Magneto",
  "operating_status": true
}
```

DELETE is the same as GET, but no body is returned. Here, the code is illustrated to show how to handle the request and response. Remember, Revel is more than a simple API framework. It is a fully-fledged web framework similar to Django (Python) or Ruby on Rails. We have got templates, tests, and many more bundled in revel.go. It is mainly used for web development, but one can also use it to quickly develop a REST API.

Make sure that you create a new Revel project for GOPATH/user, otherwise, your Revel command-line tool may not find the project while running the project.

There is middleware support in all the web frameworks we saw in this chapter. go-restful names its middleware Filters, whereas Gin names them Custom Middleware, and Revel calls its middleware, Interceptors. A middleware reads or writes the request and response before and after a function handler, respectively.

In Chapter 3, *Working with Middleware and RPC*, we have already briefly discussed middleware.

Summary

In this chapter, we built a Metro Rail API with the help of a few web frameworks available in Go. The most popular ones are `go-restful`, Gin Gonic, and `revel.go`. We have introduced a database layer in this chapter. We chose SQLite3 and tried to write a sample application using the `go-sqlite3` library.

We then explored `go-restful` and looked in detail at how to create routes and handlers. `go-restful` has the concept of building APIs on top of resources. We explained why `go-restful` is lightweight and can be used to create low-latency APIs.

Next, we introduced the Gin framework and tried to re-implement the `railAPI`. Finally, we tried to create another API on the train resource, but this time with the `revel.go` web framework. Revel is a framework that is similar to Django and Ruby on Rails. It provides scaffolding for most of the server needs such as routing, handlers, and middleware.

The main theme of this chapter is to suggest you use available frameworks for REST API development. Use `revel.go` when you have an end-to-end web application (templates and UI) in addition to the REST API, use Gin to quickly create REST services, and use `go-restful` when the performance of the API is critical.

We also worked with a relational database in the form of SQLite3. In the next chapter, we introduce a popular non-relational database called MongoDB for building an API.

Working with MongoDB and Go to Create a REST API

5

In this chapter, we are going to introduce a popular NoSQL database called MongoDB. We will learn how well MongoDB suits modern web services by storing documents instead of relations. We'll begin by learning about MongoDB collections and documents and create an example API with MongoDB as the database. While doing so, we'll use a driver package called `mongo-driver`. Then, we'll try to design a document model schema for a delivery logistics problem.

In this chapter, we are going to discuss the following topics:

- Introduction to MongoDB
- Installing MongoDB and using the shell
- Introducing `mongo-driver`, an official MongoDB driver for Go
- RESTful API with `gorilla/mux` and MongoDB
- Boosting querying performance with indexing
- Designing MongoDB documents for delivery logistics

Technical requirements

The following software needs to be pre-installed if you wish to run the code examples in this book:

- OS: Linux(Ubuntu 18.04)/Windows 10/Mac OS X >=10.13
- Dep: A dependency management tool for Go >= 0.5.3
- Go compiler >= 1.13.5
- MongoDB >= 4.2.3

You can download the code for this chapter from `https://github.com/PacktPublishing/ Hands-On-Restful-Web-services-with-Go/tree/master/chapter5`. Clone the code and use the code samples in the `chapter5` directory.

Introduction to MongoDB

MongoDB is a popular NoSQL database that is attracting a lot of developers worldwide. It is different from traditional relational databases such as MySQL, PostgreSQL, and SQLite3. The main big difference with MongoDB compared to other databases is it is schemaless and stores collections and documents. Think of MongoDB collections as tables, and documents as rows in SQL databases. However, in MongoDB, there is no relationship between collections. This schemaless design allows MongoDB to scale horizontally using a mechanism called **Sharding**. MongoDB stores data as BSON files on disk. BSON is an efficient binary format for operation and data transfer. Almost all MongoDB clients convert JSON into BSON and vice versa while inserting or retrieving documents.

Many big companies such as Expedia, Comcast, and MetLife built their applications on MongoDB. It has been proven as a vital element in modern internet businesses. MongoDB stores data in a document; think of this as a row in SQL databases. All MongoDB documents are stored in a collection, and this collection is similar to a table (in terms of SQL). Let's look at an example. A sample document for an IMDb movie has a few keys, such as name, year, and directors. The values for these keys can be a number, boolean, string, list, or a map. This would look something similar to the following:

```
{
  _id: 5,
  name: 'Star Trek',
  year: 2009,
  directors: ['J.J. Abrams'],
  writers: ['Roberto Orci', 'Alex Kurtzman'],
  boxOffice: {
    budget:150000000,
    gross:257704099
  }
}
```

The main advantages of MongoDB over relational databases are as follows:

- Easy to model (schema-free)
- Can leverage querying power
- Document structure suits modern-day web applications (**JSON**)
- More scalable than relational databases (via **Sharding**)

Now that we know what MongoDB is, let's look at it in more detail. In the next section, we will learn how to install MongoDB and try to access it from the MongoDB shell.

Installing MongoDB and using the shell

MongoDB can be easily installed on any platform. On Ubuntu 18.04, we need to perform some steps before running the `apt-get` command:

```
sudo apt-get update
sudo apt-get install -y mongodb
```

Once you've installed it, check whether the `mongo` process is running. If not, you can start the MongoDB daemon using the following command:

```
systemctl start mongod
```

If the user is root, you can drop the `sudo` keyword before each command.

 We can also download MongoDB manually from the website and copy it to `/usr/local/bin`. To do this, we have to create an init script for the server since the server stops when the system is shut down. We can use the `nohup` tool to run the server in the background. Usually, it is better to install it using `apt-get`.

To install MongoDB on Mac OS X, you'll need to use the Homebrew software. Follow these steps to do so:

1. We can easily install it using the following command:

    ```
    brew tap mongodb/brew
    brew install mongodb-community
    ```

2. After that, we need to create the `db` directory where MongoDB stores its database:

    ```
    mkdir -p /data/db
    ```

3. Then, change the permissions of that file using `chown`:

```
chown -R `id -un` /data/db
```

4. Now, MongoDB is ready. To see its logs interactively, we need to stop MongoDB as a process and run it in a shell. To stop the service, use the following command:

```
systemctl stop mongod
```

5. Now, in a Terminal window, run the following command, which starts MongoDB interactively (not in the background):

```
mongod
```

The preceding command results in the following output:

```
> mongod
2020-02-09T10:42:47.171+0100 I  CONTROL  [main] Automatically disabling TLS 1.0, to force-enable TLS 1.0 specify --sslDisabledProtocols 'none'
2020-02-09T10:42:47.193+0100 I  CONTROL  [initandlisten] MongoDB starting : pid=10615 port=27017 dbpath=/data/db 64-bit host=naren.local
2020-02-09T10:42:47.193+0100 I  CONTROL  [initandlisten] db version v4.2.3
2020-02-09T10:42:47.193+0100 I  CONTROL  [initandlisten] git version: 6874650b362138df74be53d366bbefc321ea32d4
2020-02-09T10:42:47.193+0100 I  CONTROL  [initandlisten] allocator: system
2020-02-09T10:42:47.193+0100 I  CONTROL  [initandlisten] modules: none
2020-02-09T10:42:47.193+0100 I  CONTROL  [initandlisten] build environment:
2020-02-09T10:42:47.193+0100 I  CONTROL  [initandlisten]     distarch: x86_64
2020-02-09T10:42:47.193+0100 I  CONTROL  [initandlisten]     target_arch: x86_64
2020-02-09T10:42:47.193+0100 I  CONTROL  [initandlisten] options: {}
2020-02-09T10:42:47.194+0100 I  STORAGE  [initandlisten] wiredtiger_open config: create,cache_size=3584M,cache_overflow=(file_max=0M),session_max=33000,eviction=(threads_min
=4,threads_max=4),config_base=false,statistics=(fast),log=(enabled=true,archive=true,path=journal,compressor=snappy),file_manager=(close_idle_time=100000,close_scan_interval
=10,close_handle_minimum=250),statistics_log=(wait=0),verbose=[recovery_progress,checkpoint_progress],
2020-02-09T10:42:48.051+0100 I  STORAGE  [initandlisten] WiredTiger message [1581241368:51170][10615:0x7fffa57bc380], txn-recover: Set global recovery timestamp: (0, 0)
2020-02-09T10:42:48.220+0100 I  RECOVERY [initandlisten] WiredTiger recoveryTimestamp. Ts: Timestamp(0, 0)
2020-02-09T10:42:48.305+0100 I  STORAGE  [initandlisten] Timestamp monitor starting
2020-02-09T10:42:48.308+0100 I  CONTROL  [initandlisten]
2020-02-09T10:42:48.308+0100 I  CONTROL  [initandlisten] ** WARNING: Access control is not enabled for the database.
2020-02-09T10:42:48.308+0100 I  CONTROL  [initandlisten] **          Read and write access to data and configuration is unrestricted.
2020-02-09T10:42:48.308+0100 I  CONTROL  [initandlisten]
2020-02-09T10:42:48.308+0100 I  CONTROL  [initandlisten] ** WARNING: This server is bound to localhost.
2020-02-09T10:42:48.308+0100 I  CONTROL  [initandlisten] **          Remote systems will be unable to connect to this server.
2020-02-09T10:42:48.308+0100 I  CONTROL  [initandlisten] **          Start the server with --bind_ip <address> to specify which IP
2020-02-09T10:42:48.308+0100 I  CONTROL  [initandlisten] **          addresses it should serve responses from, or with --bind_ip_all to
2020-02-09T10:42:48.308+0100 I  CONTROL  [initandlisten] **          bind to all interfaces. If this behavior is desired, start the
2020-02-09T10:42:48.308+0100 I  CONTROL  [initandlisten] **          server with --bind_ip 127.0.0.1 to disable this warning.
```

The preceding command shows the status of the database in a few columns. From these `logs`, we can figure out that the server started on port `27017`. It displays the build environment, the storage engine that was used, and so on.

On Windows, we can manually download the installer binary and launch it by adding the installation `bin` directory to the `PATH` variable. Then, we can run it using the `mongod` command. Alongside the MongoDB installation comes a client shell called Mongo. We will look at it in brief in the next section.

Working with the MongoDB shell

Whenever we start using MongoDB, the first thing we need to explore is the available commands that we can use in order to interact with it. Looking up the available databases, collections, documents, and so on can be done with a simple client tool called **MongoDB shell**. It is similar to the MySQL client. This shell program is included in the standard MongoDB server installation. We can launch it using the following command:

```
mongo
```

Refer to the following screenshot:

```
> mongo
MongoDB shell version v4.2.3
connecting to: mongodb://127.0.0.1:27017/?compressors=disabled&gssapiServiceName=mongodb
Implicit session: session { "id" : UUID("6cf90f5a-5a8a-46bb-b7b8-378f6f2cbe45") }
MongoDB server version: 4.2.3
Server has startup warnings:
2020-02-09T10:42:48.308+0100 I  CONTROL  [initandlisten]
2020-02-09T10:42:48.308+0100 I  CONTROL  [initandlisten] ** WARNING: Access control is not enabled for the database.
2020-02-09T10:42:48.308+0100 I  CONTROL  [initandlisten] **          Read and write access to data and configuration is unrestricted.
2020-02-09T10:42:48.308+0100 I  CONTROL  [initandlisten]
2020-02-09T10:42:48.308+0100 I  CONTROL  [initandlisten] ** WARNING: This server is bound to localhost.
2020-02-09T10:42:48.308+0100 I  CONTROL  [initandlisten] **          Remote systems will be unable to connect to this server.
2020-02-09T10:42:48.308+0100 I  CONTROL  [initandlisten] **          Start the server with --bind_ip <address> to specify which IP
2020-02-09T10:42:48.308+0100 I  CONTROL  [initandlisten] **          addresses it should serve responses from, or with --bind_ip_all to
2020-02-09T10:42:48.308+0100 I  CONTROL  [initandlisten] **          bind to all interfaces. If this behavior is desired, start the
2020-02-09T10:42:48.308+0100 I  CONTROL  [initandlisten] **          server with --bind_ip 127.0.0.1 to disable this warning.
2020-02-09T10:42:48.308+0100 I  CONTROL  [initandlisten]
---
```

If you see that a `session` ID has been created, as shown in the preceding screenshot, everything worked fine. If you get an error, the server is probably not running as expected. To troubleshoot, have a look at the MongoDB troubleshooting guide at `https://docs.mongodb.com/manual/faq/diagnostics`. The client provides information about MongoDB versions and other warnings. To see all the available shell commands, use the `help` command.

Let's create a new collection called `movies` and insert the preceding example document into it. Follow these steps:

1. By default, the database will be a test database:

```
> show databases

admin    0.000GB
config   0.000GB
local    0.000GB
test     0.000GB
```

The preceding `show` command lists all available databases. `admin`, `config`, `test`, and `local` are the four databases available by default.

2. To create a new database or switch to an existing database, just type `use db_name`. In our case, let's name our database `appDB`. Type the following into a MongoDB shell:

```
> use appDB
```

This switches the current database to the `appDB` database. If you try to list the available databases, `appDB` won't show up because MongoDB only creates a physical database when some data is inserted into it (first collection or document).

3. Now, we can create a new collection by inserting the first document. We can insert the sample document for IMDb movies into a collection called `movies` using the following command:

```
> db.movies.insertOne({ _id: 5, name: 'Star Trek', year: 2009,
directors: ['J.J. Abrams'], writers: ['Roberto Orci', 'Alex
Kurtzman'], boxOffice: { budget:150000000, gross:257704099 } } )
{
        "acknowledged" : true,
        "insertedId" : 5
}
```

The JSON you inserted has an ID called `_id`. We can provide it while inserting a document, or MongoDB itself can generate one for you.

4. In SQL databases, we use *auto-increment* along with an `ID` schema to increment the `ID` field. Here, MongoDB generates a unique hash `ID` rather than a sequence. Let's insert one more document about `The Dark Knight`, but this time, we won't pass the `_id` field:

```
> db.movies.insertOne({ name: 'The Dark Knight ', year: 2008,
directors: ['Christopher Nolan'], writers: ['Jonathan Nolan',
'Christopher Nolan'], boxOffice: { budget:185000000,
gross:533316061 } } )
{
        "acknowledged" : true,
        "insertedId" : ObjectId("59574125bf7a73d140d5ba4a")
}
```

As shown by the acknowledgement JSON response, `insertedId` has changed to a very lengthy `59574125bf7a73d140d5ba4a`. This is the unique hash that's generated by MongoDB.

We can also insert a batch of documents at a given time using the `insertMany` function.

5. Using the `find` function without arguments on the movies collection returns all the matched documents, like this:

```
> db.movies.find()

{ "_id" : 5, "name" : "Star Trek", "year" : 2009, "directors" : [
"J.J. Abrams" ], "writers" : [ "Roberto Orci", "Alex Kurtzman" ],
"boxOffice" : { "budget" : 150000000, "gross" : 257704099 } }
{ "_id" : ObjectId("59574125bf7a73d140d5ba4a"), "name" : "The Dark
Knight ", "year" : 2008, "directors" : [ "Christopher Nolan" ],
"writers" : [ "Jonathan Nolan", "Christopher Nolan" ], "boxOffice"
: { "budget" : 185000000, "gross" : 533316061 } }
```

6. In order to return a single document, use the `findOne` function. This returns the oldest document from multiple results:

```
> db.movies.findOne()

{ "_id" : 5, "name" : "Star Trek", "year" : 2009, "directors" : [
"J.J. Abrams" ], "writers" : [ "Roberto Orci", "Alex Kurtzman" ],
"boxOffice" : { "budget" : 150000000, "gross" : 257704099 }}
```

7. How do we query documents? Querying in MongoDB is known as filtering data and returning a result. If we need to filter for movies that were released in 2008, then we can do this:

```
> db.movies.find({year: {$eq: 2008}})

{ "_id" : ObjectId("59574125bf7a73d140d5ba4a"), "name" : "The Dark
Knight ", "year" : 2008, "directors" : [ "Christopher Nolan" ],
"writers" : [ "Jonathan Nolan", "Christopher Nolan" ], "boxOffice"
: { "budget" : 185000000, "gross" : 533316061 } }
```

The filter query from the preceding MongoDB shell statement is as follows:

```
{year: {$eq: 2008}}
```

This states that the searching criterion is the `year` and that the value should be 2008. `$eq` is called a **filtering operator**, which helps to relate the condition between the field and data. It is equivalent to the = operator in SQL. In SQL, the equivalent query can be written as follows:

```
SELECT * FROM movies WHERE year=2008;
```

8. We can simplify the previously written MongoDB shell statement to the following:

```
> db.movies.find({year: 2008})
```

This filter query and the previous filter query are the same since they return the same set of documents. The former syntax is using `$eq`, which is a query operator. From now on, we'll call a *query operator* simply an *operator*.

The other main operators are as follows:

Operator	Function
$lt	Less than
$gt	Greater than
$in	In the
$lte	Less than or equal to
$ne	Not equal to

You can find all the available operators here: `https://docs.mongodb.com/manual/reference/operator/`.

9. Now, let's pose a question to ourselves. We have a requirement to fetch all the documents whose budget is more than $150,000,000. How can we filter this with the query knowledge we gained previously? Take a look at the following code snippet:

```
> db.movies.find({'boxOffice.budget': {$gt: 150000000}})

{ "_id" : ObjectId("59574125bf7a73d140d5ba4a"), "name" : "The Dark
Knight ", "year" : 2008, "directors" : [ "Christopher Nolan" ],
"writers" : [ "Jonathan Nolan", "Christopher Nolan" ], "boxOffice"
: { "budget" : 185000000, "gross" : 533316061 } }
```

As you can see, we accessed the `budget` key within the JSON using `boxOffice.budget`. The beauty of MongoDB is that it allows us to query the JSON with a lot of freedom.

10. Can't we add two or more operators to the criteria while fetching documents? Yes, we can! Let's find all the movies in the database that were released in 2009 with a budget of more than $150,000,000:

```
> db.movies.find({'boxOffice.budget': {$gt: 150000000}, year:
2009})
```

This returns nothing because we don't have any documents that match the given criteria. By default, comma-separated query fields, such as `'boxOffice.budget': {$gt: 150000000}, year: 2009`, are combined with the AND operation.

11. Now, let's relax our condition and find any movies that were either released in 2009 or had a budget of more than $150,000,000:

```
> db.movies.find({$or: [{'boxOffice.budget': {$gt: 150000000}},
{year: 2009}]})

{ "_id" : 5, "name" : "Star Trek", "year" : 2009, "directors" : [
"J.J. Abrams" ], "writers" : [ "Roberto Orci", "Alex Kurtzman" ],
"boxOffice" : { "budget" : 150000000, "gross" : 257704099 } }
{ "_id" : ObjectId("59574125bf7a73d140d5ba4a"), "name" : "The Dark
Knight ", "year" : 2008, "directors" : [ "Christopher Nolan" ],
"writers" : [ "Jonathan Nolan", "Christopher Nolan" ], "boxOffice"
: { "budget" : 185000000, "gross" : 533316061 } }
```

Here, the query is a bit different. We used an operator called $or to find the predicate of the two conditions. The result will be the criteria for fetching the documents. $or needs to be assigned to a list (see the preceding query) of JSON condition objects. Since JSON can be nested, conditions can also be nested. This style of querying might look new to people coming from a SQL background. The MongoDB team designed it to intuitively filter data. We can also write advanced queries such as inner joins, outer joins, nested queries, and so on easily in MongoDB with the clever use of operators.

12. So far, we have explored two **Create, Read, Update**, and **Delete** (CRUD) operations in order to create and read on MongoDB documents. Now, we'll look at the update and delete operations. To update a document, use the db.collection.update method. The syntax consists of the criteria and a set operation:

```
db.movies.update(CRITERIA, SET)
```

13. Let's update Star Trek (ID: 5)'s box office budget. Our goal is to change `150000000` to `200000000`:

```
db.movies.update({"_id": 5}, {$set: {"boxOffice.budget":
200000000}})
```

The first argument for the `update` method is the filter criteria. The second argument is a `$set` operator that changes the fields/sections in the document.

14. Now, let's take a look at the delete operation. We can delete a document from a given collection using the `deleteOne` and `deleteMany` functions:

```
> db.movies.deleteOne({"_id":
ObjectId("59574125bf7a73d140d5ba4a")})
{ "acknowledged" : true, "deletedCount" : 1 }
```

The argument that's passed to the `deleteOne` function is a filter criterion, which is similar to the read and update operations. All the documents that match the given criteria will be removed from the collection. The response contains a nice acknowledgment message with a count of documents that were deleted.

This and the preceding sections discussed the basics of MongoDB with the MongoDB shell. However, how we can do the same thing from a Go program? We need to use a driver package. In the next section, we'll explore the official MongoDB driver package for Go, called `mongo-driver`. MongoDB supports official drivers for major languages such as Python, Java, Ruby, and Go.

Introducing mongo-driver, an official MongoDB driver for Go

`mongo-driver` is a rich MongoDB driver that allows developers to write applications that use MongoDB as the database. The Go application can talk easily with MongoDB for all its CRUD operations using the `mongo` driver. It is an open source implementation maintained by MongoDB and can be used and modified freely. We can think of it as a wrapper around the MongoDB API. Installing the package is similar to other `go get` commands. However, in this chapter, we'll introduce a new Go package tool called `dep`.

dep is a Go package installer tool similar to Python's pip or JavaScript's npm. Follow this web page to install the dep tool on various platforms: https://golang.github.io/dep/docs/installation.html.

Let's write a Go program that inserts The Dark Knight movie document into MongoDB. Follow these steps:

1. Create a directory for our project:

   ```
   mkdir $GOPATH/src/github.com/git-user/chapter5/intro
   ```

2. Now, traverse to the intro directory and initialize the dep tool. It creates a few files so that we can track package dependencies:

   ```
   dep init
   ```

3. Add the mongo-driver dependency to dep:

   ```
   dep ensure -add "go.mongodb.org/mongo-driver/mongo@~1.0.0"
   ```

4. Create a main file, like this:

   ```
   touch $GOPATH/src/github.com/git-user/chapter5/intro/main.go
   ```

5. This is all we need to do to set up all the files and dependencies. To represent the movie and box office, we have to create structs that imitate the BSON data. These structs look like this:

   ```go
   // Movie holds a movie data
   type Movie struct {
     Name string `bson:"name"`
     Year string `bson:"year"`
     Directors []string `bson:"directors"`
     Writers []string `bson:"writers"`
     BoxOffice `bson:"boxOffice"`
   }

   // BoxOffice is nested in Movie
   type BoxOffice struct {
     Budget uint64 `bson:"budget"`
     Gross uint64 `bson:"gross"`
   }
   ```

We used `bson` tags for the struct fields. The reason we did this is that the `mongo-driver` package uses another package called `bson` to serialize Go structs into BSON format. This `bson` package needs some meta information in the form of tags to process fields. Hence, we attach a few `helper` tags. The preceding structs represent the BSON documents in memory.

6. Now, we have to import two packages called `mongo` and `options` from `mongo-driver`. The `bson` package is required if we wish to perform queries on MongoDB collections. The import section of the program looks like this:

```
package main

import (
  "context"
  "fmt"
  "log"

  "go.mongodb.org/mongo-driver/mongo"
  "go.mongodb.org/mongo-driver/mongo/options"
  "gopkg.in/mgo.v2/bson"
)
```

7. Now, in the `main` function, we have to create a database client and connect to it. This should happen in the main block of the program. As per the `mongo-driver` API, we create an instance of `ClientOptions`. The `ClientOptions` object holds details such as the database server's information (host and port) and so on. Then, we create a client using a context and the `ClientOptions` object. The context is used as a request timeout. With the help of the client, we can ping the database using the `Ping` method. If the database ping is successful, we can fetch the reference for a collection. The logic for creating a client and pinging the server looks like this:

```
clientOptions :=
options.Client().ApplyURI("mongodb://localhost:27017")
client, err := mongo.Connect(context.TODO(), clientOptions)

if err != nil {
  panic(err)
}

err = client.Ping(context.TODO(), nil)

if err != nil {
  log.Fatal(err)
}
```

```
fmt.Println("Connected to MongoDB successfully")
collection := client.Database("appDB").Collection("movies")
```

8. Now that the collection is ready, we can insert a movie record into the database. `mongo-driver` provides a method called `InsertOne` for a collection. We can insert a struct into the database collection as follows:

```
// Create a movie
darkNight := Movie{
  Name: "The Dark Knight",
  Year: "2008",
  Directors: []string{"Christopher Nolan"},
  Writers: []string{"Jonathan Nolan", "Christopher Nolan"},
  BoxOffice: BoxOffice{
    Budget: 185000000,
    Gross: 533316061,
  },
}

// Insert a document into MongoDB
_, err := collection.InsertOne(context.TODO(), darkNight)

if err != nil {
  log.Fatal(err)
}
```

9. By doing this, a record has been inserted into the database. Let's retrieve it using a query with a filter, that is, a movie with a box office budget greater than $150 million. We should create an empty movie struct to hold the result. A filter query can be constructed using the `bson.M` struct. It is a generic map that holds `KEY:VALUE` pairs and is convenient for creating BSON queries. The `collection.FindOne` method takes a filter query and returns a `SingleResult` object. We can decode that object into the empty movie struct like so:

```
queryResult := &Movie{}
// bson.M is used for building map for filter query
filter := bson.M{"boxOffice.budget": bson.M{"$gt": 150000000}}
result = collection.FindOne(context.TODO(), filter)
err = result.Decode(queryResult)

if err != nil {
  log.Fatal(err)
}

fmt.Println("Movie:", queryResult)
```

10. Finally, we disconnect from the database once our operations have been completed:

```
err = client.Disconnect(context.TODO())
if err != nil {
  panic(err)
}
fmt.Println("Disconnected from MongoDB")
```

11. We can run the entire program using the following code:

```
go run $GOPATH/src/github.com/git-user/chapter5/intro/main.go
```

The output looks as follows:

```
Connected to MongoDB successfully
Movie: &{ObjectID("5cfd106733090c1e34713c43")}
Disconnected from MongoDB
```

The result from a query can be stored in a new struct and can be serialized into JSON so that the clients can use it too. For that, you should add JSON meta tags to the struct, along with BSON tags.

RESTful API with gorilla/mux and MongoDB

In the previous chapters, we explored all the possible ways of building a RESTful API. We used basic HTTP routers, as well as many other web frameworks. However, to keep it simple, we can use gorilla/mux with mongo-driver for the MongoDB driver. In this section, we will build an end-to-end movie API while integrating the database and HTTP router. In the previous section, we learned how to create a new MongoDB document and retrieve it using mongo-driver. By consolidating our knowledge of HTTP routers and databases, we can create a movie API.

Let's create the plan so that we can create the API:

1. Prepare structs to hold movie information and the database connection.
2. Create a server for hosting the API.
3. Prepare the routes for the API endpoints.
4. Implement handlers for the routes.

We have to follow these steps to achieve our goal:

1. Create a directory to hold our project:

   mkdir $GOPATH/src/github.com/git-user/chapter5/movieAPI

2. Add a `main.go` file in the project:

   touch $GOPATH/src/github.com/git-user/chapter5/movieAPI/main.go

 Please install the `mongo-driver` package using the `dep` tool, just like we did in the previous section.

3. Let's take a look at the structs we need to create; that is, `DB`, `Movie`, and `BoxOffice`. `Movie` and `BoxOffice` hold the movie information. The `DB` struct holds a collection in a MongoDB database that can be passed across multiple functions. The code for this is as follows:

```go
type DB struct {
  collection *mongo.Collection
}

type Movie struct {
  ID interface{} `json:"id" bson:"_id,omitempty"`
  Name string `json:"name" bson:"name"`
  Year string `json:"year" bson:"year"`
  Directors []string `json:"directors" bson:"directors"`
  Writers []string `json:"writers" bson:"writers"`
  BoxOffice BoxOffice `json:"boxOffice" bson:"boxOffice"`
}

type BoxOffice struct {
  Budget uint64 `json:"budget" bson:"budget"`
  Gross uint64 `json:"gross" bson:"gross"`
}
```

4. We need a few important packages in order to implement our API. These are `gorilla/mux`, `mongo-driver`, and a few other `helper` packages. Let's look at how to import these packages:

```go
    ...
    "go.mongodb.org/mongo-driver/bson/primitive"

    "go.mongodb.org/mongo-driver/bson"
```

```
"github.com/gorilla/mux"
"go.mongodb.org/mongo-driver/mongo"
"go.mongodb.org/mongo-driver/mongo/options"
```

We need the `primitive` package to generate an `ObjectID` from a string, the `bson` package to create query filters, and the `mongo/options` package to create a MongoDB client.

5. Let's create the `main` function, which is where we create a MongoDB client. The client is created by passing options to the `Connect` method. Once we are connected to MongoDB, which is running locally on port `27017`, we can access the collection using the `Database.Collection` method. We can delay cleaning up the connection using the `defer` keyword:

```
func main() {
  clientOptions :=
    options.Client().ApplyURI("mongodb://localhost:27017")
  client, err := mongo.Connect(context.TODO(), clientOptions)
  if err != nil {
    panic(err)
  }
  defer client.Disconnect(context.TODO())

  collection := client.Database("appDB").Collection("movies")
  db := &DB{collection: collection}
  ...
}
```

The `defer` keyword is special in a Go program. It defers a function call so that it's executed right before the enclosing outer function returns. It is commonly used for I/O connection cleanup.

In our case, the enclosing function is the `main`, and the deferred function is `client.Disconnect`. So, when `main` returns/terminates, the defer statement closes the MongoDB connection properly.

6. Next, we create a few HTTP routes for the `GET` and `POST` operations on a movie. Let's call them `GetMovie` and `PostMovie`, respectively. The code looks like this:

```
r := mux.NewRouter()
r.HandleFunc("/v1/movies/{id:[a-zA-Z0-9]*}",
 db.GetMovie).Methods("GET")
r.HandleFunc("/v1/movies", db.PostMovie).Methods("POST")
```

7. Now, we can start a server using the `http.Server` method, as shown in the following code:

```
srv := &http.Server{
  Handler: r,
  Addr: "127.0.0.1:8000",
  WriteTimeout: 15 * time.Second,
  ReadTimeout: 15 * time.Second,
}
log.Fatal(srv.ListenAndServe())
}
```

8. Now comes the actual implementation of the handlers. `GetMovie`, like any other mux handler, takes response and request objects. It receives an `ObjectId` (hex string) of the movie from the path parameters and queries a matching document from the database. We can use the `mux.Vars` map to collect path parameters.

We can't simply form a filter query using the raw ID. We have to convert the hex string that was passed into the `ObjectID` using the `primitive.ObjectIDFromHex` method from the `mongo-driver/bson/primitive` package. We should use this `ObjectID` in a `filter` query.

Then, we run a query using the `collection.FindOne` method. The result can then be decoded into a `Movie` struct literal and returned as a JSON `response`. Take a look at the following code for the `GetMovie` function handler:

```
// GetMovie fetches a movie with a given ID
func (db *DB) GetMovie(w http.ResponseWriter, r *http.Request) {
  vars := mux.Vars(r)
  var movie Movie
  objectID, _ := primitive.ObjectIDFromHex(vars["id"])
  filter := bson.M{"_id": objectID}
  err := db.collection.FindOne(context.TODO(),
   filter).Decode(&movie)

  if err != nil {
    w.WriteHeader(http.StatusInternalServerError)
```

```
    w.Write([]byte(err.Error()))
  } else {
    w.Header().Set("Content-Type", "application/json")
    response, _ := json.Marshal(movie)
    w.WriteHeader(http.StatusOK)
    w.Write(response)
  }
}
```

9. `PostMovie` has the exact same function signature as the `GET` handler function. Instead of reading from the path parameters, it reads information from the request body in JSON and un-marshalls it into the `Movie` struct. Then, we use the `collection.InsertOne` method and perform a database insert operation. The result of the JSON is sent back as an HTTP response. The code for the `PostMovie` handler function looks like this:

```
// PostMovie adds a new movie to our MongoDB collection
func (db *DB) PostMovie(w http.ResponseWriter, r *http.Request) {
  var movie Movie
  postBody, _ := ioutil.ReadAll(r.Body)
  json.Unmarshal(postBody, &movie)
  result, err := db.collection.InsertOne(context.TODO(), movie)
  if err != nil {
    w.WriteHeader(http.StatusInternalServerError)
    w.Write([]byte(err.Error()))
  } else {
    w.Header().Set("Content-Type", "application/json")
    response, _ := json.Marshal(result)
    w.WriteHeader(http.StatusOK)
    w.Write(response)
  }
}
```

10. Now, let's run the program:

```
go run $GOPATH/src/github.com/git-user/chapter5/movieAPI/main.go
```

11. Next, we open a Terminal and make a `POST` API request using `curl` or `Postman` to create a new movie:

```
curl -X POST \
 http://localhost:8000/v1/movies \
 -H 'cache-control: no-cache' \
 -H 'content-type: application/json' \
 -d '{ "name" : "The Dark Knight", "year" : "2008", "directors" : [
"Christopher Nolan" ], "writers" : [ "Jonathan Nolan", "Christopher
Nolan" ], "boxOffice" : { "budget" : 185000000, "gross" : 533316061
```

```
    }
  }'
```

This returns the following response:

```
{"InsertedID":"5cfd6cf0c281945c6cfefaab"}
```

12. Our movie has been created successfully. Next, let's retrieve it. Make a GET API request using `curl`:

```
curl -X GET
http://localhost:8000/v1/movies/5cfd6cf0c281945c6cfefaab
```

It returns the same data that we got while creating the resource:

```
{"id":"5cfd6cf0c281945c6cfefaab","name":"The Dark
Knight","year":"2008","directors":["Christopher
Nolan"],"writers":["Jonathan Nolan","Christopher
Nolan"],"boxOffice":{"budget":185000000,"gross":533316061}}
```

13. We can easily add PUT (update) and DELETE methods to/from the preceding code. We just need to define two more handlers. First, look at the `UpdateMovie` handler. It gets the `ObjectID` as a path parameter in order to update a document in MongoDB, as shown in the following code:

```
// UpdateMovie modifies the data of given resource
func (db *DB) UpdateMovie(w http.ResponseWriter, r *http.Request) {
  vars := mux.Vars(r)
  var movie Movie
  putBody, _ := ioutil.ReadAll(r.Body)
  json.Unmarshal(putBody, &movie)

  objectID, _ := primitive.ObjectIDFromHex(vars["id"])
  filter := bson.M{"_id": objectID}
  update := bson.M{"$set": &movie}
  _, err := db.collection.UpdateOne(context.TODO(), filter, update)
  ...
}
```

14. Next, the handler function is `DeleteMovie`. It gets the object ID from the path parameters and tries to delete a document with the same ID in the database using the `DeleteOne` method, like this:

```
// DeleteMovie removes the data from the db
func (db *DB) DeleteMovie(w http.ResponseWriter, r *http.Request) {
  vars := mux.Vars(r)
  objectID, _ := primitive.ObjectIDFromHex(vars["id"])
  filter := bson.M{"_id": objectID}

  _, err := db.collection.DeleteOne(context.TODO(), filter)
  ...
}
```

In these API operations, we can also simply send the status back to the client with no HTTP body.

For these handlers to be activated by `gorilla/mux`, we have to register two new HTTP endpoints to the router, like this:

```
r.HandleFunc("/v1/movies/{id:[a-zA-Z0-9]*}",
db.UpdateMovie).Methods("PUT")
r.HandleFunc("/v1/movies/{id:[a-zA-Z0-9]*}",
db.DeleteMovie).Methods("DELETE")
```

The complete code for these additions is available in the `chapter5/movieAPI_updated/main.go` file. If you run the updated program, you will have a full CRUD-based API with MongoDB as a backend.

Boosting the querying performance with indexing

We all know that, while reading a book, indexes are very important. When we try to search for a topic in the book, we scroll through the index page. If the topic is found in the index, then we go to the specific page number for that topic. But there is a drawback here. We are using additional pages for the sake of this indexing. Similarly, MongoDB needs to go through all the documents whenever we query for something. If the document stores indexes for important fields, it can give us data quickly. At the same time, we should remember that extra space is required for storing indexes.

In computing, a B-tree is an important data structure for implementing indexing because it can categorize nodes. By traversing that tree, we can find the data we need in fewer steps. We can create an index using the `createIndex` function provided by MongoDB. Take an example of students and their scores in an examination. GET operations are more frequent with sorting scores. The indexing for this scenario can be visualized as follows:

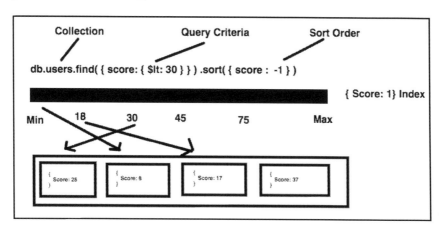

This is the official example given by the MongoDB website. The **score** is the field to be indexed because of frequent use. Once it's been indexed, the database stores the address for each document in a binary tree. Whenever someone queries this field, it checks for the range operator (in this case, it's $lt), traverses the binary tree, and gets the addresses of the documents in fewer steps. Since the score is indexed, the sort operations are less costly. So, the time that it takes for the database to return the sorted (ascending or descending) result is shorter.

Coming to our previous examples of the movies API, we can create indexes for data. By default, all the _id fields are indexed, so we are using MongoDB shell to show that. Previously, we treated the year field as a string. Let's modify that so that it's an integer and index it. Launch the MongoDB shell using the mongo command. Connect to a new database; for example, test, from a MongoDB shell and insert a document into it:

```
> db.movies.insertOne({ name: 'Star Trek',   year: 2009,   directors:
['J.J. Abrams'],   writers: ['Roberto Orci', 'Alex Kurtzman'],   boxOffice:
{      budget:150000000,      gross:257704099   } } )
{
   "acknowledged" : true,
   "insertedId" : ObjectId("595a6cc01226e5fdf52026a1")
}
```

Insert one more similar document containing different data:

```
> db.movies.insertOne({ name: 'The Dark Knight ', year: 2008, directors:
['Christopher Nolan'], writers: ['Jonathan Nolan', 'Christopher Nolan'],
boxOffice: { budget:185000000, gross:533316061 } } )
{
    "acknowledged" : true,
    "insertedId" : ObjectId("59603d3b0f41ead96110cf4f")
}
```

Now, let's add indexing to the year with the `createIndex` function:

```
db.movies.createIndex({year: 1})
```

This single line adds the magic for retrieving the database records faster. Now, all the queries related to `year` leverage the indexing:

```
> db.movies.find({year: {$lt: 2010}})
{ "_id" : ObjectId("5957397f4e5c31eb7a9ed48f"), "name" : "Star Trek",
"year" : 2009, "directors" : [ "J.J. Abrams" ], "writers" : [ "Roberto
Orci", "Alex Kurtzman" ], "boxOffice" : { "budget" : 150000000, "gross" :
257704099 } }
{ "_id" : ObjectId("59603d3b0f41ead96110cf4f"), "name" : "The Dark Knight
", "year" : 2008, "directors" : [ "Christopher Nolan" ], "writers" : [
"Jonathan Nolan", "Christopher Nolan" ], "boxOffice" : { "budget" :
185000000, "gross" : 533316061 } }
```

There is no difference in the query result. However, the lookup mechanism for documents by `MongoDB` has changed due to indexing. For a larger number of documents, this could reduce the lookup time drastically.

Indexing comes with a cost. Some queries run very slow on different fields if indexing is not done properly. We can also have compound indexes in MongoDB that can index multiple fields.

 MongoDB comes with a tool called `query planner`. To see the time of execution of a query, use the `explain` function after a `query` function, for example, `db.movies.find({year: {$lt: 2010}}).explain("executionStats")`. This explains the winning plan for a query, the time that it took in milliseconds, indexes used, and so on.

You can view the performance of indexed and non-indexed data using the `explain` function. Take a look at the MongoDB website to understand more about indexes: `https://docs.mongodb.com/manual/indexes/`.

With all the knowledge of MongoDB and the `driver` API you have under your belt, you can start developing a REST API that uses NoSQL as a backend. In the next section, we'll present a schema for delivery logistics and get you to develop a sample API.

Designing MongoDB documents for a delivery logistics API

There are many cases for which a REST API can be developed. One such case is delivery logistics. In the logistics world, many entities play an important role. To know what to implement, you need to know the terminology that's used for logistics. Here, we are going to model a few JSON documents that can be implemented for MongoDB. After going through this section, try to use this schema information as a guide to building a Logistics REST API.

The following six minimal components are essential in any delivery logistics design:

- Sender
- Receiver
- Package
- Payment
- Carrier
- Shipment

Let's look at a schema for each and every component:

1. A sender is a person sending the package:

```
{
  _id: ObjectId("5cfe142a7ba402aacb71f710"),
  first_name: "Philip",
  last_name: "Zorn",
  address: {
    type: "work"
    street: "241 Indian Spring St",
    city: "Pittsburg",
    state: "California",
    pincode: 94565,
    country: "USA"
  },
  "phone": "(xxx) yyy-zzzz"
}
```

2. A receiver receives the package from a sender:

```
{
  _id: ObjectId("5cfe142a7ba402aacb71f706"),
  first_name: "Max",
  last_name: "Charles",
  address: {
    type: "home"
    street: "Ludwig Str. 5",
    city: "Ansbach",
    state: "Bayern",
    pincode: 91522,
    country: "Deutschland"
  },
  "phone": "xx-yyyyyy-zzzzz"
}
```

3. A sender sends a package to a receiver. So, we have to model a package document that holds package information such as dimensions in centimeters and weight in grams:

```
{
  _id: ObjectId("5cfe15607ba402aacb71f711"),
  dimensions: {
    width: 21,
    height: 12
  },
  weight: 10,
  is_damaged: false,
  status: "In transit"
}
```

4. A payment transaction should be recorded when the sender buys the delivery service. It should have payment transaction details for further reference:

```
{
  _id: ObjectId("5cfe162a7ba402aacb71f713"),
  initiated_on: ISODate("2019-06-10T08:38:30.894Z"),
  successful_on: ISODate("2019-06-10T08:39:06.894Z").
  merchant_id: 112543,
  mode_of_payment: "paypal",
  payment_details: {
    transaction_token: "dfghjvbsclka76asdadn89"
  }
}
```

5. Now comes the Carrier. We have a third-party international vendor to a partner that will ship the package on our behalf:

```
{
    _id: ObjectId("5cfe1a4e7ba402aacb71f714"),
    name: "PHL International",
    carrier_code: 988,
    is_partner: true
}
```

6. Finally, with all those details, we have a shipment document that holds information about all the other stakeholders:

```
{
    _id: ObjectId("5cfe162a7ba402aacb71f712"),
    sender: ObjectId("5cfe142a7ba402aacb71f710"),
    receiver: ObjectId("5cfe142a7ba402aacb71f706"),
    package: ObjectId("5cfe15607ba402aacb71f711"),
    payment: ObjectId("5cfe162a7ba402aacb71f713"),
    carrier: ObjectId("5cfe1a4e7ba402aacb71f714"),
    promised_on: ISODate("2019-07-15T08:54:11.694Z")
}
```

A shipment contains `sender`, `receiver`, `payment`, `carrier`, and `package` details. This is a minimal document design for delivery logistics.

You can find all the previous MongoDB Shell schemas in this project's repository, that is, `chapter5/delivery_logistics`.

All the preceding schemas have been implemented to give you an idea of how a REST service can be designed for MongoDB as a storage system.

 Note that the preceding format is for MongoDB shell. Please be aware of this difference while creating the service.

Here's a coding exercise for you: *Can you create a REST service for logistics by leveraging the knowledge we gained from the initial sections of this chapter?*

Summary

We started this chapter with an introduction to MongoDB and how it solves the problems of the modern web. MongoDB is a NoSQL database that is different from traditional relational databases. Then, we learned how to install MongoDB on all platforms, how to start the MongoDB server, and we explored the features of the MongoDB shell. The MongoDB shell is a tool that can be used to quickly check or perform CRUD operations, as well as many other operations in MongoDB. We looked at operator symbols for querying. Then, we introduced Go's MongoDB driver called `mongo-driver` and learned how it's used. We created a persistent movies API with the help of `mongo-driver` and Go. Finally, we learned how to map a Go struct to a JSON document.

Not every query is efficient in MongoDB. So, for boosting query performance, we introduced the indexing mechanism, which reduces the document fetching time by arranging the documents in the order of a B-tree. We learned how to measure the execution time of a query using the `explain` command. Finally, we laid out a logistics document design by providing BSON (*MongoDB shell syntax*).

Sometimes, your REST API has to be supported with additional background services and transports. One such service is the **Remote Procedure Call** (**RPC**). When a distributed system powers a REST API, there could be thousands of RPC calls behind the scene. Those RPC calls can call different endpoints, use different data formats and transports, and so on. It is crucial to learn them if you wish to develop APIs in distributed systems. In the next chapter, we will learn how to work with an RPC method called **gRPC** and a data format called **Protocol Buffers**.

Working with Protocol Buffers and gRPC

6

In this chapter, we are going to enter the world of protocol buffers. The REST API needs support from other internal services. Those internal services can implement a **Remote Procedure Call (RPC)** and use a protocol buffer as a data exchange format. First, we will discover the benefits of using protocol buffers instead of JSON for services, and where to use both. We will use Google's `proto` library to compile protocol buffers. We will also try to write a few web services with protocol buffers that can talk to either Go, or other applications such as Python and Node.js. Then, we'll explain gRPC, an advanced simplified form of RPC. We will learn how gRPC and protocol buffers can help us build low-bandwidth services that can be consumed by different clients. Finally, we will discuss HTTP/2 and its benefits over plain HTTP/1.1-based services.

In short, we will cover the following topics:

- Introduction to protocol buffers
- Protocol buffer language
- Compiling a protocol buffer with protoc
- Introduction to gRPC
- Bidirectional streaming with gRPC

Technical requirements

You'll need to preinstall the following software in order to run the code examples in this chapter:

- OS: Linux (Ubuntu 18.04)/Windows 10/Mac OS X >=10.13
- Go's latest version compiler >= 1.13.5

You can download the code for this chapter from `https://github.com/PacktPublishing/` `Hands-On-Restful-Web-services-with-Go/tree/master/chapter6`. Clone the code and use the code samples in the `chapter6` directory.

Introduction to protocol buffers

HTTP/1.1 is the standard that is adopted by the web community. In recent times, HTTP/2 is becoming more popular because of its advantages. Some of the benefits of using HTTP/2 are as follows:

- Flow control between sender and receiver
- Better compression of HTTP headers
- Single TCP connection for bidirectional streaming
- Server push support for sending files on one TCP connection
- Support from all major browsers

The technical definition from Google about protocol buffers is as follows:

> *Protocol buffers are a flexible, efficient, automated mechanism for serializing structured data—think XML, but smaller, faster, and simpler. You define how you want your data to be structured once, then you can use the specially generated source code to easily write and read your structured data to and from a variety of data streams and using a variety of languages. You can even update your data structure without breaking deployed programs that are compiled against the "old" format.*

Let's look at this in detail. A protocol buffer is a strongly typed specification language. A tight data interface is essential for designing microservices. Protocol buffers allow us to define the data contract between multiple systems. Once a protocol buffer file has been defined, we can compile it to a target programming language. The output of this compilation will be classes and functions in the target programming language. The sender serializes data into a binary format that is transferred over the network. The receiver deserializes the data and consumes it. Basically, protocol buffers are similar to data formats such as JSON and XML, but the latter formats are text-based while protocol buffers are binary.

In Go, protocol buffers can be transported over different transports, such as HTTP/2 and **Advanced Message Queuing Protocol (AMQP)**. They are a transport format similar to JSON but strictly typed, and can only be understood between the client and the server. First, we will understand why **protocol buffers (protobufs)** exist and how to use them.

Protocol buffers have many advantages over JSON/XML for serializing structured data, such as the following:

- They have a strong interface
- They are a lot smaller than text-based data formats
- They are usually faster than JSON/XML when it comes to serialization/deserialization
- They are less ambiguous because of type and order
- They generate data access classes that are easier to use programmatically

We will prove these points while discussing a few examples later in this chapter.

Protocol buffer language

A protocol buffer is a file with minimalist language syntax. We compile a protocol buffer, and a new file is generated for a target programming language. For example, in Go, the compiled file will be a `.go` file with structs mapping the `protobuf` file. In Java, a `class` file will be created. Think of a protocol buffer as a data structure with types. The protocol buffer language provides various types that we can use to create interfaces. First, we'll discuss all the types with equivalent JSON snippets. After that, we'll implement a full example of a protocol buffer. From here on, we'll use the terms `protobuf/s` and protocol buffers interchangeably.

 Here, we are going to use `proto3` as our protobuf version. There are slight variations in versions, so please note the differences when you are using older versions.

First, let's learn how to model messages in a protobuf. A message is a resource that is transmitted to the receiver. Here, we're trying to define a simple network interface message:

```
syntax 'proto3';

message NetworkInterface {
    int index = 1;
    int mtu = 2;
    string name = 3;
    string hardwareaddr = 4;
}
```

This syntax may look new to you. In the preceding code, we were defining a message type called `NetworkInterface`. It has four fields: `index`, **maximum transmission unit** (MTU), `name`, and hardware address (MAC). If we wish to write the same in JSON, it would look like this:

```
{
    "networkInterface": {
        "index" : 0,
        "mtu" : 68,
        "name": "eth0",
        "hardwareAddr": "00:A0:C9:14:C8:29"
    }
}
```

The field names are changed to comply with the JSON style guide, but the essence and structure are the same. But what are the sequential numbers (1,2,3,4) that are given to the fields in the preceding protobuf file? They are the ordering tags that are given to serialize and deserialize protocol buffer data between two systems. It's like hinting at the protocol buffer encoding/decoding systems to write/read the data in that particular order, respectively. When the preceding protobuf file is compiled in Go as a target, the protocol buffer message will be converted into a Go struct and the fields will be filled with empty default values.

In the protobuf language, there are many basic types. Some of the important ones are as follows:

- Scalar values
- Enumerations and repeated fields
- Nested fields

We'll discuss each of them briefly in the upcoming sections.

Scalar values

The types we assigned to the fields in the `networkInterface` message are scalar types. These types are similar to Go types and match with them. For other programming languages, they will be converted into their respective types. Protobufs support many diverse types, such as `int`, `int32`, `int64`, `string`, and `bool`, which resemble Go types, but with a few variations.

They are as follows:

Go type	Protobuf type
float32	float
float64	double
uint32	fixed32
uint64	fixed64
[]byte	bytes

These types can be used while defining fields in a `protobuf` file. These fields and types in protobuf are converted into their respective Go variables and types upon being compiled. Go fills an unassigned variable with its empty value. Let's look at a few default empty values in Go for the protobuf message type:

Protobuf type	Default value
string	" "
bytes	empty bytes[]
bool	false
int, int32, int64, float, double	0
enum	0

Since protobufs make an agreement beforehand about messages and fields between end systems using a data structure, they don't take up additional space for keys like they do in JSON.

Enumerations and repeated fields

Enumerations (enum) provide the ordering of numbers for a given set of elements. The default order of values is from *0* to *n*. So, in a protocol buffer message, we can have an enumeration type. Let's look at an example of the `enum`:

```
syntax 'proto3';

message Schedule{
    enum Days{
        SUNDAY = 0;
        MONDAY = 1;
        TUESDAY = 2;
        WEDNESDAY = 3;
        THURSDAY = 4;
        FRIDAY = 5;
```

```
        SATURDAY = 6;
    }
}
```

What if we have to assign the same values for the multiple enumeration members?

Protobuf3 has an option called `allow_alias` that we can use to assign two different members the same value, like so:

```
enum EnumAllowingAlias {
    option allow_alias = true;
    UNKNOWN = 0;
    STARTED = 1;
    RUNNING = 1;
}
```

Here, `STARTED` and `RUNNING` both have a 1 tag. This means that both can have the same value in the data. If we try to remove duplicated values, we should also remove the `allow_alias` option. Otherwise, the proto compiler will throw an error (we will see what a proto compiler is shortly).

`repeated` fields are the fields in the message of a protocol buffer that represent a list of items. In JSON, we have a list of elements for a given key. Similarly, repeated fields allow us to define an array/list of elements of a particular type:

```
message Site{
    string url = 1;
    int latency = 2;
    repeated string proxies = 3;
}
```

In the preceding code, the third field is a repeated field, which means it is an array/list of proxies. The value could be something like `["100.104.112.10", "100.104.112.12"]`.

Nested fields

We can also use a message as a type of another message. It is similar to a map data structure. It is analogous to nested JSON.

For example, take a look at the following JSON code:

```
{
  "site": {
      "url": "https://example.org",
      "latency": "5ms",
```

```
    "proxies": [
      {"url": "https://example-proxy-1.org", "latency": "6ms"},
      {"url": "https://example-proxy-2.org", "latency": "4ms"}
    ]
  }
}
```

The preceding JSON contains information about a site that has a list of proxies. Each proxy is a map itself and contains details such as `url` and `latency`.

How can we model the same thing in protobufs? We can do this using the nested messages, as shown in the following code:

```
message Site {
  string url = 1;
  int latency = 2;
  repeated Proxy proxies = 3;
}

message Proxy {
  string url = 1;
  int latency = 2;
}
```

Here, we are nesting the `Proxy` type into `Site`. We will look at all of these field types soon. You can find more details about types here: `https://developers.google.com/protocol-buffers/docs/proto`.

In the next section, we'll learn about a protobuf compiler and how to use it.

Compiling a protocol buffer with protoc

So far, we have discussed how to write a protocol buffer file by defining messages and their field types. But how do we actually integrate one into our Go programs? Remember that protobufs are a format of communication between various systems, similar to JSON. But the actual data that is transferred is binary. The protoc compiler automatically generates Go structs from `.proto` files. Later, those structs can be imported to create binary data.

The following are the practical steps we follow when using protobufs in our Go programs:

1. Install the `protoc` command-line tool and the `proto` library.
2. Write a protobuf file with the `.proto` extension.
3. Compile the file so that it targets a programming language (in our case, it is Go).

4. Import structs from the generated target file and add the necessary data.
5. Serialize the data into binary format and send it to the receiver.
6. On a remote machine, the receiver deserializes the data and decodes data.

These steps can be seen in the following diagram:

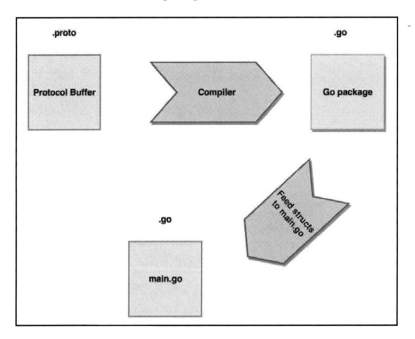

The first step is to install the protobuf compiler on our machine. For this, download the protobuf package from https://github.com/google/protobuf/releases. On Mac OS X, we can install protobuf using this command:

```
brew install protobuf
```

On Ubuntu or Linux, we can copy protoc to the /usr/bin folder:

```
# Make sure you grab the latest version
curl -OL https://github.com/protocolbuffers/protobuf/releases/download/
v3.11.3/protoc-3.11.3-linux-x86_64.zip
# Unzip
unzip protoc-3.11.3-linux-x86_64.zip -d protoc3
# Move only protoc* to /usr/bin/
sudo mv protoc3/bin/protoc /usr/bin/protoc
```

On Windows, we can just copy the executable (`.exe`) from `https://github.com/protocolbuffers/protobuf/releases/download/v3.11.3/protoc-3.11.3-win64.zip` to the `PATH` environment variable. Let's write a simple protocol buffer to illustrate how to compile and use structs from the target file. Create a folder called `protobufs` in your `GOPATH`:

```
mkdir -r $GOPATH/src/github.com/git-user/chapter6/protobufs
```

Inside protobufs, create a new directory called `protofiles`. This directory holds the compiled files from protocol buffers.

In the `protofiles` directory, create a file called `person.proto`, which models a person's information. It defines name, ID, email, and phone number. Add a few messages to it, as shown in the following code snippet:

```
syntax = "proto3";
package protofiles;

message Person {
  string name = 1;
  int32 id = 2; // Unique ID number for this person.
  string email = 3;

  enum PhoneType {
    MOBILE = 0;
    HOME = 1;
    WORK = 2;
  }

  message PhoneNumber {
    string number = 1;
    PhoneType type = 2;
  }

  repeated PhoneNumber phones = 4;
}

// Our address book file is just one of these.
message AddressBook {
  repeated Person people = 1;
}
```

Here, we created two main messages called `AddressBook` and `Person`. The `AddressBook` message contains a list of persons. A `Person` has a `name`, `id`, `email`, and `PhoneNumber`. In the second line, we declared the package as `protofiles`, like this:

```
package protofiles;
```

This tells the compiler to add the generating file in relation to the given package name. Go cannot consume this `.proto` file directly. We need to compile it to a valid Go file. When compiled, the `protofiles` package will be used to create a Go package. To compile our `person.proto` protocol buffer file, traverse to the `protofiles` directory and run the following command:

```
protoc --go_out=. *.proto
```

This command converts the given protocol buffer file(s) into the Go file(s) with the same name. After running this command, you'll see that a new file has been created in the same directory:

```
[16:20:27] git-user:protofiles git:(master*) $ ls -l
total 24
-rw-r--r-- 1 naren staff 5657 Jul 15 16:20 person.pb.go
-rw-r--r--@ 1 naren staff 433 Jul 15 15:58 person.proto
```

The new file's name is `person.pb.go`. If we open and inspect this file, we'll see that it contains automatically generated code blocks:

```
....
type Person_PhoneType int32

const (
  Person_MOBILE Person_PhoneType = 0
  Person_HOME Person_PhoneType = 1
  Person_WORK Person_PhoneType = 2
)

var Person_PhoneType_name = map[int32]string{
  0: "MOBILE",
  1: "HOME",
  2: "WORK",
}
var Person_PhoneType_value = map[string]int32{
  "MOBILE": 0,
  "HOME": 1,
  "WORK": 2,
}
.....
```

This is just one part of that file. Many getter and setter methods will be created for the given structs, such as `Person` and `AddressBook`, in the output file.

The preceding `person.pb.go` package is automatically generated boilerplate by the `proto` compiler. We need to consume that package in the main program to create protocol buffer strings. Now, we should create the `main.go` file, which uses the `Person` struct from the `person.pb.go` file like this:

```
touch -p $GOPATH/src/github.com/git-
user/chapter6/protobufs/basicExample/main.go
```

Now, for Go to serialize a struct into binary format, we need to install the Go `proto` driver. Install it using the `go get` command:

```
go get github.com/golang/protobuf/proto
```

The goal of the program we are going to create is to read the `Person` struct from the auto-generated package and serialize it into a buffer string using the `proto.Marshal` method. The fill the `main.go` like this:

```
package main

import (
  "fmt"

  "github.com/golang/protobuf/proto"
  pb "github.com/git-user/chapter6/protobufs/protofiles"
)

func main() {
  p := &pb.Person{
    Id: 1234,
    Name: "Roger F",
    Email: "rf@example.com",
    Phones: []*pb.Person_PhoneNumber{
      {Number: "555-4321", Type: pb.Person_HOME},
    },
  }

  p1 := &pb.Person{}
  body, _ := proto.Marshal(p)
  _ = proto.Unmarshal(body, p1)
  fmt.Println("Original struct loaded from proto file:", p, "\n")
  fmt.Println("Marshalled proto data: ", body, "\n")
  fmt.Println("Unmarshalled struct: ", p1)
}
```

Here, we are importing the **protocol buffer** (pb) from the `protofiles` package. We
initialized the `Person` struct with details. Then, we serialized the struct using
the `proto.Marshal` function. If we run this program, the output looks like this:

```
go run $GOPATH/src/github.com/git-
user/chapter6/protobufs/basicExample/main.go

Original struct loaded from proto file: name:"Roger F" id:1234
email:"rf@example.com" phones:<number:"555-4321" type:HOME >

Marshaled proto data: [10 7 82 111 103 101 114 32 70 16 210 9 26 14 114 102
64 101 120 97 109 112 108 101 46 99 111 109 34 12 10 8 53 53 53 45 52 51 50
49 16 1]

Unmarshaled struct: name:"Roger F" id:1234 email:"rf@example.com"
phones:<number:"555-4321" type:HOME >
```

The second output of the marshaled data is not obvious because the `proto` library serializes
data into binary bytes. Another good thing about protocol buffers in Go is that the structs
that are generated by compiling the proto files can be used to generate JSON on the fly.
Let's modify the preceding example into a new program. Call it `jsonExample`:

```
touch -p
$GOPATH/src/github.com/narenaryan/chapter6/protobufs/jsonExample/main.go
```

In this program, we'll use JSON's marshaler instead of protobuf's marshaler. The beauty of
the Go interfaces is that it allows the protocol buffer struct to be an input for different types
of marshalers. The following is the modified code for converting the `Person` struct into
JSON:

```go
package main

import (
  "fmt"

  "encoding/json"
  pb "github.com/git-user/chapter6/protobufs/protofiles"
)

func main() {
  p := &pb.Person{
    Id: 1234,
    Name: "Roger F",
    Email: "rf@example.com",
    Phones: []*pb.Person_PhoneNumber{
      {Number: "555-4321", Type: pb.Person_HOME},
    },
```

```
  }
  body, _ := json.Marshal(p)
  fmt.Println(string(body))
}
```

If we run this, it prints a JSON string that can be sent to any client that can understand JSON:

```
go run $GOPATH/src/github.com/git-
user/chapter6/protobufs/jsonExample/main.go
```

```
{"name":"Roger
F","id":1234,"email":"rf@example.com","phones":[{"number":"555-4321","type"
:1}]}
```

Any other web service/receiver can easily consume this JSON string instantly. So, what is the benefit of using protocol buffers instead of JSON? First of all, protocol buffers are intended for two backend systems to communicate with each other with a strong interface and smaller payload size. Since the size of the binary is less than the text, the protocol marshaled data is always significantly smaller than the JSON text.

 The output that's generated by a `protobuf` compiler is nothing but a plain Go struct. This allows you to convert from and protobuf into JSON easily.

Protocol buffers are just a data format. They need a mode of transport to move between systems. We saw how RPC works and also created an RPC client and server in Chapter 3, *Working with Middleware and RPC*. Now, we are going to extend that knowledge to use a **Google Remote Procedure Call** (**gRPC**) with protocol buffers to efficiently transfer data. A server and a client, in this case, can talk with each other in the protocol buffer format.

Introduction to gRPC

gRPC is a transport mechanism that sends and receives messages between two systems. Traditionally, these systems are a server and a client. As we described in the previous chapters, RPC can be implemented in Go for transferring JSON. We called it a **JSON RPC** service. Similarly, gRPC is specially designed to transfer data in the form of protocol buffers.

gRPC makes service creation easy and elegant. It provides a nice set of APIs that we can use to define services and start running them. In this section, we will focus on how to create a gRPC service and how to use it. The main advantage of gRPC is that it can be understood by multiple programming languages. Protocol buffers provide a common data structure. So, this combination enables seamless communication between various tech stacks and systems. This is the integral concept of distributed computing.

Square, Netflix, and many other giants leverage this gRPC to scale their huge traffic-prone services. Google uses gRPC heavily for their web services. We can leverage it to get better throughput between two internal services.

We need to install the `grpc` Go library and a `protoc-gen` plugin before writing the services. Install them using the following commands:

```
go get google.golang.org/grpc
go get -u github.com/golang/protobuf/protoc-gen-go
```

gRPC has the following benefits over a traditional HTTP/REST/JSON architecture:

- gRPC uses HTTP/2, which is a binary protocol.
- Header compression is possible in HTTP/2, which means less overhead.
- We can multiplex many requests on one connection.
- We can use protobufs for strict typing of data.
- Streaming requests or responses, instead of using a request/response transaction, is possible.

Take a look at the following diagram:

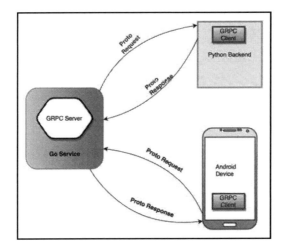

The preceding diagram clearly shows that any back-end system or mobile app can directly communicate to a gRPC server using a protocol buffer. Let's write a money transaction service in Go using gRPC and protocol buffers. A service in gRPC is an RPC contract. It takes a message and returns another message.

The steps for implementing the money transaction service are as follows:

1. Create the protocol buffer with the definitions of service and messages.
2. Compile the protocol buffer file.
3. Use the generated Go package to create a gRPC server.
4. Create a gRPC client that talks to the server.

To understand these steps, let's create the project directories for our upcoming example, like so:

```
mkdir -r $GOPATH/src/github.com/git-user/chapter6/grpcExample
mkdir -r $GOPATH/src/github.com/git-user/chapter6/grpcExample/protofiles
```

Create a file called `transaction.proto` for defining gRPC services:

```
touch -p $GOPATH/src/github.com/git-user/chapter6/grpcExample/protofiles/transaction.proto
```

Now, in the `transaction.proto` file, define the service and transaction messages, like this:

```
syntax = "proto3";
package protofiles;

message TransactionRequest {
    string from = 1;
    string to = 2;
    float amount = 3;
}

message TransactionResponse {
  bool confirmation = 1;
}

service MoneyTransaction {
    rpc MakeTransaction(TransactionRequest) returns (TransactionResponse)
{}
}
```

This is a simple protocol buffer for a money transaction on the server. We introduced the `message` keyword when we discussed protocol buffers. The new keyword, `service`, defines a gRPC service. This new keyword is solely related to gRPC, and the `protoc-gen-go` helper plugin translates it into an understandable format via the `protoc` compiler. Now, let's compile this file using `protoc` from the `grpcExample` directory:

```
protoc -I protofiles/ protofiles/transaction.proto --
go_out=plugins=grpc:protofiles
```

This command is slightly bigger than the compile command we used previously. This is because we are using the `protoc-gen-go` plugin. This command simply says to use data files as the input directory for proto files and use the same directory for outputting the target Go files. Now, if we list the `protofiles` directory, we'll see an autogenerated file called `transaction.pb.go`:

```
ls protofiles
-rw-r--r-- 1 git-user staff 6215 Jan 16 17:28 transaction.pb.go
-rw-r--r-- 1 git-user staff 294 Jan 16 17:28 transaction.proto
```

Now, we have to build a server and client that consumes previously built protobufs. Create two more directories for the server and client logic in `grpcExample`, like this:

```
mkdir grpcServer grpcClient
```

Let's create a grPC server first. Add a file called `server.go` to the `grpcServer` directory, which implements the transaction service. Our goal is to create a server that collects a transaction request from the client and returns the confirmation.

We need the help of more packages here, that is, `context` and `reflection`. `context` is used to create a `context` variable, which lives throughout an RPC request's lifetime. Both of these libraries are used by gRPC for its internal functions:

```
import (
    ...
    pb "github.com/git-user/chapter6/grpcExample/protofiles"
    "golang.org/x/net/context"
    "google.golang.org/grpc"
    "google.golang.org/grpc/reflection"
)
```

If we open the autogenerated `transaction.pb.go` package in `protofiles`, we can clearly see that there are two important things:

- The `MakeTransaction` function, as part of the `MoneyTransactionServer` interface
- The `RegisterMoneyTransactionServer` function

`MakeTransaction` is used for implementing the service. Let's take a look at the implementation. It defines a struct and a method. This method performs the money transaction using the data that's supplied via the `*pb.TransactionRequest` argument:

```
// server is used to create MoneyTransactionServer.
type server struct{}

// MakeTransaction implements MoneyTransactionServer.MakeTransaction
func (s *server) MakeTransaction(ctx context.Context, in
*pb.TransactionRequest) (*pb.TransactionResponse, error) {
  // Use in.Amount, in.From, in.To and perform transaction logic
  return &pb.TransactionResponse{Confirmation: true}, nil
}
```

`MakeTransaction` contains the RPC request details. It is basically a struct that maps to the `TransactionRequest` message we defined in the protocol buffer file. What's returned from `MakeTransaction` is `TransactionResponse`. This function signature matches with the one we defined in the protocol buffer file initially:

```
rpc MakeTransaction(TransactionRequest) returns (TransactionResponse) {}
```

Now comes the main block. Here, we have to create an instance of the gRPC server and register the server struct with it. We run this gRPC server on port `50051`:

```
const (
    port = ":50051"
)

func main() {
  lis, err := net.Listen("tcp", port)
  ...
  s := grpc.NewServer()
  pb.RegisterMoneyTransactionServer(s, &server{})
  reflection.Register(s)
  if err := s.Serve(lis); err != nil {
    log.Fatalf("Failed to serve: %v", err)
  }
}
```

Now, we need to write a client. Add a file called `client.go` in the `grpcClient` directory. The client should dial the server and acquire a connection. Using that connection, we can call remote functions and get the results. A gRPC client also uses the same protobuf boilerplate classes so that it's in sync with the server. The following is the code for the client:

```
package main

import (
  "log"

  pb "github.com/git-user/chapter6/grpcExample/protofiles"
  "golang.org/x/net/context"
  "google.golang.org/grpc"
)

const (
  address = "localhost:50051"
)

func main() {
  // Set up a connection to the server.
  conn, err := grpc.Dial(address, grpc.WithInsecure())
  ...
  // Create a client
  c := pb.NewMoneyTransactionClient(conn)
  from := "1234"
  to := "5678"
  amount := float32(1250.75)

  // Make a server request.
  r, err := c.MakeTransaction(context.Background(),
  &pb.TransactionRequest{From: from,
    To: to, Amount: amount})
  ...
}
```

This client is also using the `grpc` package. It uses an empty context called `context.Background()` to pass to the `MakeTransaction` function. The second argument of the function is the `TransactionRequest` struct:

```
&pb.TransactionRequest{From: from, To: to, Amount: amount}
```

Now, let's run both the server and the client and view the output. Open a new console and run the gRPC server by using the following command:

```
go run $GOPATH/src/github.com/git-user/chapter6/grpcExample/grpcServer/
server.go
```

The TCP server starts listening on port `50051`. Now, open one more Terminal/shell and start the client program that talks to this server:

```
go run $GOPATH/src/github.com/git-user/chapter6/grpcExample/grpcClient/
client.go
```

It prints the output of the successful transaction:

```
2020/01/10 19:13:16 Transaction confirmed: true
```

At the same time, the server logs this message to the console:

```
2020/01/10 19:13:16 Amount: 1250.750000, From A/c:1234, To A/c:5678
```

Here, the client made a single request to the gRPC server and passed details of the `From A/c` number, the `To A/c` number, and `Amount`. The server picks those details, processes them, and sends a response saying everything is fine.

> A gRPC client can request a gRPC server to perform a computation-heavy/secure operation. The client can be a mobile device too.

The full programs can be found in this chapter's project repository. In the next section, we'll look at bidirectional streaming in gRPC.

Bidirectional streaming with gRPC

The main advantage of gRPC over traditional HTTP/1.1 is that it can use a single TCP connection for sending and receiving multiple messages between the server and the client. We saw the example of a money transaction previously. Another real-world use case is a GPS installed in a taxi. Here, the taxi is the client that sends its geographical points to the server along its route. Finally, the server can calculate the total fare amount depending on the time spent between points and the total distance.

Another use case is a server pushing data to a client. This is called a server push model, where a server can send a stream of results back to the client. This is different from polling, where the client creates a new request/response cycle each and every time. The server push can be very handy for building real-time applications. Let's implement an example to illustrate this:

1. Create a project called `serverPush`, like this:

```
mkdir -r $GOPATH/src/github.com/git-user/chapter6/serverPush
mkdir -r $GOPATH/src/github.com/git-user/chapter6/serverPush/
protofiles
```

2. Now, add the transactions to `protofiles`, a protocol buffer that is similar to the one that we used in the previous gRPC money transaction example, except the return type of `MakeTransaction` is a stream:

```
syntax = "proto3";
package protofiles;

message TransactionRequest {
    string from = 1;
    string to = 2;
    float amount = 3;
}

message TransactionResponse {
    string status = 1;
    int32 step = 2;
    string description = 3;
}

service MoneyTransaction {
    rpc MakeTransaction(TransactionRequest) returns (stream
        TransactionResponse) {}
}
```

We have two messages and one service defined in the protocol buffer file. The exciting part is in the service; we are returning a stream instead of a plain response:

```
rpc MakeTransaction(TransactionRequest) returns (stream
TransactionResponse) {}
```

The use case of this project is that *the client sends a money transfer request to the server, the server does a few tasks, and then sends those step details as a stream of responses back to the server.*

3. Now, let's compile the `.proto` file:

```
protoc -I protofiles/ protofiles/transaction.proto
  --go_out=plugins=grpc:protofiles
```

This creates a new file called `transaction.pb.go` in the `protofiles` directory. We use the definitions in this file in our server and client programs, which we will create shortly.

4. Now, let's write the gRPC server code. This code is a bit different compared to the previous example because of the introduction of streams:

```
mkdir $GOPATH/src/github.com/git-user/chapter6/serverPush/
grpcServer
touch $GOPATH/src/github.com/git-user/chapter6/serverPush/
grpcServer/server.go
```

We skip the imports and look at the main logic of the program. The main function is similar to the previous gRPC example, but the most interesting thing is the handler. Let's say the handler takes the request from the client and performs three steps. At the end of each step, the server sends a notification to the client. It is a long-living connection, unlike the one-time RPC call we saw earlier. The following is the code for streaming `MakeTransaction`:

```
const (
  port = ":50051"
  noOfSteps = 3
)

// MakeTransaction implements
MoneyTransactionServer.MakeTransaction
func (s *server) MakeTransaction(in *pb.TransactionRequest, stream
pb.MoneyTransaction_MakeTransactionServer) error {
  log.Printf("Got request for money transfer....")
  log.Printf("Amount: $%f, From A/c:%s, To A/c:%s", in.Amount,
   in.From, in.To)
  // Send streams here
  for i := 0; i < noOfSteps; i++ {
    time.Sleep(time.Second * 2)
    // Once task is done, send the successful message
    // back to the client
    if err := stream.Send(&pb.TransactionResponse{Status: "good",
```

```
    Step: int32(i),
    Description: fmt.Sprintf("Performing step %d",
     int32(i))}); err != nil {
    log.Fatalf("%v.Send(%v) = %v", stream, "status", err)
   }
  }
  log.Printf("Successfully transferred amount $%v from %v to %v",
   in.Amount, in.From, in.To)
  return nil
 }
```

`MakeTransaction` takes a request and a stream as its arguments. In the function, we are looping through the number of steps (here, there are three) and performing the computation. The server is simulating the mock I/O or computation using the `time.Sleep` function. The crucial server method for sending a message is `Send`:

```
    stream.Send()
```

This function sends a stream response from the server to the client.

5. Now, let's compose the client program. This is also a bit different from the basic gRPC client that we saw in the money transaction example's client code. Create a new directory for the client program:

```
mkdir $GOPATH/src/github.com/git-user/chapter6/serverPush/
grpcClient
touch $GOPATH/src/github.com/git-user/chapter6/serverPush/
grpcClient/cilent.go
```

6. Now, the client should listen indefinitely for the stream of messages. For that, we used a `for loop` and `break`. Let's modify our previous client handler into a new one called `ReceiveStream`:

```
// ReceiveStream listens to the stream contents and use them
func ReceiveStream(client pb.MoneyTransactionClient,
 request *pb.TransactionRequest) {
  log.Println("Started listening to the server stream!")
  stream, err := client.MakeTransaction(context.Background(),
   request)
  if err != nil {
    log.Fatalf("%v.MakeTransaction(_) = _, %v", client, err)
  }
  // Listen to the stream of messages
  for {
    response, err := stream.Recv()
    if err == io.EOF {
```

```
      // If there are no more messages, get out of loop
      break
    }
    if err != nil {
      log.Fatalf("%v.MakeTransaction(_) = _, %v", client, err)
    }
    log.Printf("Status: %v, Operation: %v", response.Status,
     response.Description)
    }
  }
```

Here, `ReceiveStream` is the custom function we wrote for the sake of sending a request and receiving a stream of messages. It takes two arguments: `MoneyTransactionClient` and `TransactionRequest`. It uses the first argument to create a stream and starts listening to it. Whenever the server exhausts all the messages, the client will stop listening and terminate. Then, an `io.EOF` error will be returned if the client tries to receive messages. We are logging the responses that we collected from the gRPC server. The second argument, `TransactionRequest`, is used to send the request to the server for the first time. Running this will make this process clearer to us.

 The imports and main logic for the server and client are dropped for brevity. Please refer to this project's repository for the complete programs: `chapter6/serverPush`.

7. On the first Terminal, run the gRPC server:

```
go run $GOPATH/src/github.com/git-user/chapter6/serverPush/
grpcServer/server.go
```

It will keep on listening for incoming requests.

8. Now, run the client on the second Terminal to see it in action:

```
go run $GOPATH/src/github.com/git-user/chapter6/serverPush/
grpcClient/client.go
```

This outputs the following to the console:

```
2019/06/10 20:43:53 Started listening to the server stream!
2019/06/10 20:43:55 Status: good, Operation: Performing step 0
2019/06/10 20:43:57 Status: good, Operation: Performing step 1
2019/06/10 20:43:59 Status: good, Operation: Performing step 2
```

At the same time, the server also logs its own messages on the first Terminal:

```
2017/07/16 15:08:15 Got request for money Transfer....
2017/07/16 15:08:15 Amount: $1250.750000, From A/c:1234, To
A/c:5678
2017/07/16 15:08:21 Successfully transferred amount $1250.75 from
1234 to 5678
```

This process happens in sync with the server. The client stays alive until the last streaming message is sent back. The server can handle any number of clients at a given time. Every client request is considered an individual entity. This is an example of the server sending a stream of responses. There are other use cases that can also be implemented with protocol buffers and gRPC:

- The client sends streamed requests to get one final response from the server
- The client and server can both send streamed requests and responses at the same time

The official gRPC team has provided a nice example of routing a taxi on GitHub. You can take a look at it to learn more about the functionality of bidirectional streams at `https://github.com/grpc/grpc-go/tree/master/examples/route_guide`.

Summary

In this chapter, we started our journey by understanding the basics of protocol buffers. Then, we came across the protocol buffers language, which has many types, such as scalar, enumeration, and repeated types. We look at a few analogies between JSON and protocol buffers. We learned that protocol buffers are more memory-efficient than the plain JSON data format as the former are binary-based.

Next, we installed the `protoc` compiler to compile our files written in the protocol buffer language. Then, we learned how to compile a `.proto` file to generate a `.go` file with boilerplate code. This Go file contains all the structs and interfaces for the main program to consume. Next, we wrote a protocol buffer for an address book and person.

Then, we moved on to gRPC, an RPC technology from Google that uses protocol buffers. We saw the benefits of HTTP/2 and gRPC. Then, we defined a gRPC service and some data in the form of protocol buffers. Next, we implemented a gRPC server and gRPC with respect to the file we generated from `.proto`.

gRPC technology provides a bidirectional and full-duplex transport mechanism for stream data. This means that it can use a single TCP connection for all its message transmissions. We implemented one such scenario where the client sends a message to a server and the server replies with a stream of messages.

In the next chapter, we will learn about using PostgreSQL as backend storage for an API. There, we'll learn how to work with a relational database and Go. We'll also learn how to run a database in the form of a Docker container.

7
Working with PostgreSQL, JSON, and Go

In this chapter, we are going to take a bird's-eye view of SQL. In the previous chapters, we discussed SQLite3, which is a lightweight database for quick prototyping. But when it comes to developing an enterprise-grade application, MySQL or PostgreSQL is the preferred choice. Both are well-proven, heavy-duty databases that are open source. In this chapter, we'll pick PostgreSQL as our main subject.

First, we'll discuss the internals of PostgreSQL, and then move on to use the database with Go. The goal of this chapter is to make the reader comfortable working with PostgreSQL and Go. We'll also build a URL-shortening service that requires a database layer.

In this chapter, we will cover the following topics:

- Discussing PostgreSQL installation options
- Introducing pq, a pure PostgreSQL database driver for Go
- Implementing a URL-shortening service using PostgreSQL and pq
- Exploring the JSONStore feature in PostgreSQL

Technical requirements

The following software should be pre-installed in order to run the code samples:

- Operating system: Linux (Ubuntu 18.04)/Windows 10/MacOS X >= 10.13
- Software: Docker >= 18 (Docker Desktop for Windows and MacOS X)
- Go compiler: stable version >= 1.13.5
- PostgreSQL: stable version >= 10.8

You can download the code for this chapter from `https://github.com/PacktPublishing/Hands-On-Restful-Web-services-with-Go/tree/master/chapter7`. Clone the code, and use the code samples in the `chapter7` directory.

Discussing PostgreSQL installation options

PostgreSQL is an open source database that can be installed on multiple platforms. There are two standard options to install PostgreSQL:

- Manual server installation on a machine
- Installation in a Docker container

Manual installation on an operating system can be a universal installation. You can find instructions for installation at this official PostgreSQL link: `https://www.postgresql.org/download/`.

For MacOS X and Windows, you get straightforward installers. For the varieties of Linux, the PostgreSQL website has nice documentation with detailed instructions. The only drawback with universal installation is you are bound to install/uninstall the PostgreSQL database whenever you change the version. In container-based systems, the execution environment is isolated from the host system. Docker is one such popular container system. In the upcoming subsection, we'll look at the installation of PostgreSQL inside a Docker container.

Installing via Docker

We can also install PostgreSQL via Docker. This is the most common approach these days because of reduced complexity and an easy installation process. Assuming Docker is set up on your machine, proceed as follows:

1. The latest stable version is `10.8`. Pull a Docker image with the version as a tag, like this:

   ```
   docker pull postgres:10.8
   ```

2. See a list of all the images available with the following command:

   ```
   docker images
   ```

3. Start a PostgreSQL server on port 5432 inside a container by mapping the database file to a local file, like this:

```
docker run --name postgres-local -p 5432:5432 -v ~/.postgres-
data:/var/lib/postgresql/data  -e POSTGRES_PASSWORD=YOUR_PASSWORD -
d postgres:10.8
```

This starts the PostgreSQL server on localhost:5432. It also mounts the PostgreSQL database's data directory to a local directory named postgres-data.

Replace YOUR_PASSWORD with an actual password while running the preceding command. The -d option is used in the command to run the container as a daemon process. Now, the PostgreSQL server is running on our machine. It uses the postgres:10.8 Docker image we pulled previously.

 We can also use the docker run command without pulling the image. The docker pull command is to explicitly show that we are using the postgres image.

Once we have installed PostgreSQL, we have to create default users to access the database. We'll look at this in the next section.

Adding users and databases in PostgreSQL

Now, we can create a new user and database. For this, we are going to use Ubuntu/MacOS X as a general example. We do this in a shell called the psql shell. We can see all available commands in psql using the \? command. In order to enter the psql shell, first, change to the postgres user. On Ubuntu, for universal installation, you can enter the psql shell using the following command:

```
sudo su postgres
```

Now, it turns us into a user called postgres. Then, launch the psql shell using the following command:

```
psql
```

In the case of PostgreSQL running in a Docker container, use this command to launch the psql shell directly:

```
docker exec -i -t postgres-local-1 psql -U postgres
```

Once you are in the `psql` shell, type the `\?` help command in there, and you will see the output of all available commands, as shown in the following screenshot:

```
Informational
  (options: S = show system objects, + = additional detail)
  \d[S+]                    list tables, views, and sequences
  \d[S+]      NAME          describe table, view, sequence, or index
  \da[S]      [PATTERN]     list aggregates
  \dA[+]      [PATTERN]     list access methods
  \db[+]      [PATTERN]     list tablespaces
  \dc[S+]     [PATTERN]     list conversions
  \dC[+]      [PATTERN]     list casts
  \dd[S]      [PATTERN]     show object descriptions not displayed elsewhere
  \ddp        [PATTERN]     list default privileges
  \dD[S+]     [PATTERN]     list domains
  \det[+]     [PATTERN]     list foreign tables
  \des[+]     [PATTERN]     list foreign servers
  \deu[+]     [PATTERN]     list user mappings
```

To list all available users and their privileges, you will find the following command in the `Informational` section of the help shell:

```
\du - List roles
```

A role is the access permission given to a user. With the `\du` command, you can see that the default user is `postgres`, with the following roles attached:

```
postgres  | Superuser, Create role, Create DB, Replication, Bypass RLS
```

We need a new user to work with PostgreSQL. To add a new user, just type this `SQL` command in the `psql` shell:

```
CREATE ROLE git-user with LOGIN PASSWORD 'YOUR_PASSWORD'; # Caution: Choose
strong password here
```

This creates a new user with the name `gituser` and the password `YOUR_PASSWORD`. Now, give permission to the user to create databases and further roles, using the following command:

```
ALTER USER gituser CREATEDB, CREATEROLE;
```

In order to delete a user, use the `DROP` command in the same context, like this:

```
DROP ROLE git-user;
```

Don't try to change the password for the default `postgres` user. It is intended to be a superuser account, and should not be kept as a normal user. Instead, create a new role and give the required permissions for it. Use strong passwords.

If you don't use a **command-line interface** (**CLI**), you can install a **graphical user interface** (**GUI**) client such as **pgAdmin 4** for accessing the database.

 You can find more details about installing **pgAdmin 4** as a Docker application here: `https://hub.docker.com/r/dpage/pgadmin4/`.

Now we know how to create a role, let's see a few more **create**, **read**, **update**, and **delete** (**CRUD**) SQL commands that are common in most relational databases. Take a look at the following table:

Action	SQL command
Create a database	`CREATE DATABASE mydb;`

Create a table	`CREATE TABLE products (`
	`    product_no integer,`
	`    name text,`
	`    price numeric`
	`);`

Insert into table	`INSERT INTO products VALUES (1, 'Rice', 5.99);`
Update table	`UPDATE products SET price = 10 WHERE price = 5.99;`
Delete from table	`DELETE FROM products WHERE price = 5.99;`

These basic commands can be supported by many advanced SQL operators, such as `LIMIT`, `ORDER BY`, and `GROUP BY`. SQL has many other concepts, such as joining relations over tables.

 You can find more details about SQL queries that are supported by PostgreSQL here: `https://www.postgresql.org/docs/10/sql.html`.

In the next section, we'll see how Go programs communicate with the PostgreSQL server. We'll try to leverage a database driver called `pq`. Using that driver package, we'll see an example of how to insert a web URL into PostgreSQL.

Introducing pq, a pure PostgreSQL database driver for Go

In Chapter 4, *Simplifying RESTful Services with Popular Go Frameworks*, we used a driver package called go-sqlite3 to work with SQLite3. In the same way, pq is a database driver package available for Go. We can install that library system-wide by using the go get command, as follows:

```
go get github.com/lib/pq
```

We can also use the dep tool to install this package. We'll use it in this example. Let's look at the steps for installation here:

1. Create a new project directory called basicExample in GOPATH, as follows:

   ```
   touch -p $GOPATH/src/github.com/git-user/chapter7/basicExample
   ```

2. Now, traverse to the basicExample directory and use dep to install the pq package in the directory, like this:

   ```
   dep init
   dep ensure --add github.com/lib/pq
   ```

   This creates a few configuration files and adds a package to the vendor in the same directory. Now, we can create our program and use that pq package.

3. In order to create a new table, we should create a new database in the PostgreSQL server. To create a new database, enter the psql shell or use **pgAdmin 4**, as shown in the following command (you only have to do this once):

   ```
   CREATE DATABASE mydb;
   ```

Let's look at a short example that explains the usage of the pq driver. In the later sections, we'll implement a URL-shortening service. This a pre-step for that service. We'll create a table called web_url for our purpose by following these steps:

1. Create a directory called helper in the project, as follows:

   ```
   mkdir $GOPATH/src/github.com/git-user/chapter7/basicExample/helper
   ```

   This helps in initiating database operations such as creating a table.

2. Now, add a file called `models.go`. This file is going to have the table creation logic. We use `sql.Open` to make a connection to PostgreSQL. That function takes a database type and a database string as arguments. We can prepare a SQL statement using the `db.Prepare` command.

3. Import the necessary packages in the program, like this:

```
package helper

import (
    "database/sql"
    "fmt"
    "log"

    _ "github.com/lib/pq" // sql behavior modified
)
```

4. Now, create a few constants that hold database-connection information. A database connection needs a hostname, a port, a username, a password, and a database name, as shown in the following code block:

```
const (
    host = "127.0.0.1"
    port = 5432
    user = "git-user"
    password = "YOUR_PASSWORD"
    dbname = "mydb"
)
```

The password should be the one you passed when creating the user.

5. Next, create a function called `InitDB`. It uses a connection string to open a new database connection to PostgreSQL. After a successful connection, it should prepare a SQL statement to create a table called `web_url`. The code for the function looks like this:

```
func InitDB() (*sql.DB, error) {
    var connectionString = fmt.Sprintf("host=%s port=%d user=%s "+
        "password=%s dbname=%s sslmode=disable",
        host, port, user, password, dbname)

    var err error
    db, err := sql.Open("postgres", connectionString)

    if err != nil {
        return nil, err
    }
```

```
        stmt, err := db.Prepare("CREATE TABLE IF NOT EXISTS web_url(ID
    SERIAL PRIMARY KEY, URL TEXT NOT NULL);")

        if err != nil {
            return nil, err
        }

        _, err = stmt.Exec()

        if err != nil {
            return nil, err
        }

        return db, nil
    }
```

The `sql.Open` method opens the connection string. It then prepares and executes a `CREATE TABLE` query to create a `web_url` table if this does not already exist. `InitDB` returns an error if any operation fails on the database.

6. Let's create a `main.go` program to use the `helper` package, as follows:

   mkdir $GOPATH/src/github.com/git-user/chapter7/basicExample/main.go

7. In the `main` block, we can import an `InitDB` helper function and use it like this:

```
    package main

    import (
        "log"

        "github.com/git-user/chapter7/basicExample/helper"
    )

    func main() {
        _, err := helper.InitDB()
        if err != nil {
            log.Println(err)
        }

        log.Println("Database tables are successfully initialized.")
    }
```

This program imports the `helper` package and uses the `InitDB` function from it. We log a successful initialization message if the table was successfully created; otherwise, we log an error.

8. If you run the program, you will see this message printed:

```
go run main.go

2020/02/13 22:15:34 Database tables are successfully initialized.
```

This creates a `web_url` table in the `mydb` database.

9. We can cross-check that by entering into the `psql` shell and typing the following:

```
\c mydb \dt
```

This connects the user to the `mydb` database and lists all available tables, as shown in the following code snippet:

```
You are now connected to database "mydb" as user "postgres".
 List of relations
 Schema | Name | Type | Owner
--------+---------+-------+-------
 public | web_url | table | user
(1 row)
```

In PostgreSQL, the `AUTO_INCREMENT` type needs to be replaced by `SERIAL` while providing a schema for table creation.

As we promised earlier, in the next section, we will try to implement a URL-shortening service. We'll initially lay out the basics required for building such a service. Then, we'll move on to the implementation. The URL-shortening service will give you a clear understanding of how PostgreSQL can be used to solve problems.

Implementing a URL-shortening service using PostgreSQL and pq

Let's code the URL-shortening service to explain all the concepts we discussed in the preceding section. We need a few basics before writing an API for our service. First, we need to design a package that implements the `Base62` algorithm with encoding/decoding functions. The URL-shortening technique needs the `Base62` algorithm to convert a long URL to a short one, and vice versa. After designing the package, we'll write an example to show how this encoding works.

Defining the Base62 algorithm

The `Base62` algorithm is a number encoder that converts a given number to a string. How does it do that? The input number is mapped from 62 characters. The beauty of this algorithm is that it creates unique, shorter strings for every given number. It can generate memorable short strings, even when the inputs are big. We use this technique to pass a database ID into the `ToBase62` function—which we are going to create shortly—and get a short string out. Let's write an example for implementing the `Base62` algorithm. The logic is purely mathematical and can be implemented in different ways. Proceed as follows:

1. Create a project called `base62Example`, like this:

   ```
   mkdir $GOPATH/src/github.com/git-user/chapter7/base62Example
   ```

2. Create a package called `base62` and add a file called `encodeutils.go`, like this:

   ```
   mkdir $GOPATH/src/github.com/git-user/chapter7/base62Example/base62
   touch $GOPATH/src/github.com/git-user/chapter7/base62Example/base62
   /encodeutils.go
   ```

3. Define two functions called `ToBase62` and `ToBase10`. The first one takes an integer and generates a `base62` string, and the latter one reverses the effect, which means it takes a `base62` string and returns the original number. The program for encoding/decoding is as follows:

   ```go
   package base62

   import (
       "math"
       "strings"
   )

   const base =
   "0123456789abcdefghijklmnopqrstuvwxyzABCDEFGHIJKLMNOPQRSTUVWXYZ"
   const b = 62

   // Function encodes the given database ID to a base62 string
   func ToBase62(num int) string{
       r := num % b
       res := string(base[r])
       div := num / b
       q := int(math.Floor(float64(div)))

       for q != 0 {
           r = q % b
           temp := q / b
   ```

```
        q = int(math.Floor(float64(temp)))
        res = string(base[int(r)]) + res
    }

    return string(res)
}

// Function decodes a given base62 string to database ID
func ToBase10(str string) int{
    res := 0
    for _, r := range str {
        res = (b * res) + strings.Index(base, string(r))
    }
    return res
}
```

4. Create another program that uses these utility functions, as follows:

> **vi $GOPATH/src/github.com/git-
> user/chapter7/base62Example/base62/usebase62.go**

This program uses the imported functions from encodeutils.go and calculates an encoded string. Then, it decodes back again to the original number and prints both the number and the string, as follows:

```
package main

import (
  "log"

  "github.com/git-user/chapter7/base62Example/base62"
)

func main() {
  x := 100
  base62String := base62.ToBase62(x)
  log.Println(base62String)
  normalNumber := base62.ToBase10(base62String)
  log.Println(normalNumber)
}
```

Here, we are using the encode/decode functions from the base62 package and trying to print the conversion.

5. We can run the program using the following command:

```
go run usebase62.go
```

It prints the following:

```
2020/02/14 21:24:43 1C
2020/02/14 21:24:43 100
```

The `Base62` encoding of `100` is `1C`. This is because the number `100` shrunk to `1C` in our `base62` logic.

After learning the basics of `Base62` encoding, let's implement a URL-shortening service, whereby we'll leverage a `Base62` algorithm to generate a short URL. The implementation strategy looks like this:

1. Design an API route to collect a long URL from the client.
2. Insert that long URL in the database and get the ID of that record.
3. Use that ID to generate a `Base62` string and pass it along with the API server hostname as a shortened URL in the response.
4. Whenever a client uses that shortened URL, it hits our API server.
5. The API server then decodes the `Base62` string back to the database ID and fetches the original URL.
6. Finally, the client can use this URL to redirect to the original site.

Remember that we are building a service to support URL shorteners. These leverage our API to `encode/decode` logic to ask for a shortened URL.

We are going to write a Go API service that implements the preceding strategy. We will reuse the following files:

- `encodeutils.go` from the `base62Example` project for encoding/decoding
- `base62` and `models.go` from the `basicExample` project for database logic

We will use the `gorilla/mux` package for multiplexing the URL and `pq` for storing and retrieving results in the PostgreSQL database. Let's create the project structure, as follows:

1. The directory structure looks like this:

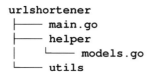

```
urlshortener
├──── main.go
├──── helper
│     └──── models.go
└──── utils
```

└──── **encodeutils.go**

2 directories, 3 files

2. Copy encodeutils.go and models.go from the preceding examples to the directories shown in the preceding code block.

3. We need two data structures in the main program: one to hold the database connection and the other one for the URL-shortener service response. Let's call the response as a Record type. Create two structs, like this:

```
type DBClient struct {
  db *sql.DB
}

type Record struct {
  ID int `json:"id"`
  URL string `json:"url"`
}
```

4. Now, create the main function, where we define two URLs to handler functions. These application routes are required to shorten the URL and retrieve the original URL respectively. The main block should create a new database connection and two mux routes. We attach GenerateShortURL and GetOriginalURL function handlers to those two mux routes.

5. Finally, we run the HTTP server, serving the API. See the following code for the main block:

```
func main() {
  db, err := models.InitDB()
  if err != nil {
    panic(err)
  }
  dbclient := &DBClient{db: db}
  if err != nil {
    panic(err)
  }
  defer db.Close()
  // Create a new router
  r := mux.NewRouter()
  // Attach an elegant path with handler
  r.HandleFunc("/v1/short/{encoded_string:[a-zA-Z0-9]*}",
   dbclient.GetOriginalURL).Methods("GET")
  r.HandleFunc("/v1/short",
   dbclient.GenerateShortURL).Methods("POST")
  srv := &http.Server{
    Handler: r,
```

```
        Addr: "127.0.0.1:8000",
        // Good practice: enforce timeouts for servers you create!
        WriteTimeout: 15 * time.Second,
        ReadTimeout: 15 * time.Second,
    }
    log.Fatal(srv.ListenAndServe())
}
```

See the POST operation. The GenerateShortURL function handler takes an HTTP request and performs the following actions:

1. Inserts the URL coming from the HTTP request body into the database and fetches the ID of a new record.

2. Uses base62 to convert the ID to a string and send it back in the HTTP response, as follows:

```
// GenerateShortURL adds URL to DB and gives back shortened string
func (driver *DBClient) GenerateShortURL(w http.ResponseWriter,
r *http.Request) {
    var id int
    var record Record
    postBody, _ := ioutil.ReadAll(r.Body)
    err := json.Unmarshal(postBody, &record)
    err = driver.db.QueryRow("INSERT INTO web_url(url)
     VALUES($1) RETURNING id", record.URL).Scan(&id)
    responseMap := map[string]string{"encoded_string":
     base62.ToBase62(id)}

    if err != nil {
        w.WriteHeader(http.StatusInternalServerError)
        w.Write([]byte(err.Error()))
    } else {
        w.WriteHeader(http.StatusOK)
        w.Header().Set("Content-Type", "application/json")
        response, _ := json.Marshal(responseMap)
        w.Write(response)
    }
}
```

The client thinks the original URL is shortened, but in reality, the ID is mapped to a shorter string using the base62 algorithm.

Now comes the GET operation. The GetOriginalURL function handler takes the shortened URL and converts it back to the original one. The logic is to convert a base62 string (a shortened string) to a number and use that number to fetch records from the PostgreSQL database. We parse the input request and collect the encoded_string parameter. We use that to retrieve the original URL from the database. See the following code for the GetOriginalURL function handler:

```go
// GetOriginalURL fetches the original URL for the given encoded(short)
string
func (driver *DBClient) GetOriginalURL(w http.ResponseWriter,
r *http.Request) {
    var url string
    vars := mux.Vars(r)
    // Get ID from base62 string
    id := base62.ToBase10(vars["encoded_string"])
    err := driver.db.QueryRow("SELECT url FROM web_url
     WHERE id = $1", id).Scan(&url)
    // Handle response details
    if err != nil {
        w.WriteHeader(http.StatusInternalServerError)
        w.Write([]byte(err.Error()))
    } else {
        w.WriteHeader(http.StatusOK)
        w.Header().Set("Content-Type", "application/json")
        responseMap := map[string]interface{}{"url": url}
        response, _ := json.Marshal(responseMap)
        w.Write(response)
    }
}
```

The DBClient struct is needed in order to pass the database driver between various functions. Run the program, like this:

```
go run $GOPATH/src/github.com/git-user/chapter7/urlshortener/main.go
```

Another option is to install a binary. If your $GOPATH/bin is already in the system PATH variable, we can first install the binary and run it like this:

```
go install $GOPATH/src/github.com/git-user/chapter7/urlshortener/main.go
```

Use the binary name, as follows:

```
./urlshortener
```

It is a best practice to install the binary because it is available system-wide. But for smaller programs, we can run `main.go` from the directory of the program.

Now, it runs the HTTP server on port `8000` and starts collecting requests for the URL-shortening service. Open the console and type these `curl` commands:

```
curl -X POST \
  http://localhost:8000/v1/short \
  -H 'cache-control: no-cache' \
  -H 'content-type: application/json' \
  -d '{
  "url":
"https://www.packtpub.com/eu/game-development/unreal-engine-4-shaders-and-e
ffects-cookbook"
  }'
```

It returns the shortened string, as follows:

```
{
  "encoded_string": "1"
}
```

The encoded string is just `"1"`. The `Base62` algorithm starts allocating shorter strings, starting from `"1"` up to a combination of alphanumeric letters. Now, if we need to retrieve the original URL, we can perform a `GET` request, like this:

```
curl -X GET http://localhost:8000/v1/short/1
```

It returns the following JSON code:

```
{
"url":"https://www.packtpub.com/eu/game-development/unreal-engine-4-shaders
-and-effects-cookbook"
}
```

So, the service can use this result to redirect the user to the original URL (site). Here, the generated string doesn't depend on the length of the URL because the database ID is the only criterion for encoding.

The package imports in `urlshortener` are left out, for brevity. Please refer to the project code from the `chapter7` GitHub repository.

The RETURNING keyword needs to be added to the INSERT SQL command in PostgreSQL to fetch the last inserted database ID. This is not the case with the MySQL or SQLite3 INSERT INTO web_url( ) VALUES($1) RETURNING id, record.URL query. This database query returns the last inserted record's ID. If we drop that RETURNING keyword, the query returns nothing.

In the next section, we'll look at an important feature of PostgreSQL called JSONStore. PostgreSQL, unlike other relational databases, can allow JSON to be stored in the form of fields. It also provides a query language for JSON.

Exploring the JSONStore feature in PostgreSQL

PostgreSQL >9.2 has a prominent feature called JSONStore. PostgreSQL introduced two new data types for 9.2">storing JSON data. PostgreSQL allows users to insert JSON data as a json field or a jsonb field. It is quite useful for modeling real-world data that has to be more flexible in its structure. PostgreSQL draws on the best of both worlds by allowing us to store JSON strings as well as relational types.

The main difference between json and jsonb is that the json field stores data as plaintext whereas jsonb stores that same data as a binary field. Each has its own benefits. For example, the json field commonly takes up less space than jsonb because it is a straightforward insert, but the jsonb field indexes JSON for better querying. You should choose the right field depending on whether the JSON document is fetched as a whole or queried on internal keys.

In this section, we will try to understand a few of the JSON models that we defined for the logistics use case in the previous chapter, but here, we'll use the jsonb field to store and retrieve items in PostgreSQL. For accessing PostgreSQL's JSONStore, the normal pq library is very tedious. So, in order to handle that better, we can use an **Object Relational Mapper (ORM)** called **Grails Object Relational Mapping (GORM)**. In the next section, we will discuss this briefly.

Introducing GORM, a powerful ORM for Go

GORM provides methods for all operations that can be done in the `database/sql` package. We can install GORM using the `dep` tool. In this section, we will look at with examples of how to insert, retrieve, and query PostgreSQL `JSON` using the `GORM` package.

For the full documentation about this ORM, visit `http://jinzhu.me/gorm/`. Let's write a program that implements the `Shipment` and `Package` types as JSON models. We'll use the same models that we defined in the previous chapter for logistics. Let's look at the steps:

1. Create a new directory called `jsonstore` in `$GOPATH/src/github.com/git-user/chapter7` and create the files, like this:

   ```
   mkdir jsonstore
   mkdir jsonstore/helper
   touch jsonstore/helper/models.go
   ```

2. Install all dependencies via `dep` in the `jsonstore` directory, like this:

   ```
   dep init
   dep ensure --add "github.com/gorilla/mux" "github.com/jinzhu/gorm"
   "github.com/lib/pq"
   ```

3. Now, edit the `helper.go` file to add `Shipment` and `Package` models. Every model (table) we create should be represented as a struct in `gorm`. That is the reason we created two structs: `Package` and `Shipment`. The first line should be `gorm.Model`. The other fields are the fields of the table. By default, an auto-increment ID will be created in the documents inserted into the database. See the following code:

   ```go
   package helper

   import (
     "github.com/jinzhu/gorm"
     _ "github.com/lib/pq"
   )

   type Shipment struct {
     gorm.Model
     Packages []Package
     Data string `sql:"type:JSONB NOT NULL DEFAULT '{}'::JSONB"
   json:"-"`
   }
   ```

```
type Package struct {
  gorm.Model
  Data string `sql:"type:JSONB NOT NULL DEFAULT '{}'::JSONB"`
}

// GORM creates tables with plural names.
// Use this to suppress it
func (Shipment) TableName() string {
  return "Shipment"
}

func (Package) TableName() string {
  return "Package"
}
```

If you notice, in the preceding code block, Data is the jsonb field created for the Shipment and Package tables.

4. After finishing the definitions of structs, we can write a table initialization logic that migrates these structs into tables in the PostgreSQL database. In order to do that, utilize the Open method from the GORM package to get the database connection. We can then run the AutoMigrate method with the structs we created previously, to save them to the database. See the following code for migration:

```
func InitDB() (*gorm.DB, error) {
  var err error
  db, err := gorm.Open("postgres",
   "postgres://git-user:YOUR_PASSWORD@
   localhost/mydb?sslmode=disable")
  if err != nil {
    return nil, err
  }
  db.AutoMigrate(&Shipment{}, &Package{})
  return db, nil
}
```

This InitDB logic looks similar to the logic we defined using the pq library. This helper file migrates the tables and returns the database connection back to whoever calls the InitDB function. In the next section, we'll leverage this connection to interact with the Shipment and Package tables.

Implementing the logistics REST API

Before jumping in, let's design the API specification table that shows the REST API signatures for various URL endpoints. Refer to the following table:

Endpoint	Method	Description
`/v1/shipment/id`	`GET`	Get a shipment from ID
`/v1/package/id`	`GET`	Get a package from ID
`/v1/package?weight=n`	`GET`	Get a package with a given weight in grams
`/v1/shipment`	`POST`	Create a new shipment
`/v1/package`	`POST`	Create a new package

To implement the preceding API, we need a main program that registers API routes to handler functions. Add one more file to our `jsonstore` project, like this:

```
touch jsonstore/main.go
```

In this program, we will try to implement the `POST` and `GET` endpoints for `Package`. We suggest implementing the remaining two endpoints of `Shipment` as an assignment for the reader. Follow these steps:

1. The program structure follows the same style as all the programs we have seen until now. We collect the database connection from the helper package and use it to create `DBClient`. We use `gorilla/mux` as our HTTP router and the `gorm` package for database operations. We should have these routes and handlers in our program, as follows:

```go
type DBClient struct {
    db *gorm.DB
}

func main(){
    ...
    db, err := models.InitDB()
    dbclient := &DBClient{db: db}

    r.HandleFunc("/v1/package/{id:[a-zA-Z0-9]*}",
     dbclient.GetPackage).Methods("GET")
    r.HandleFunc("/v1/package",
     dbclient.PostPackage).Methods("POST")
    r.HandleFunc("/v1/package",
     dbclient.GetPackagesbyWeight).Methods("GET")
    ...
}
```

2. The POST handler function saves a package object into the database. It returns an ID of the inserted record. The code for the PostPackage handler looks like this:

```
// PostPackage saves the package information
func (driver *DBClient) PostPackage(w http.ResponseWriter,
 r *http.Request) {
  var Package = models.Package{}
  postBody, _ := ioutil.ReadAll(r.Body)
  Package.Data = string(postBody)
  driver.db.Save(&Package)
  responseMap := map[string]interface{}{"id": Package.ID}
  w.Header().Set("Content-Type", "application/json")
  response, _ := json.Marshal(responseMap)
  w.Write(response)
}
```

This function is reading the POST body from the response and making an ORM function call to save the package data, like this:

```
driver.db.Save(&Package)
```

After saving the package successfully to the database, the preceding function is returning the ID as part of the response.

3. Now, let's write the code for the GetPackage handler function. It is similar to the preceding handler except that it uses a different database function. In this code, instead of reading the request body, we have to read the PATH variable and use that for querying data. See the following code:

```
type PackageResponse struct {
    Package helper.Package `json:"Package"`
}

// GetPackage fetches the original URL for the given
// encoded(short) string
func (driver *DBClient) GetPackage(w http.ResponseWriter,
r *http.Request) {
  var Package = models.Package{}
  vars := mux.Vars(r)

  driver.db.First(&Package, vars["id"])
  var PackageData interface{}

  json.Unmarshal([]byte(Package.Data), &PackageData)
  var response = PackageResponse{Package: Package}
  w.WriteHeader(http.StatusOK)
```

```
w.Header().Set("Content-Type", "application/json")
respJSON, _ := json.Marshal(response)
w.Write(respJSON)
}
```

In this case, the query is as follows:

```
driver.db.First(&Package, vars["id"])
```

4. Now comes another `GET` operation. The `GetPackagebyWeight` handler function queries the database for a package with a given weight. Here, we use a JSON query on the `data` field. We use a special syntax of `column ->> field`, as shown in the following handler code:

```
// GetPackagesbyWeight fetches all packages with given weight
func (driver *DBClient) GetPackagesbyWeight(w http.ResponseWriter,
r *http.Request) {
  var packages []models.Package
  weight := r.FormValue("weight")
  // Handle response details
  var query = "select * from \"Package\" where data->>'weight'=?"
  driver.db.Raw(query, weight).Scan(&packages)
  w.WriteHeader(http.StatusOK)
  w.Header().Set("Content-Type", "application/json")
  respJSON, _ := json.Marshal(packages)
  w.Write(respJSON)
}
```

 There are many other variations for querying JSON in PostgreSQL. You can find them here: `https://www.postgresql.org/docs/10/functions-json.html`.

In the `GetPackagesbyWeight` handler function, we are making a raw query to the database by using the `db.Raw` method. It returns all packages as a list of those matching the weight criteria . For this `GET` API, the weight criteria list is being sent by the client as a query parameter.

There are four important aspects in this JSONStore example, as follows:

- We replaced the traditional driver, `pq`, with the GORM driver.
- We used GORM functions for CRUD operations.
- We inserted JSON into PostgreSQL and retrieved results.
- We executed raw SQL and filtered fields on JSON.

This completes the important logic for our program. Please refer to the `chapter7` repository for the complete code.

Now, run the program using the following command:

```
go run jsonstore/main.go
```

It runs a Go server. Make a few `curl` commands to see the API response, as follows:

1. Create the package (POST), as follows:

```
curl -X POST \
  http://localhost:8000/v1/package \
  -H 'cache-control: no-cache' \
  -H 'content-type: application/json' \
  -d '{
      "dimensions": {
       "width": 21,
        "height": 12
      },
      "weight": 10,
      "is_damaged": false,
      "status": "In transit"
      }'
```

It returns the inserted record in the database, as follows:

```
{
  "id": 1
}
```

2. Now, we need to GET the details of the inserted package, as follows:

```
curl -X GET http://localhost:8000/v1/package/1
```

It returns all the details about a package with ID:1, as follows:

```
{"Package":{"ID":1,"CreatedAt":"2020-02-15T11:14:52.859073Z","Updat
edAt":"2020-02-15T11:14:52.859073Z","DeletedAt":null,"Data":"{\"sta
tus\": \"In transit\", \"weight\": 10, \"dimensions\": {\"width\":
21, \"height\": 12}, \"is_damaged\": false}"}}
```

3. Let's test our second `GET` API, as follows:

```
curl -X GET 'http://localhost:8000/v1/package?weight=10'
```

This returns all the packages with a weight of 10 gms, as follows:

```
[{"ID":1,"CreatedAt":"2020-02-15T11:14:52.859073Z","UpdatedAt":"202
0-02-15T11:14:52.859073Z","DeletedAt":null,"Data":"{\"status\":
\"In transit\", \"weight\": 10, \"dimensions\": {\"width\": 21,
\"height\": 12}, \"is_damaged\": false}"}]
```

The goal of this project is to show how JSON can be stored in and retrieved from PostgreSQL. This concludes our journey through PostgreSQL. There is a lot more to explore in PostgreSQL, but it is out of the scope of this book. PostgreSQL brings together the best of both worlds by allowing us to store relational as well as JSON data in the same table. It also allows us to query JSON data.

Summary

In this chapter, we started our journey by introducing PostgreSQL. We saw how to run PostgreSQL in Docker, and then listed out a few basic SQL queries for CRUD operations. We learned how to add new users and roles in PostgreSQL. We then discussed pq, a PostgreSQL driver package for Go, with an example.

We designed a URL-shortening service using the Base62 algorithm. We leveraged pq and `gorilla/mux` for implementing that service.

PostgreSQL also allows **JSON storage (JSONStore)** from version 9.2 onward. It allows developers to insert and retrieve JSON documents in a database. It combines the power of both relational and non-relational databases with JSONStore.

We also introduced GORM, a well-known ORM for Go. Using an ORM, database operations can be easily managed. GORM provides a few useful functions—such as `AutoMigrate` (creating a table if one doesn't exist)—for writing intuitive Go code over the traditional `database/sql` driver.

Finally, we implemented a REST API for logistics using GORM. PostgreSQL is a well-established, open source relational database that can be a good storage backend for Go. With pq and GORM, driver support for Go is exceptional. The primary goal of this chapter was to make you feel comfortable working with PostgreSQL and Go for REST API development.

So far, we have looked at about building servers that provide REST APIs. Sometimes, developers need client-side tools to consume a REST API. It is also useful to understand how clients can consume a REST API to create a better API. In the next chapter, we will learn generally about how client software is built in Go. There, we also develop API clients for a GitHub REST API.

Building a REST API Client in Go

8

In this chapter, we are going to discuss how Go client applications work in depth. We will explore `grequests`, a Python requests-style library that allows us to make API calls from the Go code. Then, we'll write some client software that uses the GitHub API. While doing that, we'll try to learn about two Go libraries called `cli` and `cobra`. After learning about the fundamentals of those packages, we'll write an API testing tool for the command line. Then, we'll introduce Redis, an in-memory database that we can use to cache the API responses to back up the data.

In this chapter, we will cover the following topics:

- Plan for building a REST API client
- Basics for writing a command-line tool in Go
- `grequests` – a REST API package for Go
- Getting comfortable with the GitHub REST API
- Cobra, an advanced CLI library
- Creating a CLI tool as an API client for the GitHub REST API
- Using Redis to cache the API data

Technical requirements

The following software needs to be pre-installed so that you can run the code samples in this chapter:

- OS: Linux(Ubuntu 18.04)/ Windows 10/Mac OS X >=10.13
- Go stable version compiler >= 1.13.5
- Dep: A dependency management tool for Go >= 0.5.3

You can download the code for this chapter from `https://github.com/PacktPublishing/Hands-On-Restful-Web-services-with-Go/tree/master/chapter8`. Clone the code and use the code samples in the `chapter8` directory.

Plan for building a REST API client

So far, we've mainly focused on writing server-side REST APIs. Basically, these are server programs. In a few cases, such as gRPC, we need a client. A client program takes input from the user and executes some logic. For developing a Go client, we should know about the `flag` library in Go. Before that, we should be aware of how to make requests for an API from a Go program. In the previous chapters, we used different clients such as cURL, Browser, Postman, and so on. But how can we turn a Go program into a client?

Command-line tools are equally important as web user interfaces to perform system tasks. In **business-to-business (B2B)** companies, the software is packaged as a single binary instead of having multiple different packages. As a Go developer, you should know how to achieve the goal of writing apps for the command line. Then, that knowledge can be invested in creating REST API-related web clients easily and elegantly.

Let's explore the basics of how we can write **command-line interface (CLI)** tools in Go.

Basics for writing a command-line tool in Go

Go provides a built-in library called `flag` for writing CLI tools. It refers to the command-line flags. Since it is already packed with the Go distribution, there is no need to install anything externally. The `flag` package has multiple functions, such as `Int` and `String`, to handle the respective type input that's supplied as a command-line flag. Let's suppose that we collect a name from the user and print it back to the console.

To do this, we can use the `flag.String` method, as shown in the following code snippet:

```
import "flag"
var name = flag.String("name", "stranger", "your wonderful name")
```

Let's write a short program to illustrate the `flag` API in more detail:

1. Create a file called `flagExample.go` in the GOPATH, as follows:

   ```
   mkdir -p $GOPATH/src/github.com/git-user/chapter8/basic/
   touch $GOPATH/src/github.com/git-user/chapter8/basic/flagExample.go
   ```

2. Now, we can use the `flag` package's `String` method to receive a string from the command line as an option, like so:

   ```
   package main

   import (
       "flag"
       "log"
       )

   var name = flag.String("name", "stranger", "your wonderful name")

   func main(){
       flag.Parse()
       log.Printf("Hello %s, Welcome to the command line world",
        *name)
   }
   ```

   In this program, we are creating a flag called name. It is a string pointer.
   `flag.String` takes three arguments. The first argument is the name of the
   option. The second and third method arguments are the default values of that flag
   and the help text, respectively. We have asked the program to parse all the flag
   pointers in the main block.

   When we run the program, it maps the values supplied from the command-line
   options to the respective variables. To access the value of a flag in code, we use *,
   which is a pointer value reference; for example *name in the preceding code
   block.

3. Build and then run the program using the following command:

   ```
   go build $GOPATH/src/github.com/git-user/chapter8/basic/
   flagExample.go
   ```

This creates a binary in the `basic` directory.

4. We can run it like a normal executable, as follows:

```
./flagExample
```

It gives us the following output:

```
Hello stranger, Welcome to the command line world
```

As you may have noticed, we didn't pass the `name` argument to the command. However, we did assign the default value to that argument. Go's flag takes the default value and proceeds further.

5. Now, in order to see what options are available and to find out about them, we need to ask for help, like this:

```
./flagExample -h
```

```
Output
=========
Usage of ./flagExample:
  -name string
        your wonderful name (default "stranger")
```

This is the reason why we passed the help text as the third argument for the flag command.

In Windows, `.exe` will be generated when we build a `.go` file. After that, from the command line, we can run the program by calling the program name.

6. Now, try to pass the `name` option with a value:

```
./flagExample -name Albert
(or)
./flagExample -name=Albert
```

Both styles work fine and the output prints the supplied value:

```
Hello Albert, Welcome to the command line world
```

7. If we wish to pass multiple options, modify the preceding program in the `basic` directory to add age, and call it `flagExampleMultipleParam.go`:

```
package main

import (
    "flag"
    "log"
    )

var name = flag.String("name", "stranger", "your wonderful name")
var age = flag.Int("age", 0, "your graceful age")

func main(){
    flag.Parse()
    log.Printf("Hello %s (%d years), Welcome to the command line
    world", *name, *age)
}
```

8. This takes two options, with the addition of a different type. If we build and run this, we'll see the following output:

```
./flagExampleMultiParam -name Albert -age 24

Hello Albert (24 years), Welcome to the command line world
```

This is exactly what we expected.

9. Instead of using pointers, we can bind a variable to the parsed output. This binding is done through the `init()` function, which runs in a Go program, irrespective of whether the main function exists or not:

```
var name String

func init() {
    flag.StringVar(&name, "name", "stranger", "your wonderful name")
}
```

In this way, the value will be directly stored in the variable.

10. Completely rewriting the preceding program to create a new one using the `init()` function can be seen in the following code snippet:

```
basic/initFlag.go

    package main
```

```
import (
    "flag"
    "log"
    )

var name string
var age int

func init() {
    flag.StringVar(&name, "name", "stranger", "your wonderful
     name")
    flag.IntVar(&age, "age", 0, "your graceful age")
}

func main(){
    flag.Parse()
    log.Printf("Hello %s (%d years), Welcome to the command
     line world", name, age)
}
```

The output is exactly the same as it was for the preceding program. Here, instead of using pointers, we are able to load data directly into our variables.

In Go, execution starts from the main program. However, a Go program can have any number of init functions. If a package has an init function in it, that will be executed before the main function.

This flag library is very basic to work with. However, in order to write advanced client applications, we need to take the help of a CLI package. In the next section, we'll explore a package called cli that will do just this.

CLI – a package for building beautiful clients

The cli package is the next step for a Go developer after working with the flag package. It provides an intuitive API for creating command-line applications with ease. It allows a Go program to collect arguments and flags. It's quite handy for designing complex applications.

First, create a directory for our example programs. For our basic CLI example, create the following directory:

```
mkdir -p $GOPATH/src/github.com/git-user/chapter8/cli/example1
```

To install the package, we use the `dep` tool. Initialize the tool first and then add the `cli` package as the dependency:

```
dep init
dep ensure --add github.com/urfave/cli
```

Now, we can write a program that does exactly the same job as the preceding flag example. Create a file called `example1/main.go`.

The `cli` package provides three major elements:

- App
- Flag
- Action

Apps are used for defining namespaces in applications. A **flag** is an actual container that stores options passed. **Action** is a function that executes on collected options. Let's look at the following example code for further insight. Here, we're trying to use the `cli` API to create App, Flags, and Action. We have to import the package into our program:

```go
package main

import (
  "log"
  "os"

  "github.com/urfave/cli"
)

func main() {
  // Create new app
  app := cli.NewApp()

  // add flags with three arguments
  app.Flags = []cli.Flag {
    cli.StringFlag{
      Name: "name",
      Value: "stranger",
      Usage: "your wonderful name",
    },
    cli.IntFlag{
      Name: "age",
      Value: 0,
      Usage: "your graceful age",
    },
  }
```

```
    // This function parses and brings data in cli.Context struct
    app.Action = func(c *cli.Context) error {
      // c.String, c.Int looks for value of given flag
      log.Printf("Hello %s (%d years), Welcome to the command line world",
       c.String("name"), c.Int("age"))
      return nil
    }
    // Pass os.Args to cli app to parse content
    app.Run(os.Args)
  }
```

This is lengthier than the one we saw previously, but it is more expressive. Here, we created a new app using the `cli.NewApp` function. This creates a new struct. We need to attach parameters to this struct, specifically the `Flags` struct and the `Action` function. The `Flags` struct is a list that defines all possible flags for this application.

The structure of `Flag` from GoDoc (`https://godoc.org/github.com/urfave/cli#Flag`) is as follows:

```
  type Flag interface {
      fmt.Stringer
      // Apply Flag settings to the given flag set
      Apply(*flag.FlagSet)
      GetName() string
  }
```

The inbuilt structs, such as `StringFlag` and `IntFlag`, implement this `Flag` interface. The `Name`, `Value`, and `Usage` fields are straightforward. They are similar to the ones we used in the `flag` package. The `Action` function takes the `cli.Context` argument.

The context object holds any information regarding flags and command-line arguments. The `c.String`, `c.Int`, and other functions are used to look up the flag variables. For example, in the preceding program, `c.String("name")` fetches a flag variable whose name is `name`. This program runs the same as the previous flag example. You can build and run the program like so:

```
go build example1/main.go

./main -name "Albert" # Run program
```

That's it regarding the basic usage of the `cli` package. This package also provides advanced combinations of flags and arguments. We'll look at this in the next section.

Collecting command-line arguments in the CLI

In bash terminology, there is a difference between command-line arguments and flags. The following diagram clearly specifies the distinction between them:

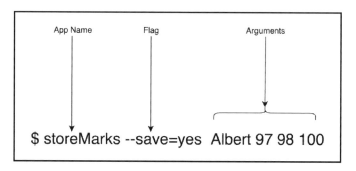

Suppose that we have a command-line app called storeMarks for saving the marks of a student. It has a flag (called save) to specify whether details should be persisted or not. The arguments that are given are the name and actual marks of the student. We already saw how to collect the flag values in the program. In this section, we will learn how to collect program arguments in an expressive way. Follow these steps:

1. For collecting arguments, we use the c.Args function, where c is the cli context of the Action function. Add a new directory called example2 for our project:

   ```
   mkdir -p $GOPATH/src/github.com/git-user/chapter8/cli/example2
   ```

   Then, create a program file called example2/main.go.

2. Define the app in the main block cli.NewApp creates a new application:

   ```
   app := cli.NewApp()
   ```

3. Next, we define the flags on the app.cli.Flag takes a few predefined flags, such as integer flag or string flag. Here, we need a string flag:

   ```
   app.Flags = []cli.Flag{
     cli.StringFlag{
       Name:  "save",
       Value: "no",
       Usage: "Should save to database (yes/no)",
     },
   }
   ```

4. Now, we have to define actions on the app. Actions are the control structures that define the dynamics of logic upon given flags. These options are as follows:

- --save=no, which skips saving arguments to the database
- --save=yes (or) no flag, which saves arguments to the database:

```
app.Version = "1.0"
// define action
app.Action = func(c *cli.Context) error {
  var args []string
  if c.NArg() > 0 {
    // Fetch arguments in a array
    args = c.Args()
    personName := args[0]
    marks := args[1:len(args)]
    log.Println("Person: ", personName)
    log.Println("marks", marks)
  }
  // check the flag value
  if c.String("save") == "no" {
    log.Println("Skipping saving to the database")
  } else {
    // Add database logic here
    log.Println("Saving to the database", args)
  }
  return nil
}
```

All the preceding statements will go into the main function.

5. We have to run the app using app.Run to make the tool run and collect arguments:

```
package main

import (
  "github.com/urfave/cli"
  "log"
  "os"
)

func main() {
  // Here goes app, flags, actions
  app.Run(os.Args)
}
```

`c.Args` stores all the arguments supplied with the command. Since we know the order of the arguments, we deduced that the first argument is the name, and the remaining values are the marks. We are checking a flag called `save` to save those details in a database or not (we don't have database logic here, for simplicity). `app.Version` sets the version of the tool. Everything else remains the same as the previous `cli` introductory example.

First, let's build the program:

```
go build $GOPATH/src/github.com/git-user/chapter8/cli/example2
```

Now, from the `example2` directory, run the built tool by passing the flag and its arguments:

```
./main --save=yes Albert 89 85 97

2017/09/02 21:02:02 Person: Albert
2017/09/02 21:02:02 marks [89 85 97]
2017/09/02 21:02:02 Saving to the database [Albert 89 85 97]
```

If we don't give a flag, the default is `save=no`:

```
./main Albert 89 85 97

2017/09/02 21:02:59 Person: Albert
2017/09/02 21:02:59 marks [89 85 97]
2017/09/02 21:02:59 Skipping saving to the database
```

So far, everything looks good. But how can we make the command-line tool display help text when a user needs it? The `cli` library creates a nice help section for the given app. If you type in any of these commands, some help text will be auto-generated:

- `./storeMarks -h`
- `./storeMarks -help`
- `./storeMarks --help`
- `./storeMarks help`

A nice help section appears, like the one shown in the following code, which shows version details and available flags (global options), commands, and arguments:

```
NAME:
    storeMarks - A new cli application

USAGE:
    storeMarks [global options] command [command options] [arguments...]
```

```
VERSION:
   1.0

COMMANDS:
      help, h Shows a list of commands or help for one command

GLOBAL OPTIONS:
   --save value Should save to database (yes/no) (default: "no")
   --help, -h show help
   --version, -v print the version
```

The `cli` package simplifies client application development. It is much faster and intuitive than the internal `flag` package.

 Command-line tools are binaries that are generated after building the program. They need to be run with the options. It is like any system program and not related to the Go compiler anymore. Make sure you build them for the target architecture where you want to run them.

We can use the `flag` package or `cli` to build a REST API client. However, for advanced applications, we might need a robust library with rich features. In the next section, we'll explore such a library called `cobra`, which is used to create command-line tools.

Cobra, an advanced CLI library

Like `cli`, `cobra` is a package for writing client binaries but takes a different approach. In cobra, we have to create separate commands and use them in our main app. We can install `cobra` using dep. Let's create our cobra project repository:

```
mkdir -p $GOPATH/src/github.com/git-user/chapter8/cobraCLI
```

Now, let's create another directory called `cmd` in the project for defining commands. In cobra apps, there will be a root command. This can have multiple subcommands. We can implement the same example we used for the flag package. Input the name and age from the command line using cobra.

Let's define a root command:

```
var rootCmd = &cobra.Command{
    Use:   "details",
    Short: "This project takes student information",
    Long: `A long string about description`,
    Args:  cobra.MinimumNArgs(1),
    Run: func(cmd *cobra.Command, args []string) {
```

```
        name := cmd.PersistentFlags().Lookup("name").Value
        age := cmd.PersistentFlags().Lookup("age").Value
        log.Printf("Hello %s (%s years), Welcome to the command line
          world", name, age)
    },
}
```

This creates a command with "details" as a command. It has few properties, such as `Use`, `Short`, `Long`, `Args` and, `Run`. See the following table to find their exact meaning:

Parameter	Meaning
Use	Name of the command
Short	Short description
Long	Long description
Args	Number of arguments expected
Run	Process inputs after collection

In the `Run` command, we are expecting two arguments: `name` and `age`. However, in order to collect them, we have to define them. Where can we define them? Cobra asks the developer to define them in a special function called `Execute`:

```
// Execute is Cobra logic start point
func Execute() {
    rootCmd.PersistentFlags().StringP("name", "n", "stranger", "Name of
      the student")
    rootCmd.PersistentFlags().IntP("age", "a", 25, "Age of the student")

    if err := rootCmd.Execute(); err != nil {
        fmt.Println(err)
        os.Exit(1)
    }
}
```

We need to use the previously defined root command to attach the flags. `PersistentFlags` has various types that can be used to collect flags. Now, create the main program and import this command:

touch $GOPATH/src/github.com/git-user/chapter8/cobraCLI/main.go

Now, in this file, you can import the command and call the `Execute` function:

```
package main

import "github.com/git-user/chapter8/cobraExample/cmd"
```

```
func main() {
    cmd.Execute()
}
```

That's it. We have a client application that can be used to collect the name and age of the student. When we build this, it generates a binary:

```
go build $GOPATH/src/github.com/git-user/chapter8/cobraCLI
```

Now, we can run that binary as a client tool:

```
./cobraExample details -n Albert -a 23
```

It prints a log to the console:

```
Hello Albert (23 years), Welcome to the command line world
```

We can also pass flags in a different order:

```
./cobraExample details --age=23 --name=Albert
```

We can also create many subcommands on top of this command and do a lot more. This is just a basic example. We will look at an advanced example in the next section, where you will implement the same with cobra.

Later in this chapter, we'll discuss creating REST clients in Go. Before that, you should know how to make HTTP requests from a Go program. Although this is possible with Go's built-in `net/http` package, we need a more intuitive package. In the next section, we'll look at `grequests`, a similar package to Python's `Requests` for making HTTP requests.

grequests a REST API package for Go

The developers who worked on Python know about the `Requests` library. It is a clean, short library that is not included in the standard library of Python.

The Go `grequests` package is inspired by `Requests`. It provides a simple set of functions, using which we can make API requests such as `GET`, `POST`, `PUT`, and `DELETE` from our Go code. Using `grequests` allows us to encapsulate the in-built HTTP request and response.

Create the project directory and install `grequests` using the `dep` tool:

```
mkdir -p $GOPATH/src/github.com/git-user/chapter8/requestExample/
touch $GOPATH/src/github.com/git-user/chapter8/requestExample/
basicRequest.go
```

To install the `grequests` package for Go, run the following `dep` command:

```
dep init
dep ensure --add github.com/levigross/grequests
```

Now, let's write a basic program illustrating the use of the `grequests` library to make a GET request to a REST API. It uses the `Get` method from the `grequests` library:

```
package main

import (
  "github.com/levigross/grequests"
  "log"
)

func main() {
  resp, err := grequests.Get("http://httpbin.org/get", nil)
  // You can modify the request by passing an optional
  // RequestOptions struct
  if err != nil {
    log.Fatalln("Unable to make request: ", err)
  }
  log.Println(resp.String())
}
```

The `grequests` package contains methods for performing all REST actions. The preceding program uses the `Get` function from the package. It takes two function arguments. The first one is the URL of the API, while the second one is the request parameters object. Since we are not passing any request parameters, the second argument is `nil` here. `resp` is returned from the request, and it has a function called `String()` that returns the response body:

```
go run requestExample/basicRequest.go
```

The output is the JSON response that's returned by `httpbin`:

```
{
  "args": {},
  "headers": {
    "Accept-Encoding": "gzip",
    "Connection": "close",
    "Host": "httpbin.org",
```

```
      "User-Agent": "GRequests/0.10"
    },
    "origin": "116.75.82.9",
    "url": "http://httpbin.org/get"
}
```

Here, we understood how to use grequests. However, to leverage its power, we should be aware of its API (functions).

In the next section, we'll look at the grequests library in more detail. We'll learn how request parameters and response properties are configured.

API overview of grequests

The most important thing to explore in grequests is not the HTTP functions, but the RequestOptions struct. It is a very big struct that holds various kinds of information regarding the type of API method being used. If the REST method is GET, RequestOptions holds the Params property. If the method is a POST, the struct will have a Data property. Whenever we make a request to a URL endpoint, we get a response back. Let's look at the structure of the response. From the official documentation, the response looks like this:

```
type Response struct {
    Ok bool
    Error error
    RawResponse *http.Response
    StatusCode int
    Header http.Header
}
```

The Ok property of the response holds information about whether a request was successful or not. If something went wrong, an error will be found in the Error property. RawResponse is the Go HTTP response that will be used by other functions of the grequests response. StatusCode and Header store the status codes of the response and header details, respectively. There are a few functions in Response that are useful

- Response.JSON()
- Response.XML()
- Response.String()
- Response.Bytes()

The data from the response can be filled into a generic map by the preceding functions. Let's take a look at an example, that is `requestExample/jsonRequest.go`:

```
package main

import (
  "github.com/levigross/grequests"
  "log"
)

func main() {
  resp, err := grequests.Get("http://httpbin.org/get", nil)
  // You can modify the request by passing an optional
  // RequestOptions struct
  if err != nil {
    log.Fatalln("Unable to make request: ", err)
  }
  var returnData map[string]interface{}
  resp.JSON(&returnData)
  log.Println(returnData)

}
```

Here, we declared an interface to hold the JSON values. Then, we populated `returnData` (empty interface) using the `resp.JSON` function. This program prints the map instead of plain JSON.

 You can find out about all the available options by looking at the project documentation: `https://godoc.org/github.com/levigross/grequests`.

In the next section, we'll understand how GitHub API version 3 works and use our knowledge of command-line arguments to develop a client that fetches useful information from the GitHub API.

Getting comfortable with the GitHub REST API

GitHub provides a well-written, easy to consume REST API. It opens up the data about users, repositories, repository statistics, and so on to the clients through well-formed API. The current stable version is v3. The API documentation can be found at `https://developer.github.com/v3/`. The root endpoint of the API is `https://api.github.com`.

All GitHub API routes will be appended to this root endpoint. Let's learn how to make a few queries and get data. For an unauthenticated client, the rate limit is 60/hour, whereas, for clients who are passing `client_id` (we can get it from their GitHub account console), it is 5,000/hour.

If you have a GitHub account (if not, it is highly recommended that you create one), you can find the access tokens in the **Your Profile | Personal Access Tokens** section or by visiting https://github.com/settings/tokens. Create a new access token using the **Generate new token** button. You'll be asked for various permissions for different resources. Tick the `repo` and `gist` options. A new personal token string will be generated for you. Save it somewhere safe and private. The token that was generated can now be used to access the GitHub API (for a longer rate limit).

The next step is to export that access token as an environment variable, `GITHUB_TOKEN`. You can set it using the `export` command, like so:

```
export GITHUB_TOKEN=YOUR_GITHUB_ACCESS_TOKEN
```

`YOUR_GITHUB_ACCESS_TOKEN` is what was generated and saved from the GitHub account. You can also add the preceding export command to your `~/.bashrc` file to make it persistent from the next shell launch.

Let's write a program for fetching all the repositories of a user:

1. Create a new directory and program, like so:

   ```
   mkdir -p $GOPATH/src/github.com/git-user/chapter8/githubAPI
   touch $GOPATH/src/github.com/git-user/chapter8/githubAPI/main.go
   ```

   We should use this logic to make a GET request from a Go program. This program fetches repository information from the GitHub API.

2. Create a struct that will hold the repository's information. Let's call it `Repo`. We will also define an environment variable that will fetch `GITHUB_TOKEN`. Now, we can create request options from that token. For GitHub to authenticate the origin of the GET request, we should pass an argument called `Auth` to the `RequestOptions` struct. This can be seen in the following code block:

   ```
   var GITHUB_TOKEN = os.Getenv("GITHUB_TOKEN")
   var requestOptions = &grequests.RequestOptions{Auth:
   []string{GITHUB_TOKEN, "x-oauth-basic"}}

   type Repo struct {
       ID int `json:"id"`
       Name string `json:"name"`
   ```

```
    FullName string `json:"full_name"`
    Forks int `json:"forks"`
    Private bool `json:"private"`
}
```

3. Now, define a function handler that takes a URL as input and returns the GitHub API `Response`. It makes a simple GET request to the given URL location. We use the `grequests` package to make API calls to GitHub:

```
func getStats(url string) *grequests.Response{
    resp, err := grequests.Get(url, requestOptions)
    // You can modify the request by passing an optional
RequestOptions struct
    if err != nil {
        log.Fatalln("Unable to make request: ", err)
    }
    return resp
}
```

4. Now, define the main block, which passes a GitHub link to the preceding function and stores the response in the `Repo` struct:

```
package main

import (
  "github.com/levigross/grequests"
  "log"
  "os"
)

func main() {
  var repos []Repo
  var repoUrl = "https://api.github.com/users/torvalds/repos"
  resp := getStats(repoUrl)
  resp.JSON(&repos)
  log.Println(repos)
}
```

`Response` consists of multiple repositories, so we have to load the response JSON into an array of `Repo`.

5. If you run the preceding program, you will receive the following output:

```
go run $GOPATH/src/github.com/git-user/chapter8/githubAPI/main.go

2019/07/03 17:59:41 [{79171906 libdc-for-dirk torvalds/libdc-for-
dirk 10 false} {2325298 linux torvalds/linux 18274 false} {78665021
```

```
subsurface-for-dirk torvalds/subsurface-for-dirk 16 false}
{86106493 test-tlb torvalds/test-tlb 25 false}]
```

The preceding program illustrates how we can query the GitHub API and load that data into our custom struct called `Repo`. The JSON that's returned contains many fields, but for simplicity's sake, we are just picking a few important fields.

So far, we've seen how to make HTTP requests to the GitHub API. In the next section, we'll create a client that makes HTTP requests to the GitHub API based on user commands.

Creating a CLI tool as an API client for the GitHub REST API

After looking at this example, we'll be able to easily access the GitHub API from our Go client. We can combine both of the techniques we've learned about in this chapter to come up with a command-line tool that consumes the GitHub API. Let's create a new command-line application that does the following:

- Provides options to get repository details by username
- Uploads a file to GitHub gist (text snippets) with a given description
- Authenticates using a personal access token

We'll use the `cli` package and `grequests` to build this tool. You can re-implement the same example in cobra too.

 Gist are snippets provided by GitHub that store text content. For more details, visit `https://gist.github.com`.

Create a directory called `gitTool` in this chapter's directory and add the `main` file to it, like so:

```
mkdir -p $GOPATH/src/github.com/git-user/chapter8/gitTool
touch $GOPATH/src/github.com/git-user/chapter8/gitTool/main.go
```

First, let's define the main block with a few `cli` commands so that we can input commands for repository details and gist upload actions. Here, we're using `app` from the `cli` package and creating `Commands`. We're defining two commands here:

```
func main() {
    app := cli.NewApp()
```

```go
// define command for our client
app.Commands = []cli.Command{
    {
        Name:    "fetch",
        Aliases: []string{"f"},
        Usage:   "Fetch the repo details with user. [Usage]: githubAPI
         fetch user",
        Action: func(c *cli.Context) error {
            if c.NArg() > 0 {
                // Github API Logic
                var repos []Repo
                user := c.Args()[0]
                var repoUrl = fmt.Sprintf("https://api.github.com/
                 users/%s/repos", user)
                resp := getStats(repoUrl)
                resp.JSON(&repos)
                log.Println(repos)
            } else {
                log.Println("Please give a username. See -h to
                 see help")
            }
            return nil
        },
    },
    {
        Name:    "create",
        Aliases: []string{"c"},
        Usage:   "Creates a gist from the given text.
         [Usage]: githubAPI name 'description' sample.txt",
        Action: func(c *cli.Context) error {
            if c.NArg() > 1 {
                // Github API Logic
                args := c.Args()
                var postUrl = "https://api.github.com/gists"
                resp := createGist(postUrl, args)
                log.Println(resp.String())
            } else {
                log.Println("Please give sufficient arguments.
                 See -h to see help")
            }
            return nil
        },
    },
}

app.Version = "1.0"
app.Run(os.Args)
}
```

As you can see, `getStats` and `createGist` are the functions that are used for actual API calls. We'll define these next, but, before we do, we should prepare a few data structures that hold information about the following:

- The repository
- The file to upload as a gist
- Gist on GitHub (list of files)

Now, we need to create three structs that hold the preceding information, as follows:

```go
// Struct for holding response of repositories fetch API
type Repo struct {
    ID        int     `json:"id"`
    Name      string  `json:"name"`
    FullName  string  `json:"full_name"`
    Forks     int     `json:"forks"`
    Private   bool    `json:"private"`
}

// Structs for modelling JSON body in create Gist
type File struct {
    Content string `json:"content"`
}

type Gist struct {
    Description string          `json:"description"`
    Public      bool            `json:"public"`
    Files       map[string]File `json:"files"`
}
```

Now, create a request option that builds a header and uses GitHub tokens from environment variables:

```go
var GITHUB_TOKEN = os.Getenv("GITHUB_TOKEN")
var requestOptions = &grequests.RequestOptions{Auth: []string{GITHUB_TOKEN,
"x-oauth-basic"}}
```

Now, it's time to write the `getStats` and `createGist` functions. Let's code `getStats` first:

```go
// Fetches the repos for the given Github users
func getStats(url string) *grequests.Response {
    resp, err := grequests.Get(url, requestOptions)
    // you can modify the request by passing an optional
    // RequestOptions struct
    if err != nil {
        log.Fatalln("Unable to make request: ", err)
    }
```

```
        return resp
    }
```

This function makes a GET request and returns the response object. The code is simple and is a generic GET request.

Now, let's look at createGist. Here, we have to do more. A gist contains multiple files. Due to this, we need to do the following in our program:

1. Get the list of files from command-line arguments.
2. Read the file content and store it in a map of files with the filename as the key and content as the value.
3. Convert this map into JSON.
4. Make a POST request to the Gist API with the preceding JSON as the body.

We have to make a POST request to the Gist API. The createGist function takes a URL string and other arguments. The function should return the response of the POST request:

```
// Reads the files provided and creates Gist on github
func createGist(url string, args []string) *grequests.Response {
    // get first two arguments
    description := args[0]
    // remaining arguments are file names with path
    var fileContents = make(map[string]File)
    for i := 1; i < len(args); i++ {
        dat, err := ioutil.ReadFile(args[i])
        if err != nil {
            log.Println("Please check the filenames. Absolute path
              (or) same directory are allowed")
            return nil
        }
        var file File
        file.Content = string(dat)
        fileContents[args[i]] = file
    }
    var gist = Gist{Description: description, Public: true,
     Files: fileContents}
    var postBody, _ = json.Marshal(gist)
    var requestOptions_copy = requestOptions
    // Add data to JSON field
    requestOptions_copy.JSON = string(postBody)
    // make a Post request to Github
    resp, err := grequests.Post(url, requestOptions_copy)
    if err != nil {
        log.Println("Create request failed for Github API")
    }
```

```
        return resp
    }
```

We are using `grequests.Post` to pass files to GitHub's Gist API. It returns `Status: 201 Created` on successful creation with gist details in the response body.

Now, let's build the command-line tool:

```
go build $GOPATH/src/github.com/git-user/chapter8/gitTool
```

This creates a binary in the same directory. If we type in `./gitTool -h`, it shows us the following:

```
NAME:
    gitTool - A new cli application

USAGE:
    gitTool [global options] command [command options] [arguments...]

VERSION:
    1.0

COMMANDS:
        fetch, f Fetch the repo details with user. [Usage]: goTool fetch user
        create, c Creates a gist from the given text. [Usage]: goTool name
        'description' sample.txt
        help, h Shows a list of commands or help for one command

GLOBAL OPTIONS:
    --help, -h show help
    --version, -v print the version
```

If you take a look at the help commands, you'll see two commands, `fetch` and `create`. The `fetch` command fetches the repositories of a given user, while the `create` command creates a `gist` with the supplied files. Let's create two sample files in the same directory of the program to test the `create` command:

```
echo 'I am sample1 file text' > githubAPI/sample1.txt
echo 'I am sample2 file text' > githubAPI/sample2.txt
```

Run the tool with the first command:

```
./gitTool f torvalds
```

This returns all the repositories that belong to the great Linus Torvalds. The log message prints the struct that was filled:

```
[{79171906 libdc-for-dirk torvalds/libdc-for-dirk 10 false} {2325298 linux
torvalds/linux 18310 false} {78665021 subsurface-for-dirk
torvalds/subsurface-for-dirk 16 false} {86106493 test-tlb torvalds/test-tlb
25 false}]
```

Now, let's check the second command. This creates the `gist` with the given description and a set of files as arguments:

```
./gitTool c "I am doing well" sample1.txt sample2.txt
```

It returns JSON details about the created gist. It is a very lengthy JSON, so the output has been skipped here. Now, if you open your `gist.github.com` account, you will see the created `gist`:

Remember, the GitHub `gists` API expects JSON data as a body in the following format:

```
{
  "description": "the description for this gist",
"public": true,
"files": {
"file1.txt": {
"content": "String file contents"
  }
```

```
    }
}
```

 For any Go program to read and comprehend quickly, follow the `main` function and then step into the other functions. By doing this, we can read the code from the whole application.

As an exercise, build a command-line tool for the preceding requirements in `cobra`.

Using Redis to cache the API data

Redis is an in-memory database that can store key/value pairs. It best suits the use case of storing heavy read-intensive data. For example, news agencies such as the BBC and The Guardian show the latest news articles on their dashboard. Their traffic is high and, if documents are to be fetched from the database, they have to maintain a huge cluster of databases at all times.

Since the given set of news articles does not change (for hours), an agency can maintain a cache of articles. When the first customer visits the page, a copy is pulled from the DB, placed in the Redis cache, and then sent to the browser. Then, for another customer, the news agency server reads content from Redis instead of hitting the DB. Since Redis runs in the primary memory, latency is minimal. As a result, the customer sees faster page loads. The benchmarks on the web can tell us more about how efficiently a site can optimize its contents.

What if data is no longer relevant in Redis? (For example, the agency updated its top stories.) Redis provides a way to expire the `keys:values` stored in it. We can run a scheduler that updates Redis whenever the expiration time has passed.

Similarly, we can cache the third-party API responses for the given request (`GET`). We need to do this because third-party systems such as GitHub have a rate limit (telling us to be conservative). For a given `GET URL`, we can store the `URL` as a key and the `Response` as a value. Whenever the same request is given within the next time (before key expiration), just pull the response out of Redis instead of hitting the GitHub servers.

This method is applicable to our REST API, too. The most frequent and unchanged REST API responses can be cached in order to reduce the load on the primary database.

There is a wonderful library available for Go that can talk to Redis. It can be found at `https://github.com/go-redis/redis`. It is a well-known library that many developers recommend. The following diagram illustrates this concept very well:

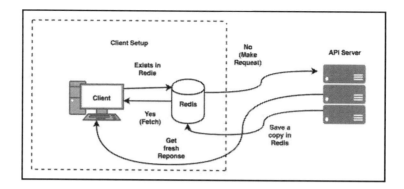

One caveat here is the expiration of the API. A real-time API should not be cached because of its dynamic nature. Caching brings performance optimization to our plate, as well as a few headaches regarding data syncing.

 Be careful while caching. Always implement a robust cache-busting method. There are many better practices available globally. Please go through them to get an understanding of the various architectures.

We'll discuss Redis in more detail in the next chapter, where we'll discuss strategies that can be used to develop asynchronous APIs.

Summary

We started this chapter with understanding client software: how a software client works and how we can create a few. We saw the basics of writing a command-line application. cli is a third-party package that allows us to create beautiful command-line applications. After installing it, we learned how to collect command-line arguments through the tool. We also explored commands and flags in our CLI application. Next, we looked into grequests, a package similar to Python requests that's used to make API requests from Go code. We learned how to make GET, POST, and other requests from the client programs. We looked at a fresh package called cobra for creating commands/sub-commands.

Then, we explored the GitHub API and how to fetch details about repositories. With the knowledge of both concepts, we developed a client that lists the repositories for a given user and also creates a gist (a set of text snippets on GitHub). Finally, we introduced the Redis architecture and how caching can help us handle the rate-limited API.

In the next chapter, we'll discuss strategies for building asynchronous APIs with the help of queuing and caching.

Asynchronous API Design

9

In this chapter, we are going to discuss how to design an asynchronous API for clients. We will look into strategies such as queuing tasks and publish/subscribe paradigms. A synchronous request waits on the server to compute the result. On the other hand, an **asynchronous (async)** request receives a response immediately with the information about the eventual result. The real world is composed of many synchronous and asynchronous events.

Asynchronous events are very popular in browsers. An async API mimics the same behavior as an event loop in modern browsers. In this chapter, we'll look at the difference between the request types. We'll also write a few clients in Go that can consume an asynchronous API.

In this chapter, we will cover the following topics:

- Understanding sync/async API requests
- Fan-in/fan-out of services
- Delaying API jobs with queuing
- Long-running task design
- Caching strategies for APIs
- Event-driven API

Technical requirements

You will need to install the following software to run the code samples in this chapter:

- OS: Linux (Ubuntu 18.04)/Windows 10/Mac OS X >=10.13
- Go stable version compiler >= 1.13.5
- Dep: A dependency management tool for Go >= 0.5.3
- Docker version >= 18.09.2

You can download the code for this chapter from `https://github.com/PacktPublishing/Hands-On-Restful-Web-services-with-Go/tree/master/chapter9`. Clone the code and use the code samples in the `chapter9` directory.

Understanding sync/async API requests

A synchronous request is an HTTP request that blocks the server until the response is returned. The majority of the services on the web run in this fashion. Nowadays, with the advent of distributed systems and loose coupling, API requests can also be asynchronous. In other words, an asynchronous request returns with information that can be used to fetch the information of a process. These asynchronous requests on a server are closely related to how concurrently the server can execute a job for multiple clients. Let's look at what a synchronous request looks like:

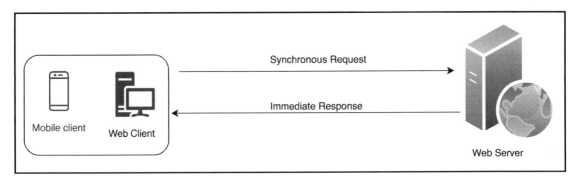

In this type of request, the web server performs all the actions and returns an **Immediate Response** to the **Web client/Mobile client**. The drawback of this approach is that if the server takes too much time to render the result, the client is blocked on the server's action.

An asynchronous request instantly returns a response but not with the result. It issues a ticket for finding the status of the requested operation. A client can use that ticket (a different response) to check the status and the final result of the operation:

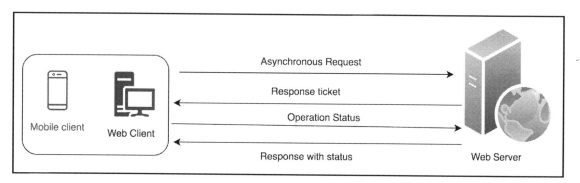

As shown in the preceding diagram, the client is sending a request to the server and the server returns a response to the client. This response is not something the client can consume instantly. Long-running tasks/jobs can be made asynchronous by the server. The client can then use the received response to find out the status of the job. Once the job is done, either the server can notify the client or the client can poll the result by looking at the status. So far, we have only built a synchronous API. This chapter will discuss its implementation in detail.

In the next section, we'll discuss how APIs can diverge into multiple or submerge into a single call. These techniques are called fan-out and fan-in, respectively.

Fan-in/fan-out of services

Let's take a real-world example of an e-commerce website integrating itself with a third-party payment gateway. Here, the website uses an API from the payment gateway to pop up the payment screen and enters security credentials. At the same time, the website may call another API called analytics to record the attempt of payment. This process of forking a single request into multiple is called **fan-out**. In the real world, there can be many fan-out services involved in a single client request.

Another example is **MapReduce**. Map is a fan-in operation, while Reduce is a fan-out operation. A server can fan out a piece of information to the next set of services (API) and ignore the result or can wait until all the responses from those servers are returned. As shown in the following diagram, an incoming request is being multiplexed by the server into two outgoing requests:

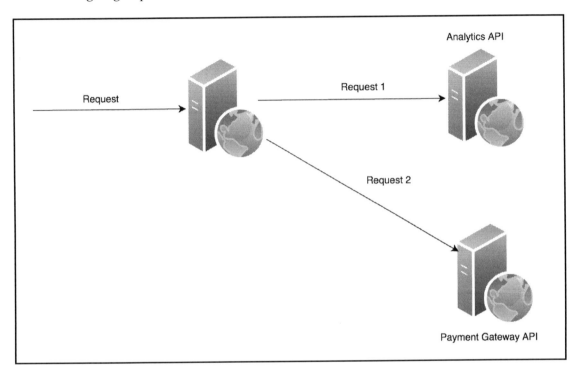

This process is a simple fan-out.

Fan-in is an operation where two or more incoming requests converge into a single request. This scenario is how an API aggregates results from multiple backend services and returns the result on the fly to a client. For example, think about a hotel price aggregator or flight ticket aggregator that fetches requested information about multiple hotels or flights from various data providers and displays them. The following diagram shows how a fan-in operation combines multiple requests and prepares a final response that's consumed by a client:

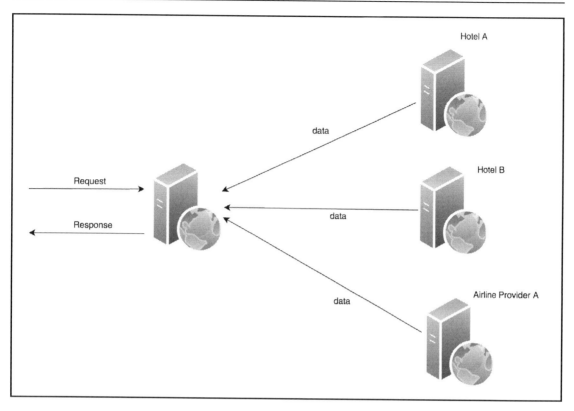

The client can also be a server that serves further clients. As shown in the preceding diagram, the left-side hand server is collecting the responses from **Hotel A**, **Hotel B**, and **Airline Provider A** and preparing another response for a different client. Therefore, fan-in and fan-out operations are not always completely independent of each other. Mostly, it will be a hybrid scenario where both fan-in and fan-out operations fit with each other.

Please remember that the fan-out operation to the next set of servers can be asynchronous too. This may not be true with fan-in requests. A fan-in operation is sometimes called an API call.

In this section, we've seen how fan-in and fan-out work. To use these techniques, we need to know how to implement an asynchronous service (API). In the next section, we'll try to implement such a service using a mechanism called job queuing.

Delaying API jobs with queuing

In synchronous APIs, the blocking code plays a crucial role in preparing the response that is sent to the client. However, in the asynchronous design, non-blocking is key. A queue and workers can be helpful in achieving non-blocking code. A server can have multiple workers running in parallel who can exhaust the contents of a queue and work on them. Whenever a client requests an operation through an asynchronous API, the server can put that request in a job queue, and all the workers can pick up a task whenever their turn comes.

This approach can offload an API server and focus on its business logic instead of getting blocked on parallel/independent tasks such as sending emails, contacting third-party services, and so on.

A few use cases of queuing are as follows:

- Compress images and email the final result
- Automatic back pressuring (limiting the load on the server to predictable amounts)

To explain this concept in detail, let's formulate an example and try to implement it.

Let's develop an asynchronous API server that can perform two different kinds of jobs:

- Logging given information to the database
- Sending an email

The condition is that it should not block other operations. The API should return a Job ID ticket to the client who can use that information to fetch the running information of the job.

Before jumping into the implementation, we should know about a few basics of enabling queuing to our service. We can implement queue/worker from scratch, but there are many good open source queuing systems such as RabbitMQ or ZeroMQ to choose from.

We, as part of implementing the preceding problem, will use RabbitMQ due to its popularity and the maturity of Go bindings.

RabbitMQ, a powerful message queue

RabbitMQ implements a messaging protocol called **Advanced Message Queueing Protocol (AMQP)**. It uses it to support worker queues. It also supports many other data exchange patterns, such as the following:

- Publish/Subscribe
- Topic/Subscription
- Routing messages
- **Remote Procedure Call (RPC)**

In this section, we'll focus on the messaging functionality of RabbitMQ. We can install RabbitMQ on our system using Docker, like so:

```
docker run --hostname rabbitmq-host --name rabbitmq-server -p 5672:5672 -p
15672:15672 rabbitmq:3
```

It starts the RabbitMQ broker with the given hostname, `rabbitmq-host`, and container name, `rabbitmq-server`. We use `rabbitmq:3` as the base image for our server. Docker pulls the image from the Docker hub and creates a container. You will see an output similar to this:

```
                Starting broker...
2019-08-10 08:19:20.371 [info] <0.223.0>
  node            : rabbit@rabbitmq-host
  home dir        : /var/lib/rabbitmq
  config file(s)  : /etc/rabbitmq/rabbitmq.conf
  cookie hash     : tUgaG2zTrSrf/yZv3KRV5Q==
  log(s)          : <stdout>
  database dir    : /var/lib/rabbitmq/mnesia/rabbit@rabbitmq-host

....
2019-08-10 08:19:20.873 [info] <0.497.0> started TCP listener on [::]:5672
```

RabbitMQ uses default port `5672` for its operations. You can change this using the initial settings for the Docker command.

The preceding RabbitMQ broker runs in the foreground. However, in production, you have to run it in the background. This means you need to pass the -d flag to the Docker command to run it in the background, like so:

```
docker run -d --hostname rabbitmq-host --name rabbitmq-
server -p 5672:5672 -p 15672:15672 rabbitmq:3
```

By default, if we don't pass user credentials while launching the container (`docker run ...`), a default <guest:guest> user's credentials are created for the broker. You can reset them at any time or pass them while launching a container. You can find out more at https://hub.docker.com/_/rabbitmq.

Communicating with RabbitMQ in Go

Now, we have a message broker (RabbitMQ). Before building an asynchronous API, we should learn how a Go program can talk to the message broker and send/receive the messages. While doing so, we'll create clients for production and consumption.

First, we have to create a connection to dial to the broker. If the connection is successful, a Channel needs to be created out of the connection. It has the API for performing operations on the message broker. Then, we can define a queue that messages are sent to. Finally, we publish a message to the queue.

We use an open source Go package called amqp for working with RabbitMQ.

Let's create our first program of this chapter:

1. Create a directory like this for a message sender:

   mkdir -p $GOPATH/src/github.com/git-user/chapter9/basicSender

2. Install the amqp package using the dep tool:

   dep ensure --add "github.com/streadway/amqp"

   This creates the Gopkg.toml and Gopkg.lock files in the directory.

Now, we are ready to go. We're going to look at an example that creates a queue in RabbitMQ and sends a message to it:

1. First, let's import the necessary packages/libraries inside `main.go`. These are `log` and `amqp`:

```
package main

import (
    "log"

    "github.com/streadway/amqp"
)
```

2. Now, we need a handler to handle errors that will be generated from every step. Go's error handling can be messy, which hampers readability. To have a clean code structure, we need to handle errors in one single place:

```
func handleError(err error, msg string) {
    if err != nil {
        log.Fatalf("%s: %s", msg, err)
    }
}
```

This function takes an error and a message and logs the information to `STDOUT`.

3. Now, let's write the logic for sending and receiving messages. In the program's main block, create a connection and channel. Then, dial to RabbitMQ using a connection string that contains user credentials. Once the connection is successful, obtain the `Channel` object to push messages. The code looks like this:

```
func main() {
    conn, err := amqp.Dial("amqp://guest:guest@localhost:5672/")
    handleError(err, "Dialing failed to RabbitMQ broker")
    defer conn.Close()

    channel, err := conn.Channel()
    handleError(err, "Fetching channel failed")
    defer channel.Close()
}
```

This is the connection string:

```
amqp://guest:guest@localhost:5672/
```

It is formed with the details of `protocol ://user:password@host:port`, where `host`, `port`, `user`, and `password` are the credentials of the RabbitMQ server.

 You should never use the default credentials for RabbitMQ in production. Please set strong passwords for all your sensitive information, including – RabbitMQ.

4. Declare a queue called `test` for publishing the messages:

```
testQueue, err := channel.QueueDeclare(
    "test", // Name of the queue
    false,  // Message is persisted or not
    false,  // Delete message when unused
    false,  // Exclusive
    false,  // No Waiting time
    nil,    // Extra args
)

handleError(err, "Queue creation failed")
```

5. Now, we have a queue. Let's prepare an `amqp` message (RabbitMQ message) to push it into the queue. Let's say the message body is a log of server time:

```
serverTime := time.Now()
message := amqp.Publishing{
    ContentType: "text/plain",
    Body:        []byte(serverTime.String()),
}
```

6. Publish the preceding message to the predefined queue, that is `testQueue`:

```
err = channel.Publish(
    "",             // exchange
    testQueue.Name, // routing key(Queue)
    false,          // mandatory
    false,          // immediate
    message,
)

handleError(err, "Failed to publish a message")
log.Println("Successfully published a message to the queue")
```

The `Publish` method publishes a given message into a RabbitMQ queue.

We've finished creating a sender. Now, if we run this program, it pushes a message instantly.

Now, let's write a receiver (worker) to consume those messages:

1. The logic is to define a `Consumer` and receive the messages. The code for the worker is mostly the same as it was previously:

```
mkdir -p $GOPATH/src/github.com/git-user/chapter9/basicReceiver
touch $GOPATH/src/github.com/git-user/chapter9/basicReceiver/
main.go
```

2. Dial to RabbitMQ using the connection string, fetch the `Channel`, and create a representation for `testQueue`:

```
package main

import (
    "log"

    "github.com/streadway/amqp"
)

func handleError(err error, msg string) {
    if err != nil {
        log.Fatalf("%s: %s", msg, err)
    }
}

func main() {
    conn, err := amqp.Dial("amqp://guest:guest@localhost:5672/")
    handleError(err, "Dialing failed to RabbitMQ broker")
    defer conn.Close()

    channel, err := conn.Channel()
    handleError(err, "Fetching channel failed")
    defer channel.Close()

    testQueue, err := channel.QueueDeclare(
        "test", // Name of the queue
        false,  // Message is persisted or not
        false,  // Delete message when unused
        false,  // Exclusive
        false,  // No Waiting time
        nil,    // Extra args
    )
```

```
    handleError(err, "Queue creation failed")

}
```

3. We need to add some extra functionality to consume. Just after `handleError` in the main section, we need to define which queue to consume and its properties:

```
messages, err := channel.Consume(
    testQueue.Name, // queue
    "",             // consumer
    true,           // auto-acknowledge
    false,          // exclusive
    false,          // no-local
    false,          // no-wait
    nil,            // args
)

handleError(err, "Failed to register a consumer")
```

4. `messages` is a consumable that can be read for messages that are pushed into `testQueue`. Let's see how we can read it:

```
go func() {
    for message := range messages {
        log.Printf("Received a message from the queue: %s",
        message.Body)
    }
}()
```

This runs a go-routine that spawns a function that runs an infinite loop to collect messages and process them. A go-routine is a lightweight thread that's managed by Go's runtime engine. We can spawn a go-routine from a function. Here, we are simply logging the message to STDOUT in our go-routine. If we don't block the main program, the whole process ends, quickly killing the go-routine.

5. Let's create a channel and read from it to block the main program:

```
log.Println("Worker has started")
wait := make(chan bool)
<-wait
```

In this way, we have a worker.

6. Let's run both programs to see how they work. First, run the worker. It creates a Queue called "text" if it doesn't exist. Then, run the sender to send a message to the queue on a Terminal:

```
go run $GOPATH/src/github.com/git-user/chapter9/basicReceiver/
main.go
2019/08/10 16:02:29 Worker has started
```

7. In another window of the Terminal (shell), run the sender program, which pushes a server time log into the queue:

```
go run $GOPATH/src/github.com/git-user/chapter9/basicSender/
main.go
2019/08/10 16:03:15 Successfully published a message to the queue
```

8. If you check the first Terminal, you'll see the following message:

```
2019/08/10 16:03:15 Received a message from the queue: 2019-08-10
16:03:15.367476 +0200 CEST m=+0.014980319
```

This means the worker is successfully able to retrieve the messages from the queue. This functionality can be leveraged by API servers to put long-running jobs into message queues and let dedicated workers handle them.

After grasping the basics of queuing and how it can help us build asynchronous APIs, we should implement a real-world problem. In the next section, we'll define the problem statement and try to design a long-running task that performs various functions at the same time.

Long-running task design

So far, we've learned about the basics of queuing and how to delay jobs. Now, we're going to design a solution to a problem regarding asynchronous APIs. The problem is that we want to build a system that can handle requests for the following scenarios:

- The server should save information to the database as one operation.
- It should send an email to the given email address.
- It should perform a long-running job and POST the result to a callback. This is known as a web-hook.

Let's say these three operations are asynchronous and long-running. We need a mechanism to facilitate a long-running process that has the following characteristics:

- The client can fire an API and receive a job ID back.
- The job is pushed onto a queue with the respective message format.
- A worker picks the job and starts performing it.
- Finally, the worker saves the result on various endpoints and sends the status to the database.

The following diagram shows the preceding requirements in detail:

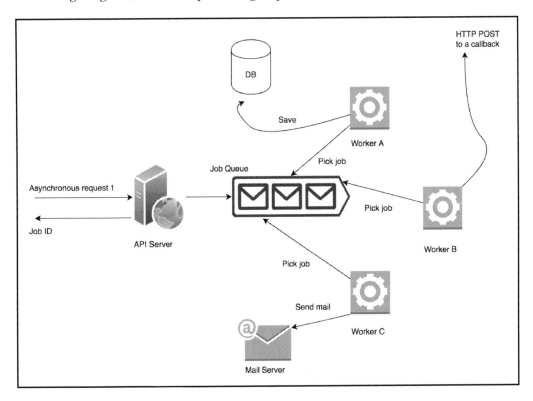

The preceding diagram shows a few engaging entities:

- **API server**
- **Database server**
- **Queue**
- **Workers**

API Server is accepting asynchronous requests from the client and pushing those jobs into a message queue. Then, the workers are picking those jobs and performing some action on them.

Worker A saves the information from the message into a database. **Worker B** picks a job. After working on the message, it posts some information to a callback that was received as part of a request. **Worker C**'s job is to send an email.

For the sake of simplicity, we'll mock the end actions (DB insert, Email sending, and Callback). We're doing this in order to focus on the asynchronous API design over concrete actions.

To design this flow, we need to reuse the same message and make it fit all use cases. JSON is a better format for storing information about a job.

We need to create some structs that hold information about the jobs, as follows:

- **Job**: Global storage for a job
- **Log**: Information dedicated to Job A
- **CallBack**: Information dedicated to Job B
- **Mail**: Information dedicated to Job C

A, B, and C are the worker types mentioned in the previous diagram.

Now, let's define our project. Creating a project directory and developing each piece shown in the preceding architecture is part of this process:

1. Create the project:

   ```
   mkdir -p $GOPATH/src/github.com/git-user/chapter9/longRunningTaskV1
   ```

   We're naming it V1 (Version 1) because it is our first attempt to achieve asynchronicity. We'll add more features with more versions in the upcoming sections.

2. We need to store our structs in the `models` directory. Create a package called `models` and add a new file to store the preceding structs:

   ```
   mkdir -p $GOPATH/src/github.com/git-user/chapter9/longRunningTaskV1
   /models
   touch $GOPATH/src/github.com/git-user/chapter9/longRunningTaskV1
   /models/job.go
   ```

3. For the fields, we have UUID to track the job, type to distinguish between jobs, and extra data that is specific to respective jobs. We use Google's UUID package to generate a UUID string and set a Job ID. type could be "A", "B", or "C".Log is used for time-related operations, so it needs a time field. callback needs a callback URL to post data. mail needs an email address to send a message to. The struct file contains the following constructs:

```go
package models

import (
    "time"

    "github.com/google/uuid"
)

// Job represents UUID of a Job
type Job struct {
    ID        uuid.UUID   `json:"uuid"`
    Type      string      `json:"type"`
    ExtraData interface{} `json:"extra_data"`
}

// Worker-A data
type Log struct {
    ClientTime time.Time `json:"client_time"`
}

// CallBack data
type CallBack struct {
    CallBackURL string `json:"callback_url"`
}

// Mail data
type Mail struct {
    EmailAddress string `json:"email_address"`
}
```

The important field from the preceding file is ExtraData:

```go
ExtraData interface{} `json:"extra_data"`
```

We define it as an interface and make it a placeholder for Log, Callback, and Mail. We instantiate the respective structs when we publish the message.

4. In the main program, we have to define a few helper functions and constants. We add these to our project's main file:

```
touch $GOPATH/src/github.com/git-user/chapter9/longRunningTaskV1
/main.go
```

5. Define the queue name, the address that the HTTP server runs on, and an error handler that handles any errors:

```
const queueName string = "jobQueue"
const hostString string = "127.0.0.1:8000"

func handleError(err error, msg string) {
    if err != nil {
        log.Fatalf("%s: %s", msg, err)
    }
}
```

This is done to avoid duplicate code.

We have to bake a few more components in our project:

- An HTTP server
- Workers
- URL handlers

A `Handler` takes an incoming request and tries to create an instant Job ID. Once it successfully places the job in the queue, it returns the Job ID to the caller. Now, the workers who are already started and listening to the job queue pick those tasks and execute them concurrently.

6. Create a file for the worker:

```
touch $GOPATH/src/github.com/git-user/chapter9/longRunningTaskV1
/worker.go
```

`Workers` is a `struct` that holds a connection to the message queue. Using that connection, all the workers read from the queue:

```
type Workers struct {
    conn *amqp.Connection
}
```

At some point, we need to start the workers. To do this, we need to define a run method that initiates/boots workers. The worker should listen to the message queue for messages and consume them.

7. Once there is an incoming message, check the type of work and delegate it to the respective functions, that is, dbWork, callbackWork, and emailWork:

```go
func (w *Workers) run() {
    log.Printf("Workers are booted up and running")
    channel, err := w.conn.Channel()
    handleError(err, "Fetching channel failed")
    defer channel.Close()

    jobQueue, err := channel.QueueDeclare(
        queueName, // Name of the queue
        false,     // Message is persisted or not
        false,     // Delete message when unused
        false,     // Exclusive
        false,     // No Waiting time
        nil,       // Extra args
    )
    handleError(err, "Job queue fetch failed")

    messages, err := channel.Consume(
        jobQueue.Name, // queue
        "",            // consumer
        true,          // auto-acknowledge
        false,         // exclusive
        false,         // no-local
        false,         // no-wait
        nil,           // args
    )
    go func() {
        for message := range messages {

            job := models.Job{}
            err = json.Unmarshal(message.Body, &job)

            log.Printf("Workers received a message from the queue:
             %s", job)
            handleError(err, "Unable to load queue message")

            switch job.Type {
            case "A":
                w.dbWork(job)
            case "B":
                w.callbackWork(job)
```

```
            case "C":
                w.emailWork(job)
            }
        }
    }()
    defer w.conn.Close()
    wait := make(chan bool)
    <-wait // Run long-running worker
}
```

8. At the end of the function, we closed the channel and blocked the worker since go-routines are running in the background.

9. Now, we can mock the actual work of the workers with delays for three functions: dbWork, callbackWork, and emailWork. We use delays to simulate the background work and log messages accordingly. We will define those functions on the workers struct so that the functions are tightly attached:

```
func (w *Workers) dbWork(job models.Job) {
    result := job.ExtraData.(map[string]interface{})
    log.Printf("Worker %s: extracting data..., JOB: %s",
     job.Type, result)
    time.Sleep(2 * time.Second)
    log.Printf("Worker %s: saving data to database...,
     JOB: %s", job.Type, job.ID)
}

func (w *Workers) callbackWork(job models.Job) {
    log.Printf("Worker %s: performing some long running process...,
     JOB: %s", job.Type, job.ID)
    time.Sleep(10 * time.Second)
    log.Printf("Worker %s: posting the data back to the given
     callback..., JOB: %s", job.Type, job.ID)
}

func (w *Workers) emailWork(job models.Job) {
    log.Printf("Worker %s: sending the email..., JOB: %s",
     job.Type, job.ID)
    time.Sleep(2 * time.Second)
    log.Printf("Worker %s: sent the email successfully,
     JOB: %s", job.Type, job.ID)
}
```

These workers work independent of the main program. They listen to the message queue and process incoming messages according to their type. By doing this, we have defined the endpoints/workers.

10. Now, it's time to define a few endpoints for our HTTP server that accept the API requests and publish messages to the queue. These will go into a new file called `handlers.go`:

```
touch $GOPATH/src/github.com/git-user/chapter9/longRunningTaskV1
/handlers.go
```

11. Our handlers also need access to the message queue's connection, which is a channel where we can publish messages. Due to this, it is better to have a struct for the server and define the handlers as methods. Let's call it `JobStruct`:

```
// JobServer holds handler functions
type JobServer struct {
    Queue    amqp.Queue
    Channel  *amqp.Channel
    Conn     *amqp.Connection
}
```

12. We should attach a method called `publish` to the preceding struct. All the handlers can use this method to publish a JSON body to the message queue. It is similar to the logic we explored when we introduced the RabbitMQ channel:

```
func (s *JobServer) publish(jsonBody []byte) error {
    message := amqp.Publishing{
        ContentType: "application/json",
        Body:        jsonBody,
    }
    err := s.Channel.Publish(
        "",          // exchange
        queueName,   // routing key(Queue)
        false,       // mandatory
        false,       // immediate
        message,
    )

    handleError(err, "Error while generating JobID")
    return err
}
```

Now, let's define three handlers that will work on three types of jobs, as follows:

- The first handler creates a job for work type A– saving client time to the database.
- The second handler creates a job for work type B– a callback to the URL after some time.
- The third handler creates a job for work type C– sending an email.

For the first handler, we take a query parameter called `client_time` from an HTTP request and use it to save in the DB. We use `json` and `strconv` to make required data conversions. Once we have the necessary information for the worker, we can compose the JSON and publish it to the queue:

```
func (s *JobServer) asyncDBHandler(w http.ResponseWriter,
r *http.Request) {
    jobID, err := uuid.NewRandom()
    queryParams := r.URL.Query()
    // Ex: client_time: 1569174071
    unixTime, err := strconv.ParseInt(queryParams.Get("client_time"),
     10, 64)
    clientTime := time.Unix(unixTime, 0)
    handleError(err, "Error while converting client time")

    jsonBody, err := json.Marshal(models.Job{ID: jobID,
        Type:       "A",
        ExtraData: models.Log{ClientTime: clientTime},
    })
    handleError(err, "JSON body creation failed")

    if s.publish(jsonBody) == nil {
        w.WriteHeader(http.StatusOK)
        w.Header().Set("Content-Type", "application/json")
        w.Write(jsonBody)
    } else {
        w.WriteHeader(http.StatusInternalServerError)
    }
}
```

As you can see, this function handler composes a message that is required for the worker that processes "A"(database job). Extra information is passed inside the `ExtraData` field. As we mentioned previously, the interface can fit any kind of new struct in it. So, at runtime, we set what could fit into `ExtraData`.

The other two handlers look exactly the same, except for the composition of `jsonBody`.

The JSON message for handler 2 is as follows:

```
    jsonBody, err := json.Marshal(models.Job{ID: jobID,
        Type:       "B",
        ExtraData: "", // Can be custom data, Ex: {"client_time":
                       // "2020-01-22T20:38:15+02:00"}
    })
```

The JSON message for handler 3 is as follows:

```
jsonBody, err := json.Marshal(models.Job{ID: jobID,
    Type:      "C",
    ExtraData: "", // Can be custom data, Ex: {"email_address":
                   // "packt@example.org"}
})
```

Next is the main program. We have to glue workers, handlers, and structs using our main logic. Previously, we added the constants, but now we have to extend this to bring the workers and API to life.

Finally, we should glue everything we have built so far together. Follow these steps to do so:

1. We need a function that returns a `JobServer` object. Let's add that function, called `getServer`, to the `main.go` file. The job server holds a connection and a queue. The code looks like this:

```
func getServer(name string) JobServer {
    /*
        Creates a server object and initiates
        the Channel and Queue details to publish messages
    */
    conn, err := amqp.Dial("amqp://guest:guest@localhost:5672/")
    handleError(err, "Dialing failed to RabbitMQ broker")

    channel, err := conn.Channel()
    handleError(err, "Fetching channel failed")

    jobQueue, err := channel.QueueDeclare(
        name,  // Name of the queue
        false, // Message is persisted or not
        false, // Delete message when unused
        false, // Exclusive
        false, // No Waiting time
        nil,   // Extra args
    )
    handleError(err, "Job queue creation failed")
    return JobServer{Conn: conn, Channel: channel, Queue: jobQueue}
}
```

Using this server, we can link URL endpoints to handler functions. These functions use the instantiated connection properties of RabbitMQ/Message Queue.

2. Now, get a `JobServer` by calling the preceding function with `queueName`, which we defined as a constant:

```
func main() {
    jobServer := getServer(queueName)

    // Rest of the code goes here....
}
```

3. Next, we should start the workers. If we start them normally, they'll block the main execution thread. Therefore, we have to make them goroutines:

```
// Start Workers
go func(conn *amqp.Connection) {
    workerProcess := Workers{
        conn: jobServer.Conn,
    }
    workerProcess.run()
}(jobServer.Conn)
```

4. To take client requests and make our application possible, we have to attach handlers to the URL. The Gorilla Mux router can be used for this. We discussed it extensively in Chapter 2, *Handling Routing for our REST Services*. We'll reuse the same pattern we used there to attach the routes to the handlers:

```
router := mux.NewRouter()
// Attach handlers
router.HandleFunc("/job/database", jobServer.asyncDBHandler)
router.HandleFunc("/job/mail", jobServer.asyncMailHandler)
router.HandleFunc("/job/callback", jobServer.asyncCallbackHandler)

httpServer := &http.Server{
    Handler:      router,
    Addr:         hostString,
    WriteTimeout: 15 * time.Second,
    ReadTimeout:  15 * time.Second,
}

// Run HTTP server
log.Fatal(httpServer.ListenAndServe())
```

This starts an HTTP server and routes requests to the URL we defined previously. As you may have noticed, we are using a job server's handlers as endpoints.

5. Last but not least, we should safely close the connection and channel:

```
// Cleanup resources
defer jobServer.Channel.Close()
defer jobServer.Conn.Close()
```

This completes our example. Let's build the Go project from the project root (`longRunningTask`) and see the output:

 Make sure your RabbitMQ server isn't down. Our job server uses RabbitMQ as a message queue.

1. Run the `go build` command:

   ```
   go build .
   ```

2. This generates an executable with the same name as the project, that is, `longRunningTaskV1`. We can start our HTTP server like so:

   ```
   ./longRunningTaskV1
   2019/09/22 20:36:06 Workers are booted up and running
   ```

3. The server is now running on port `8000`. Make a few `curl GET` requests to the server:

   ```
   > curl -X GET
   http://localhost:8000/job/database\?client_time\=1569177495
   {"uuid":"9dfbc374-a046-4b29-
   b6f8-5414a277aaa2","type":"A","extra_data":{"client_time":"2019-09-
   22T20:38:15+02:00"}}

   > curl -X GET http://localhost:8000/job/callback
   {"uuid":"ac297c92-74ec-4fcb-
   b3e6-6dfb96eb45e0","type":"B","extra_data":""}

   > curl -X GET http://localhost:8000/job/mail
   {"uuid":"4ed59a6f-24d8-4179-8432-
   fe4adcdd4f51","type":"C","extra_data":""}
   ```

4. Instead of blocking the requests, the server returns quickly with a Job ID for the tasks. Let's take a look at the server logs:

   ```
   2019/09/22 20:39:56 Workers received a message from the queue:
   {9dfbc374-a046-4b29-b6f8-5414a277aaa2 A
   map[client_time:2019-09-22T20:38:15+02:00]}
   ```

```
2019/09/22 20:39:56 Worker A: extracting data..., JOB:
map[client_time:2019-09-22T20:38:15+02:00]
2019/09/22 20:39:58 Worker A: saving data to database..., JOB:
9dfbc374-a046-4b29-b6f8-5414a277aaa2
2019/09/22 20:40:29 Workers received a message from the queue:
{ac297c92-74ec-4fcb-b3e6-6dfb96eb45e0 B }
2019/09/22 20:40:29 Worker B: performing some long running
process..., JOB: ac297c92-74ec-4fcb-b3e6-6dfb96eb45e0
2019/09/22 20:40:39 Worker B: posting the data back to the given
callback..., JOB: ac297c92-74ec-4fcb-b3e6-6dfb96eb45e0
2019/09/22 20:40:39 Workers received a message from the queue:
{4ed59a6f-24d8-4179-8432-fe4adcdd4f51 C }
2019/09/22 20:40:39 Worker C: sending the email..., JOB:
4ed59a6f-24d8-4179-8432-fe4adcdd4f51
2019/09/22 20:40:41 Worker C: sent the email successfully, JOB:
4ed59a6f-24d8-4179-8432-fe4adcdd4f51
```

There is a two second delay in sending the mail, but the client is not blocked on that decision. This is how an asynchronous API works by design.

Always prepare a design upfront for an asynchronous API. Since there is no silver bullet for a given problem, you have to explore various architectures, such as message queues.

Okay, but how can a client retrieve the status of a job, whether it is started, in progress, or done? To enable that feature, we have to store the state of a job somewhere. This can be a database or a temporary cache. Modern applications make a lot of read operations by polling the API for the job status. Redis is a good caching solution for these kinds of problems. We can extend this example with Redis to solve `find the status of a job ID`.

In the next section, we'll introduce Redis, which includes installing Redis and linking it to a Go program. After that, we'll construct an extended version of a long-running task with a job status.

Caching strategies for APIs

Redis is a wonderful open source solution for caching high-read configuration/information. It is a key/value pair store and has faster reads thanks to its in-memory storage. An example of a key/value pair store is a media website where a few articles are set fixed on their home page for a few hours.

Instead of letting every reader hit their database to fetch a record, a media house can use Redis to store article content. That is one of many applications of Redis.

Job status is temporary information that becomes irrelevant once the job is finished and status is logged to log storage. Due to this, Redis is the best choice for implementing job status caching. We plan to do the following things:

- Write a job status
- Read a job status

Both actions are performed by our job server but at different times. The status can be in three forms:

- Started
- In Progress
- Done

Redis provides a rich collection of data structures to hold information temporarily. Out of them, we use a simple `Key:String` for our job status. Job ID can be a key and status is its value. In simple notation, it looks like this:

```
{ '4ed59a6f-24d8-4179-8432-fe4adcdd4f51': 'In Progress'
```

We can easily run a Redis instance with Docker. Just run a Redis container and expose port `6379`:

```
> docker run --name some-redis -p 6379:6379 -d redis
```

The preceding command runs a Redis server on localhost on port `6379`. The process will be run as a daemon with the `-d` option. To check which container is for Redis, you can simply run the following Docker command:

```
> docker ps
CONTAINER ID        IMAGE               COMMAND                     CREATED
STATUS              PORTS
NAMES
2f0b2b457ed7        redis                       "docker-entrypoint.s..."    8 minutes
ago        Up 8 minutes        0.0.0.0:6379->6379/tcp
some-redis
c3b2a0a0295d        rabbitmq:3                  "docker-entrypoint.s..."    6 weeks
ago        Up 11 hours             4369/tcp, 0.0.0.0:5672->5672/tcp, 5671/tcp,
25672/tcp, 0.0.0.0:15672->15672/tcp    rabbitmq-server
```

`redis-cli` is a tool that can be used to quickly inspect the Redis server. You don't have to install it separately. Your Redis Docker instance already has it built in. You just have to execute a command against the Redis container, like this:

```
> docker exec -i -t some-redis redis-cli
127.0.0.1:6379>
```

You can get all the available keys stored in Redis with the following command:

```
127.0.0.1:6379> KEYS *
```

You can also set a key to a value with an expiration date in the CLI, like this:

```
127.0.0.1:6379> SET topic async
OK
```

The preceding command sets a key called `topic` to `async`. The server returns `OK` for a successful insert. The CLI is easy to use, but in most cases, you can also access Redis from applications. In the next section, we'll learn how to do this from Go programs.

go-redis, a Go client for communicating with Redis

There is a widely used type-safe Go client that's used to talk to Redis servers called `go-redis`. We can use it to connect to a Redis server by creating a client similar to RabbitMQ. Let's look at the steps for doing this:

1. First, we need to create a simple project called `redisIntro` for illustrating its basic usage:

   ```
   mkdir -p $GOPATH/src/github.com/git-user/chapter9/redisIntro
   ```

2. Initialize the necessary dependencies and install the `go-redis` package using the `dep` tool from your project's root:

   ```
   dep init
   dep ensure --add "github.com/go-redis/redis"
   ```

3. Now, create a small client that calls the default PING command and gets PONG back:

```
touch $GOPATH/src/github.com/git-user/chapter9/redisIntro/main.go
```

4. A client can be created using the redis.NewClient method from the go-redis package:

```
package main

import (
    "fmt"

    "github.com/go-redis/redis"
)

func main() {
    client := redis.NewClient(&redis.Options{
        Addr:     "localhost:6379",
        Password: "", // no password set
        DB:       0,  // use default DB
    })

    pong, _ := client.Ping().Result() // Ignoring error
    fmt.Println(pong)
}
```

5. The Redis client can perform commands on the server. One such command is PING. A SET or GET command works the same way. Now, let's run the program:

```
> go run $GOPATH/src/github.com/git-user/chapter9/redisIntro/
main.go
PONG
```

This prints out the PONG message, which is a response that's given by the Redis server. With this, we can confirm that our program is successfully connected to the server and that the queries are working fine.

Job status cache with Redis

Now that we've introduced Redis and the Redis client for Go, let's quickly add the feature of job status to our previously designed asynchronous API. We need to make the following changes to that project:

1. Add a new route to collect the job ID from a client
2. Add a new handler to fetch the job status from Redis
3. Whenever someone adds a new job, we need to write status to Redis in every stage of the job life cycle

We'll create a new project for this feature. It has a similar structure to `longRunningTaskV1`, which we created previously. The code and files are the same. You can clone the project and rename it `longRunningTaskV2`.

Let's take a look at the implementation, which includes dependency installs and modifications we have to make to the previous project. We won't go through the complete code, to avoid any redundancy:

1. To make sure you have all the necessary dependencies, run the `dep` command:

   ```
   dep ensure
   ```

2. Add the Redis package to the cache in order to store/retrieve the status of a job:

   ```
   dep ensure --add github.com/go-redis/redis
   ```

   The first change is to add a route to access the job status. The status could be any one of these three:

   - STARTED
   - IN PROGRESS
   - DONE

3. Let's add one more property to the `JobServer` struct, called `redisClient`. This stores the client connection to the Redis container, which is already up and running:

   ```
   vi $GOPATH/src/github.com/git-user/chapter9/longRunningTaskV2
   /handlers.go
   ```

4. Add the Redis package and modify its struct:

```
import (
    ...
    "github.com/go-redis/redis"
)


// JobServer holds handler functions
type JobServer struct {
    Queue       amqp.Queue
    Channel     *amqp.Channel
    Conn        *amqp.Connection
    redisClient *redis.Client
}
```

5. Now, add a handler function that accepts a UUID as a parameter and constructs a response by fetching the job status from Redis:

```
...
func (s *JobServer) statusHandler(w http.ResponseWriter,
r *http.Request) {
    queryParams := r.URL.Query()
    // fetch UUID from query
    uuid := queryParams.Get("uuid")
    w.Header().Set("Content-Type", "application/json")
    jobStatus := s.redisClient.Get(uuid)
    status := map[string]string{"uuid": uuid, "status":
     jobStatus.Val()}
    response, err := json.Marshal(status)
    handleError(err, "Cannot create response for client")
    w.Write(response)
}
```

This handler uses the Redis client Get function to fetch the value of a key from the Redis server. After this happens, the HTTP JSON response is sent back to the client.

6. Now, change the main.go file and add a new route:

```
import (
    ...
    "github.com/go-redis/redis" // Add redis import
)

func main() {
    jobServer := getServer(queueName)
    // Create a client and attach to job server
```

```
jobServer.redisClient = redis.NewClient(&redis.Options{
    Addr:     "localhost:6379",
    Password: "", // no password set
    DB:       0,  // use default DB
})

...

router := mux.NewRouter()
// Attach handlers
router.HandleFunc("/job/database", jobServer.asyncDBHandler)
router.HandleFunc("/job/mail", jobServer.asyncMailHandler)
router.HandleFunc("/job/callback",
 jobServer.asyncCallbackHandler)
// Add a new route here
router.HandleFunc("/job/status", jobServer.statusHandler)
}
```

This imports the Redis package and creates a new Redis client. It also adds a new route for collecting UUID job strings from clients. The new route is `"job/status"`, and we attach the newly created handler, `statusHandler`, to it.

7. We can make an API call to get the status of a job, but the pending functionality is to write a job status in Redis whenever a new job is executed. For that, we have to modify our workers a bit. The file we'll be modifying is as follows:

    vi $GOPATH/src/github.com/git-user/chapter9/longRunningTaskV2 /worker.go

Here, we should change the worker struct so that it holds one more Redis connection so that it can write the statuses of jobs in the cache. Our plan is to store the job ID as a key and the status as a value.

8. Add the Redis package to import `NewClient`:

    ```
    import (
        ...
        "github.com/go-redis/redis"
    }
    ```

9. Modify the `Worker` struct to add `redisClient`. This will hold a new connection to the Redis server:

    ```
    // Workers do the job. It holds connections

    type Workers struct {
        conn        *amqp.Connection
        redisClient *redis.Client
    ```

```
    }
```

10. In the `run` function, create a concrete connection to the Redis client:

```
func (w *Workers) run() {
    ...
    // Create a new connection
    w.redisClient = redis.NewClient(&redis.Options{
        Addr:     "localhost:6379",
        Password: "", // no password set
        DB:       0,  // use default DB
    })
    ...
}
```

11. Modify the worker functions to add the status messages. For example, let's look at `dbWork`:

```
...
func (w *Workers) dbWork(job models.Job) {
    result := job.ExtraData.(map[string]interface{})
    w.redisClient.Set(job.ID.String(), "STARTED", 0)
    log.Printf("Worker %s: extracting data..., JOB: %s",
     job.Type, result)
    w.redisClient.Set(job.ID.String(), "IN PROGRESS", 0)
    time.Sleep(2 * time.Second)
    log.Printf("Worker %s: saving data to database..., JOB: %s",
     job.Type, job.ID)
    w.redisClient.Set(job.ID.String(), "DONE", 0)
}
...
```

We are writing messages into a Redis key with the message as a value. The same key is overwritten when the process shifts to the next phase. This is achieved by calling the Redis `redisClient.Set()`. function.

If you're wondering why the third argument is provided, it's because it's the expiration time of a key on the Redis server. We can also set a key that lives only for some time. For now, we want to persist our keys, so the expiration is set to `zero`, which means no expiration in Redis.

We can apply the same process for the other two worker functions, that is, `callbackWork` and `emailWork`.

Now, it's time to test our new feature:

1. Build the `longRunningTaskV2` project and call a job using curl. Now, find the status of that job using the new endpoint that we added:

```
go build .

./longRunningTaskV2
```

2. Create a new job, like this:

```
curl -X GET
http://localhost:8000/job/database\?client_time\=1569177495
```

3. This returns the following JSON, which contains job details:

```
{"uuid":"07050695-
ce75-4ae8-99d3-2ab068cafe9d","type":"A","extra_data":{"client_time"
:"2019-09-23T00:08:15+05:30"}}
```

4. Now, we can find the status of a job with `uuid`:

```
curl -X GET
http://localhost:8000/job/status\?uuid\=07050695-ce75-4ae8-99d3-2ab
068cafe9d
```

5. This returns the following status:

```
{"uuid":"07050695-ce75-4ae8-99d3-2ab068cafe9d","status":"DONE"}
```

This message varies according to when the client calls the API. But it is a transparent way to give the status of asynchronous jobs to clients.

There is one more category of API that realizes asynchronous behavior. That is known as the event-driven API. Servers and clients can listen to broadcasted events rather than explicitly requesting them. This approach is different from traditional asynchronous implementations. We'll take a look at this in the next section.

Event-driven API

The strategies we've explained so far are instances of the request/response protocol where the client makes an API call to execute a job. There are many other architectures like this, such as the event-driven API, where a system generates a series of events that other systems can listen to and receive updates from. For a client to receive events, they should be subscribed.

This is similar to callbacks in some languages, such as JavaScript, where an event loop runs continuously and collects events. This type of approach is good for non-blocking clients and servers.

A trivial example includes a client registering an HTTP endpoint with an API. The server can trigger the API as an event whenever some useful information is available. A few practical examples are as follows:

- A weather station sending a series of events to subscribed clients (for example, mobiles)
- Amazon's **Simple Notification Service** (**SNS**) publishing a message to an endpoint
- A slack webhook that is registered to an API to get events; for example, a code pipeline failing

A few protocols that implement the event-driven architecture are as follows:

- Publish/Subscribe
- WebSocket communication
- Webhooks/ REST hooks
- Server push (SSE)

These protocols are used in different places according to the use case at hand. We'll discuss Publish/Subscribe briefly in `Chapter 11`, *Scaling our REST API Using Microservices*. There, we'll learn how to build an event-driven system, consume events from another party, and more.

Summary

In this chapter, we introduced the asynchronous API. First, we explained the key difference between a synchronous API and an asynchronous API. Then, we learned how multiple API requests lead to the fan-in or fan-out of services.

After that, we introduced a queuing system called RabbitMQ. A queue can hold jobs and allows servers to work on them. We learned how to create a queue and write a job into it. We also created a few RabbitMQ clients that can pick jobs from the queue and process them.

We also designed a long-running task with multiple workers and a queue. The workers always listen to the queue and accept jobs. We defined three kinds of workers: DB, Email, and Callback.

Redis is an in-memory database that stores key/value pairs. We can use it as a cache to store the status of jobs. We extended our long-running task to add status information by storing job statuses in Redis.

Finally, we introduced the event-driven API and learned that, using Publish/Subscribe and WebSockets, we can set up event-driven data exchange between clients and servers.

In the next chapter, we will take a look at the basics of GraphQL, as well as examples of writing a GraphQL client and a server in Go.

10
GraphQL and Go

In this chapter, we'll introduce a new query language called GraphQL. The traditional API definitions have failed to address the under-fetching and over-fetching APIs. An under-fetching API is an API that provides a minimum set of details for a given request. The drawback of this is that a developer should always create a new API or update the existing one. To overcome this, they can provide extra data that the clients can ignore safely. This causes another side effect; that is, it increases the payload size of the response. This situation is known as **over-fetching**. An over-fetching API provides unnecessary or unwanted data for clients. The response size is crucial when there are limitations regarding network bandwidth when designing APIs for clients.

GraphQL is a query language that solves this problem. In this chapter, we'll learn how a client can efficiently query data from an API using GraphQL. As with every framework, GraphQL also has a few limitations, but its positives outweigh them.

In this chapter, we'll cover the following topics:

- What is GraphQL?
- Over-fetching and under-fetching problems in the REST API
- GraphQL basics
- Creating GraphQL clients in Go
- Creating GraphQL servers in Go

Technical requirements

The following software needs to be pre-installed in order to run the code samples in this chapter:

- OS: Linux (Ubuntu 18.04)/Windows 10/Mac OS X >=10.13
- Go stable version compiler >= 1.13.5
- Dep: A dependency management tool for Go >= 0.5.3
- Docker version >= 18.09.2

You can download the code for this chapter from `https://github.com/PacktPublishing/Hands-On-Restful-Web-services-with-Go/tree/master/chapter10`. Clone the code and use the code samples in the `chapter10` directory.

What is GraphQL?

GraphQL is a query language that provides a set of rules. Using those rules and constructs, we can design an API that is efficient. According to the official documentation, the definition of GraphQL is as follows:

> *"GraphQL provides a complete and understandable description of the data in your API, gives clients the power to ask for exactly what they need and nothing more, makes it easier to evolve APIs over time, and enables powerful developer tools."*

> `-https://graphql.org/`

GraphQL provides a few features out of the box:

- Schema (a type system)
- Versionless API
- Schema to Code

A GraphQL schema is a syntax for defining the boundaries of an API. The boundaries contain information about what server resources are exposed via the API. Since it allows an on-the-fly update of the schema without failing all the clients, it helps us create a versionless API. GraphQL provides client and server libraries for handling the resources defined in a schema.

GraphQL is a language, not a runtime. So, someone has to translate a GraphQL schema to the code that a programming language can understand. A few GraphQL client and server libraries can do some automatic code generation from the schema definitions.

Regarding its functionality, let's look at the differences between a traditional API and a GraphQL-powered API.

For example, in e-commerce, a cart page or a wish list page fetches almost the same resources (most of the fields), such as product link, image, and cost. A few things do vary, however. For example, the cart page needs a shipping address but the wish list doesn't.

The API's flow looks like this:

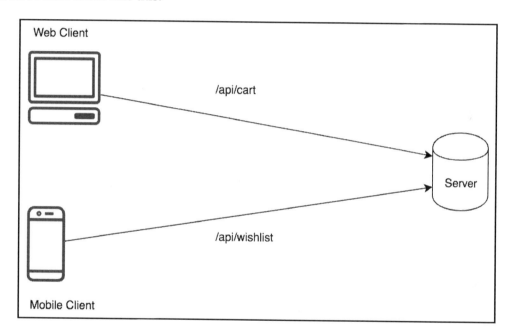

Let's say that the responses for the preceding requests appear as follows:

Cart page (web):

```
{
    'product': 'shoe',
    'cost': '20$',
    'link': 'http://example-product/1',
    'image': 'http://example-image.com'
    'shipping_address': 'some_square, Germany'
}
```

Wish list (mobile):

```
{
   'product': 'shoe',
   'cost': '20$',
   'link': 'http://example-product/1',
   'image': 'http://example-image.com'
   'related_products': ['sports_band']
}
```

The API developer usually defines two endpoints, one for the cart and another for the wish list. If the content of both the responses contains almost the same data, they can merge them into one for maintainability. There could be a problem with over-fetching for one of the API calls.

GraphQL gives the clients exactly what they need. The data that is passed over the wire is always as per the client's request. The following diagram shows this in more detail:

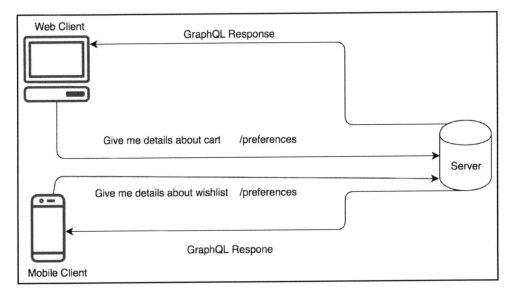

The same API endpoint can be used for multiple clients that are accepting the same resources but not the difference in data fields. That is the beauty of GraphQL. We will look at more practical examples in the upcoming sections.

In the next section, we'll show you a solid example of how over-fetching and under-fetching can occur in an API.

Over-fetching and under-fetching problems in the REST API

Over-fetching happens by an API when a server sends data that is not required by the client. The API is defined in advance and a client only needs to follow the API documentation. The drawback of this is that bandwidth is wasted. Let's take a look at an example.

You are trying to make use of a GitHub user's REST API to create a user tile display. The main intention here is to look at their followers, their public gist, their starred repositories, and the company name. However, when you make an API call to the GitHub API (https://developer.github.com/v3/users/#get-a-single-user) with the user octocat, it returns a JSON that looks like this:

```
{
  "login": "octocat",
  "id": 1,
  "node_id": "MDQ6VXNlcjE=",
  "avatar_url": "https://github.com/images/error/octocat_happy.gif",
  "gravatar_id": "",
  "url": "https://api.github.com/users/octocat",
  "html_url": "https://github.com/octocat",
  "followers_url": "https://api.github.com/users/octocat/followers",
  "following_url":
    "https://api.github.com/users/octocat/following{/other_user}",
  "gists_url": "https://api.github.com/users/octocat/gists{/gist_id}",
  "starred_url":
    "https://api.github.com/users/octocat/starred{/owner}{/repo}",
  "subscriptions_url":
    "https://api.github.com/users/octocat/subscriptions",
  "organizations_url": "https://api.github.com/users/octocat/orgs",
  "repos_url": "https://api.github.com/users/octocat/repos",
  "events_url": "https://api.github.com/users/octocat/events{/privacy}",
  "received_events_url":
    "https://api.github.com/users/octocat/received_events",
  "type": "User",
  "site_admin": false,
  "name": "monalisa octocat",
  "company": "GitHub",
  "blog": "https://github.com/blog",
  "location": "San Francisco",
  "email": "octocat@github.com",
  "hireable": false,
  "bio": "There once was...",
  "public_repos": 2,
```

```
    "public_gists": 1,
    "followers": 20,
    "following": 0,
    "created_at": "2008-01-14T04:33:35Z",
    "updated_at": "2008-01-14T04:33:35Z",
    "private_gists": 81,
    "total_private_repos": 100,
    "owned_private_repos": 100,
    "disk_usage": 10000,
    "collaborators": 8,
    "two_factor_authentication": true,
    "plan": {
      "name": "Medium",
      "space": 400,
      "private_repos": 20,
      "collaborators": 0
    }
  }
```

This is a big JSON file with spaces and newlines when you only need the aforementioned data fields. So, out of 37 fields, we are only going to consume four fields and ignore the rest.

Ignoring isn't a problem, but all the data traveled over the network to reach the client. This is an unwanted waste of bandwidth. This is called **over-fetching**.

Under-fetching is where a response that's sent by an API server is not sufficient for making decisions for a client. That leads to the following conditions:

- A client has to make subsequent API calls to different endpoints to procure data.
- A client has to compute manually on top of procured data and then merge it.

This is a very inefficient approach as clients have very few resources compared to servers. For example, if a mobile device has to compute costly operations because of under-fetching, the API has to change its strategy to provide sufficient data. That can lead to over-fetching. Finding the right balance is always tricky.

Let's take the previous example of fetching user information from the GitHub API. To get the starred repositories, we have to call `User` and then use the `starred_url` API endpoint to make a further query:

```
    "starred_url":
    "https://api.github.com/users/octocat/starred{/owner}{/repo}",
```

This is a classical under-fetching problem that limited the GitHub API until version 3 (V3). They mitigated this problem by introducing GraphQL API V4 (`https://developer.github.com/v4`).

GraphQL solves this problem by taking a whole new approach. It thinks about each entity as a resource and tries to build an API around it. This gives GraphQL the flexibility to compose data on the fly.

In the next section, we will look at the basics of GraphQL, such as syntax and definitions. This includes types, queries, and functions for manipulating data.

GraphQL basics

A GraphQL schema is composed of many building blocks. These building blocks are as follows:

- Types
- Queries
- Functions
- Aliases
- Variables
- Mutations

All these blocks are essential for building a functional GraphQL API. We can divide all of these components into two main categories:

- Schemas and types
- Queries and mutations

There are many features in each category, but we will only discuss the most important ones that can help you understand GraphQL. Let's take an example of fetching a user record from an API.

Note: All the snippets we show from here on are present in the intro directory of `Chapter10`, *GraphQL and Go*.

A typical GraphQL schema looks like this:

```
type Query {
  user: Person
}

type Person {
  name: String,
```

```
    address: [Address]
  }

  type Address {
    city: String,
    street: String,
    postalCode: Float
  }
```

This is a GraphQL schema with three types: one special type called Query and two other custom types called Person and Address.

This schema is the specification of the API. It defines what types of resources are available for querying. It also defines one special type called Query, which is used by clients to query for data. In the preceding GraphQL schema, only a user of the Person type can be queried.

A client query to the /api/users endpoint looks like this:

```
{
  user {
    name
    address {
      city
      street
      postalCode
    }
  }
}
```

The server then sends sufficient information for the previously requested fields:

```
{
  "data": {
    "user": {
      "name": "alice",
      "address": [{
        "city": "Munich",
        "street": "Marianplatz",
        "postalCode": "80331"
      }]
    }
  }
}
```

If the client doesn't need the `address` field and only needs the `name` field, it can only request the `name` to the same endpoint, that is, `/api/users`:

```
{
    user {
        name
    }
}
```

The server's response may be as follows:

```
{
    "data": {
        "user": {
            "name": "alice"
        }
    }
}
```

This response has only retained the `name` field and omitted the `address` field. This can save a lot of bandwidth.

 The shape of the GraphQL response directly matches the query, so clients can predict what they get back.

We will learn about types and queries in the next section.

Types and queries

GraphQL has a type system that a server should know about in order to prepare the schema. There are four types of high-level:

- Object level
- Field level
- Non-nullable
- Enumeration

Let's look at each type in detail.

Object-level types

Object-level types are used to define object-level constructs such as queries and resources. They are useful for defining what resources and queries are allowed on an API. The following is what we saw in the previous example, where we defined a query:

```
type Query {
  user: Person
}
```

These are special types and should not be confused with types in a programming language.

Field-level types

As the name suggests, field-level types are defined on a resource/query field. They are similar to the types in a programming language. It tells us what data type is going to be returned from the API. It can be further divided into two types:

- Scalar types (String, Int, Float, Boolean, ID)
- Custom types (Address)

In the previous example, the Person object-level type has the following fields:

- name
- address

The Go struct for the Person resource looks like this:

```
type Person {
 name: String,
 address: [Address]
}
```

The name field has a type called String, while the address field has a type called [Address], which is a list of addresses.

Non-nullable types

This is a special type that uses normal field types with special syntax and makes fields mandatory. When a type has a field with a non-nullable type, it should return non-empty data to the client. The type is defined with ! (*exclamatory*) at the end.

Take the `Person` type, for example:

```
type Person {
  name: String,
  address: [Address]
}
```

If we make the `name` field a non-nullable, it will look like this:

```
type Person {
  name: String!,
  address: [Address]
}
```

This means that if the client requests some data, the response must return a non-empty value for the `name` field. It cannot be null. We can also have a non-nullable list, like this:

```
address: [Address]!
```

The preceding syntax can return zero or more elements of the `Address` type in the response.

If we need at least one address to be returned, then we can apply the non-nullable rule to list elements too:

```
address: [Address!]!
```

The preceding rule creates an address field with a list of the `Address` type. That list should return at least one address to the clients.

Next, we'll introduce another important type called `Enumeration`.

Enumerations

Enumerations (Enums) are special types that give flexibility in defining a range of scalar types. They can be helpful for passing a range of information to the client. It brings the following benefits to an API:

- It allows an API to validate the field with a set of types.
- Without throwing out the type system, it communicates that the accessible field value will be in a finite set.

Let's take a look at an example schema:

```
type Query {
  vehicle: Vehicle
}

enum Vehicle {
  Car
  Bus
}

type Car {
  name: String,
  wheels: Int
}

type Bus {
  name: String,
  wheels: Int
}
```

In this GraphQL schema, we have a query type defined with `vehicle` as a field. `Vehicle` is an `Enum`. The vehicle has `Car` and `Bus` as its members. This means the query to this schema can expect either a `Car` or a `Bus`. This gives us flexibility over the predefined type systems.

In this section, we covered the basics for defining a schema and what types we can define. In the next section, we'll learn how to write advanced queries from the client while fetching data.

Queries and mutations

So far, we've seen how the client GraphQL query works. It describes the fields regarding the data that should be supplied. But what if we need data about certain criteria? Can we query with some values? Yes! GraphQL is built on querying and it provides a variety of options we can use while querying.

Let's go back to the initial example we showcased, that is, a user's API with `name` and `address`. The client query looks like this:

```
{
  user {
    name
    address {
      street
```

```
      }
    }
  }
```

The preceding query fetches all the users from the GraphQL server. We can also query a record by using the name. The query syntax uses curved brackets and parenthesis (:) on a field. Let's retrieve users whose name is "alice". The preceding client query should be modified using parenthesis, like this:

```
{
  user {
    name(name: "alice")
    address {
      city
      street
    }
  }
}
```

This query only fetches a record/records whose name is "alice". This construct is similar to a function call in programming languages. name: "alice" is called an argument for the query.

The GraphQL client can query using query arguments. The values for arguments can be scalar values, custom types, or even enumerations. We can also query on multiple levels. For example, let's search for a user with name "alice" that comes from city: "Munich":

```
{
  user(name: "alice"){
    name
    address(city: "Munich") {
     city
      street
    }
  }
}
```

Querying on multiple levels avoids the concept of multiple API endpoint fetches. The same API endpoint can flexibly change the data that is returned.

Mutations and inputs

A REST API has methods such as GET, POST, PUT, and DELETE. The method itself describes the operation of the API call. Does GraphQL have something similar? Yes – mutations. A **mutation** is a GraphQL client query that updates the state of a resource on the server.

Let's look at an example of a counter API. A counter API allows clients to increment and return the counter value. In REST, this is a POST method call. In GraphQL, we have to define mutations in the client query to create-then-fetch results from the server.

Say the GraphQL schema looks like this:

```
type Query {
  counter: Count
}

type Count {
  id: Int
  value: Int
}
```

The client query can fetch the count value for an id:

```
{
  counter(id: "250") {
    value
  }
}
```

This query fetches the counter value for id: "250". It returns the following JSON if the count is 1 in the server (storage):

```
{
  "data": {
    "counter": {
      "value": 1
    }
  }
}
```

But how can this API be transformed into a create-then-fetch API? This can be done using GraphQL mutations and inputs.

A special type called input defines a query argument type on the GraphQL server. So far, we've only seen scalar types as arguments. We can also create custom types and pass them into a client query. Input is used as an argument of a mutation.

The syntax for input looks like this:

```
input CounterInput {
  value: Int
}
```

After defining `input`, we can define a mutation that updates the state:

```
type Mutation {
  updateCounter(id: Int!, input: CounterInput)
}
```

This mutation defines a query function that inputs `CounterInput` and updates its `value`. Let's update our schema so that it includes these changes:

```
input CounterInput {
  value: Int
}

type Query {
  getCounter(id: Int!): Count
}

type Count {
  id: Int
  value: Int
}

type Mutation {
  updateCounter(id: Int!, input: CounterInput)
}
```

Now, a client should call a query in order to update a new value for `id: "250"`:

```
mutation {
  updateCounter(id: "250", CounterInput: {value: 2}) {
    id
    value
  }
}
```

This client query updates a counter (`id: "250"`) value with `2` and returns the updated record's ID and value. This is how GraphQL performs a create-then-fetch operation.

A GraphQL query is equivalent to REST's `GET`.

A GraphQL mutation is equivalent to REST's `PUT`, `POST`, and `DELETE`.

The knowledge you've gained regarding types, schemas, queries, and mutations should be enough for you to understand how GraphQL functions.

In the next section, we'll create a client query in Go and access GitHub's GraphQL API. This will confirm the theoretical knowledge we have gained so far.

Creating GraphQL clients in Go

When the Go program is a client for the GraphQL server, the client should understand how to compose GraphQL queries correctly and send them to the server. Go cannot do that natively, but it can with the help of an external package called `machinebox/graphql`. This is a lightweight client that allows developers to send queries and mutations to servers.

We can install the package using the `dep` tool:

```
dep ensure -add github.com/machinebox/graphql
```

Let's write a tool for fetching data from GitHub's GraphQL API. For that, create a project directory called `graphqlClient`:

```
mkdir -p $GOPATH/src/github.com/git-user/chapter10/graphqlClient
touch $GOPATH/src/github.com/git-user/chapter10/graphqlClient/main.go
```

The goal here is to fetch the details of all the available licenses for GitHub projects. GitHub provides an API to fetch all available licenses, but let's say we are only interested in the `Apache2.0` license. So, we proceed with the GitHub GraphQL API to fetch the license resource. To make API calls to GitHub, you should add a bearer token in the headers, along with the request.

We worked with the GitHub API in Chapter 8, *Building a REST API Client in Go*, to create a CLI client. There, we used a `GITHUB_TOKEN`, which acts as a personal access token or bearer token for API requests. An access token is a string that's passed to authenticate a user. We assume that you have the access token at hand (Chapter 8, *Building a REST API Client in Go*, to find out how and where to get it).

First, import the necessary packages. We need the `graphql` package and some other standard packages such as `os` to read the access token and `log` to print the response:

```
package main

import (
    "context"
    "log"
```

```
    "os"

    "github.com/machinebox/graphql"
)
```

We imported the `graphql` package as it is. If it is not available, run the following command:

```
dep init
dep ensure -add github.com/machinebox/graphql
```

The response for the GitHub license looks like this (from the documentation: `https://developer.github.com/v4/object/license/`):

```
{
  "data": {
    "license": {
      "name": "string",
      "description": "string"
    }
  }
}
```

There are many fields in the schema, but let's assume we are only interested in name and description. So, create a struct in our main program that holds this data structure:

```
// Response of API
type Response struct {
    License struct {
        Name        string `json:"name"`
        Description string `json:"description"`
    } `json:"license"`
}
```

The `graphql` package provides a function called `NewClient` for creating a GraphQL client. It takes a GraphQL server endpoint as the only argument.

Once the client has been declared, we can create a new GraphQL client request using the `graphql.NewRequest` function. It takes a client query string as the argument:

```
func main() {
    // create a client (safe to share across requests)
    client := graphql.NewClient("https://api.github.com/graphql")

    // make a request to GitHub API
    req := graphql.NewRequest(`
        query {
            license(key: "apache-2.0") {
```

```
                name
                description
            }
        }
    `)
    // Next code goes here....
}
```

Once we have both the client and request objects, we can make queries. However, the GitHub API is secured and needs an access token for authorization. For that, we should add a header called `Authorization` with the `'bearer'` token. The header can be calculated like this:

```
Authorization: 'bearer' + personal_access_token
```

We should concatenate the GitHub access token with the `'bearer  '` string (*note the space after "r"*) to form a bearer token. We should pass the whole string as a header to the GitHub GraphQL server. The code for this looks like this:

```
var GithubToken = os.Getenv("GITHUB_TOKEN")
req.Header.Add("Authorization", "bearer "+GithubToken)
```

Here, we are reading a personal access token from the environment variable and putting it into the `Authorization` header. After this, we should create a context and actually fire the request to the server using the `client.Run` function. To do this, we can declare an instance of the `Response` struct and pass it to the `Run` function. When the query is successful, the JSON response is loaded into the struct instance so that we can access the result:

```
// define a Context for the request
ctx := context.Background()

// run it and capture the response
var respData Response
if err := client.Run(ctx, req, &respData); err != nil {
    log.Fatal(err)
}
log.Println(respData.License.Description)
```

Here, `respData` is the result struct that holds the response from the GraphQL server. Once we receive the response, we can log the description of the `Apache2.0` license to the console.

Let's run the program and see the output:

```
go run github.com/git-user/chapter10/graphqlClient/main.go
```

This prints the license description to the console:

```
2019/12/15 23:16:25 A permissive license whose main conditions require
preservation of copyright and license notices. Contributors provide an
express grant of patent rights. Licensed works, modifications, and larger
works may be distributed under different terms and without source code.
```

This is how a Go client can interact with a GraphQL server. Client queries can be changed but the procedure always remains the same.

In the next section, we will learn how to implement a server that is similar to the GitHub GraphQL server that is powering API V4. We'll take a simple example of a multiplayer game and try to define a schema API.

Creating GraphQL servers in Go

So far, we've seen how to create a REST API. But how can we create a GraphQL API in Go or any other programming language? We can't do this directly. We need the help of a few packages to build GraphQL servers that can handle requests from clients. Clients can be web-based or mobile. We need two vital things to build a GraphQL server:

- Schema
- Resolvers

The Schema is what we discussed in the early stage of this chapter. Resolvers, on the other hand, are solid entities that generate HTTP responses. The Schema only validates and routes the request to the corresponding resources; revolvers do the actual logic of computing the result, a database query, or any other backend operation.

In this section, we'll create a simple server that responds to queries for player data in a multiplayer game. Let's get started:

1. Let's say the schema looks like this:

    ```
    query {
      players {
        highScore
        id
        isOnline
        levelsUnlocked
      }
    }
    ```

Let's say the server should return this information. Let's start implementing the service. We are going to mock data into our multiplayer game API. The same data can be queried from the database or can be fetched from a file. First, install the necessary packages. We need two packages:

- `graphql-go`: For creating the schema and adding resolvers
- `graphql-go-handler`: For running a server that can route requests to resolvers

2. Let's create the project repository:

```
mkdir -p $GOPATH/src/github.com/git-user/chapter10/graphqlServer
touch $GOPATH/src/github.com/git-user/chapter10/graphqlServer/
main.go
```

3. We can install both packages using the `dep` tool:

```
dep init
dep ensure -add "github.com/graphql-go/graphql"
dep ensure -add "github.com/graphql-go/handler"
```

4. Now, let's write our `main.go` file. It should contain all the necessary imports. The main imports are from the packages we installed along with `net/http`:

```
import (
    "net/http"

    "github.com/graphql-go/graphql"
    "github.com/graphql-go/handler"
)
```

5. Now, let's define our dummy data, which we serve through resolvers. Define a struct that returns the response for the preceding client query:

```go
// Player holds player response
type Player struct {
    ID             int        `json:"int"`
    Name           string     `json:"name"`
    HighScore      int        `json:"highScore"`
    IsOnline       bool       `json:"isOnline"`
    Location       string     `json:"location"`
    LevelsUnlocked []string   `json:"levelsUnlocked"`
}

var players = []Player{
    Player{ID: 123, Name: "Pablo", HighScore: 1100, IsOnline: true,
     Location: "Italy"},
```

```
        Player{ID: 230, Name: "Dora", HighScore: 2100, IsOnline: false,
        Location: "Germany"},
    }
```

The previously defined constructs are a simple Go struct and a list. We'll use this information later.

6. Now, define a player object using the `graphql.NewObject` function. This takes a `graphql.ObjectConfig` instance that defines the fields and their types for the object.

7. The `graphql` package provides scalar types and composite types such as lists. The following is the definition of the player object:

```
var playerObject = graphql.NewObject(
    graphql.ObjectConfig{
        Name: "Player",
        Fields: graphql.Fields{
            "id": &graphql.Field{
                Type: graphql.Int,
            },
            "name": &graphql.Field{
                Type: graphql.String,
            },
            "highScore": &graphql.Field{
                Type: graphql.String,
            },
            "isOnline": &graphql.Field{
                Type: graphql.Boolean,
            },
            "location": &graphql.Field{
                Type: graphql.String,
            },
            "levelsUnlocked": &graphql.Field{
                Type: graphql.NewList(graphql.String),
            },
        },
    },
)
```

These object fields will be mapped to the struct `Player` fields we defined previously.

8. Next comes our main function. Here, we have to define three things:

   - Root query
   - Schema Config
   - Schema

A root query defines the root object while querying. A schema defines the structure of the GraphQL response. A new schema can be created from the schema config. Our main function does all these things.

9. Then, we create a `fields` section and attach it to the root query. These fields have a `resolver` that gets called whenever a client makes a query. Let's say we return all the players when someone queries the root object:

```
func main() {
    // Schema
    fields := graphql.Fields{
        "players": &graphql.Field{
            Type:        graphql.NewList(playerObject),
            Description: "All players",
            Resolve: func(p graphql.ResolveParams) (interface{},
             error) {
                return players, nil
            },
        },
    }
    rootQuery := graphql.ObjectConfig{Name: "RootQuery",
     Fields: fields}
    schemaConfig := graphql.SchemaConfig{Query:
     graphql.NewObject(rootQuery)}
    schema, _ := graphql.NewSchema(schemaConfig)
    ...
}
```

10. Now, we have a schema. But in order to serve it via HTTP, we should pass this schema to the `graphql-go` package's `handler.New` function. We can also create an interactive GraphQL browser called `GraphiQL`. Let's see how to do this in code:

```
h := handler.New(&handler.Config{
    Schema:   &schema,
    Pretty:   true,
    GraphiQL: true,
```

```
  })

  http.Handle("/graphql", h)
  http.ListenAndServe(":8000", nil)
```

`handler.New` takes a schema as well as the option to prettify the GraphQL response. The GraphiQL option is used to enable the documentation and the interactive browser editor for the exposed API.

11. Now, run the program, like this:

```
go run $GOPATH/src/github.com/git-user/chapter10/graphqlServer/
main.go
```

This starts a GraphQL server on `localhost:8000`.

12. Open a browser and visit `http://localhost:8000`. You should see the interactive GraphQL editor. Now, paste the following client query into the left-hand pane:

```
query {
  players {
    highScore
    id
    isOnline
    levelsUnlocked
  }
}
```

You'll see the response that's served by our GraphQL server in the right-hand pane:

```
{
  "data": {
    "players": [
      {
        "highScore": "1100",
        "id": 123,
        "isOnline": true,
        "levelsUnlocked": []
      },
      {
        "highScore": "2100",
        "id": 230,
        "isOnline": false,
        "levelsUnlocked": []
      }
```

```
            ]
        }
    }
```

The response contains mock data, but this data should be dynamically generated in a real-world API. For more details about creating advanced queries and mutations within the server, refer to the `graphql-go` documentation (`https://github.com/graphql-go/graphql`).

You can use `GraphiQL` (an interactive GraphQL editor) as an API documentation service for your GraphQL schema. It is similar to the Swagger API specification. See the GitHub interactive API editor for inspiration: `https://developer.github.com/v4/explorer/`.

Summary

In this chapter, we understood the semantics of APIs. An API can over-fetch or under-fetch results for clients. This can cause additional noise in the data. Bandwidth wastage can be a big issue too. To overcome this problem, GraphQL offers a flexible approach for requesting data from APIs. This allows developers to write pragmatic APIs that do exactly what is requested by the client.

Then, we explored GraphQL in depth by understanding queries, mutations, schema, and types. We introduced many examples and saw what a GraphQL server response looks like.

Finally, we implemented a Go client for the Github API using a package called `machinebox/graphql`. After that, we created a server that responds to a client query.

In the next chapter, we will discuss scaling APIs using microservices.

11
Scaling our REST API Using Microservices

Building a REST API is easy in terms of the concept. But scaling it to accept huge traffic is a challenge. Till now, we've looked into the details of creating REST API structures and sample REST APIs. In this chapter, we are going to explore Go Micro, a wonderful, idiomatic Go package for building microservices.

This is the age of microservices, where huge applications are commonly broken down into loosely coupled components. The microservice architecture allows companies to quickly iterate in parallel. We will start by defining the term *microservices*, and then move on to Go Micro by creating **Remote Procedure Call** (**RPC**)-/REST-style microservices.

In this chapter, we will cover the following topics:

- What are microservices?
- Monoliths versus microservices
- Introducing Go Micro, a package for building microservices
- Adding logging to the microservices

Technical requirements

The following software should be pre-installed for running code samples:

- OS: Linux (Ubuntu 18.04)/Windows 10/Mac OS X >= 10.13
- Go stable version compiler >= 1.13.5
- Dep: A dependency management tool for Go >= 0.5.3
- Docker version >= 18.09.2

You can download the code for this chapter from `https://github.com/PacktPublishing/` `Hands-On-Restful-Web-services-with-Go/tree/master/chapter11`. Clone the code, and use the code samples in the `chapter11` directory.

What are microservices?

What are microservices? This is the question the enterprise world is asking the computing world. The sustainability of a product depends on how easily modifiable it is. Huge products should retire at some point in time if they cannot be maintained properly. The microservice architecture replaces the traditional monolith with granular services that talk to each other in some kind of agreement.

Microservices bring the following benefits to the table:

- Small teams can iterate in parallel by working on a small set of features.
- Adaptability is easy for new developers.
- They allow **Continuous Integration** (**CI**) and **Continuous Delivery** (**CD**) for individual components of a system.
- They offer easily replaceable software with a loosely coupled architecture.
- The architecture is not coupled to a specific technology

In a monolithic application (*traditional application*), a single application serves the incoming requests by sharing the computing power. It is good because we have everything in one place, and it is easily manageable. But there are few problems with monoliths, such as the following:

- A tightly coupled architecture.
- A single point of failure.
- The velocity of adding new features and components.
- The fragmentation of work is limited to teams.
- **Continuous Delivery (CD)** is tough because an entire application needs to be redeployed for a small change.

In a monolithic application, the entire software is treated as a single entity. If the database fails, the app fails. If a bug in the code crashes the software application, the entire connectivity with clients goes down. This requirement paved the way for microservices.

Let's take a scenario. A company run by Bob uses the traditional monolith model, where developers work around the clock to add new features. At the time of a software release, people need to test the code overall for every small component. The project moves from development to testing, when all changes are done.

Another company on the next street, run by Alice, uses a microservices architecture. The software developers in Alice's company work on individual services, who in turn test their individual components. The developers talk with each other's REST/RPC API to add new features. They can easily shift their stack from one technology to another, as compared to Bob's team.

This example shows that Alice's company is highly flexible than Bob's.

Orchestration and service discovery are very important aspects to consider when talking about microservices. A tool such as Kubernetes can be used to orchestrate the Docker containers. Generally, it is a good practice to have a Docker container per microservice.

Service discovery is the automatic detection of the IP address of a microservice instance on the fly. This removes the potential threat of hardcoding the IP addresses, which can cause a lack of connectivity between services. In the next section, we'll use a diagram to understand what is the crucial difference between a monolith and microservice.

Monoliths versus microservices

It is a common practice to begin a software application as a monolith, and then break it down into microservices in the long run. This actually helps to focus on the application delivery, instead of blindly following the microservice pattern. Once the product is stabilized, then developers should find a way to break down product features. Take a look at the following diagram for the difference between a monolith and microservices:

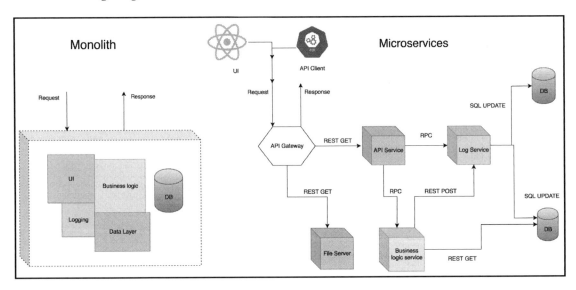

This diagram depicts the structure of monolithic and microservices architectures. A monolith has everything wrapped in a single system. It is called a **tightly coupled** architecture. In contrast, microservices are individual entities that are easy to replace and modifiable. Each microservice can talk to one another through various transport mechanisms, such as HTTP, REST, or RPC. The data format exchanged between services could be either JSON or Protocol buffers. Microservices can also handle various request entry points, such as **UI** and **API clients**.

Microservices can be implemented in any technology (Java, Go, Python, and so on), and can be replaced with any technology because of their loosely coupled nature.

In the next section, we explore how to create microservices in Go using a lightweight framework called Go Micro. There, we see how to develop mini services that can talk to each other.

Introducing Go Micro, a package for building microservices

Netflix's Eureka and Spring Boot from the Java community are famous for building microservices. The Go Micro package provides the same set of features. It is a toolkit for building microservices in Go. It is lightweight, which means start small and go big.

It has a Go style of adding services, which makes developers feel good. In the upcoming sections, we will see how to create a microservice with the steps defined by Go Micro. Go Micro provides requirements to implement RPC and **event-driven architectures (EDAs)**. It also has a pluggable interface where we can plug any external functionality.

The main features supported by Go Micro are as follows:

- Request/response
- Service discovery
- Load balancing
- Message encoding
- Async messaging
- Pluggable interfaces

Request/response is a plain HTTP/RPC call. **Service discovery** is useful for finding microservice instances at runtime. **Load balancing** is for routing requests to multiple same-type applications. **Message encoding** is essential for services to understand each other. **Async messaging** involves the generation and consumption of events. Go Micro's **pluggable interfaces** provide functionality such as codecs for translation, and brokers for storage systems.

Install Go Micro using the `dep` tool in any project in this way:

```
> dep init
> dep ensure -add  "github.com/micro/go-micro"
```

In the next section, we lay down the plan for our first microservice. We see how to encrypt and decrypt messages in Go. We will then build an encrypting/decrypting service using Go Micro.

Understanding encryption

We all know about the encryption of messages. **Encryption** is a process that uses a base message and a key to produce an encoded message through a mathematical algorithm that can only be decoded using the original key. That message can be passed over the wire. The recipient decrypts the message with a key and gets back the original message. We are going to create a microservice that provides both encryption and decryption.

See the plan for the development of our first microservice:

1. Develop utility functions for encryption/decryption.
2. Then, integrate it with Go Micro to produce a service.

Go comes with packages for encrypting messages. We need to import encrypting algorithms from those packages and use them. For that, we create a project that uses the **Advanced Encryption Standard (AES)**, as in the following steps:

1. Create a directory called `encryptString` in your `GOPATH/src/github.com` directory, as follows:

   ```
   > mkdir -p $GOPATH/src/github.com/git-user/chapter11/encryptString
   cd $GOPATH/src/github.com/git-user/chapter11/encryptString
   ```

2. Then, add one more file in the new directory, called `utils`. Add `main.go` in the project directory and `utils.go` in the new `utils` directory. The directory structure looks like this:

   ```
   └── encryptString
       ├── main.go
       └── utils
           └── utils.go
   ```

3. Now, let's add the logic of encryption in our `utils.go` file. We create two functions, one for encryption and another for the decryption of a message. First, import the necessary packages, `crypto` and `encoding`, as shown in the following code block:

   ```
   package utils
   import (
       "crypto/aes"
       "crypto/cipher"
       "encoding/base64"
   )
   ```

4. The AES algorithm takes an initialization vector. The vector is an arbitrary byte array that can be used along with a secret key for data encryption. Define it like this:

```
/* Initialization vector for the AES algorithm
More details visit this link
https://en.wikipedia.org/wiki/Advanced_Encryption_Standard */
var initVector = []byte{35, 46, 57, 24, 85, 35, 24, 74, 87, 35, 88,
98, 66, 32, 14, 05}
```

The values in the vector can also be generated randomly. Here, we use a predefined vector.

5. Now, let's implement the logic for encryption. It declares a new cipher using the `aes.NewCipher` and `aes.NewCFBEncryptor` functions. Then, we execute a function called `XORKeyStream` on the cipher to get the encrypted string. Then, we need to do a `base64` encoding to generate the protected string, like so:

```
// EncryptString encrypts the string with given key
func EncryptString(key, text string) string {
    block, err := aes.NewCipher([]byte(key))
    if err != nil {
        panic(err)
    }
    plaintext := []byte(text)
    cfb := cipher.NewCFBEncrypter(block, initVector)
    ciphertext := make([]byte, len(plaintext))
    cfb.XORKeyStream(ciphertext, plaintext)
    return base64.StdEncoding.EncodeToString(ciphertext)
}
```

6. Next, in the same way, let's define a `DecryptString` function that takes a key and `ciphertext` and generates an original message. In the `DecryptString` function, first, decode the `base64` encoded text and create a cipher block with the key. Pass this cipher block with the initialization vector to `NewCFBEncrypter`.

7. Then, use `XORKeyStream` to load content from `ciphertext` to `plaintext`. Basically, it is a process of swapping the encrypted and decrypted messages in `XORKeyStream`. The code looks like this:

```
// DecryptString decrypts the encrypted string to original
func DecryptString(key, text string) string {
    block, err := aes.NewCipher([]byte(key))
    if err != nil {
        panic(err)
    }
```

```
        ciphertext, _ := base64.StdEncoding.DecodeString(text)
        cfb := cipher.NewCFBEncrypter(block, initVector)
        plaintext := make([]byte, len(ciphertext))
        cfb.XORKeyStream(plaintext, ciphertext)
        return string(plaintext)
}
```

This completes the definition of utility files for encryption and decryption.

8. Now, let's edit the `main.go` file to leverage the preceding `utils` package and its functions. The `main` function should encrypt a message using the `EncryptString` function, and then decrypt a message using the `DecryptString` function, like this:

```
package main
import (
    "log"
    "github.com/git-user/chapter11/encryptString/utils"
)
// AES keys should be of length 16, 24, 32
func main() {
    key := "111023043350789514532147"
    message := "I am A Message"
    log.Println("Original message: ", message)
    encryptedString := utils.EncryptString(key, message)
    log.Println("Encrypted message: ", encryptedString)
    decryptedString := utils.DecryptString(key, encryptedString)
    log.Println("Decrypted message: ", decryptedString)
}
```

The original message should not change.

9. Here, we are importing the `encrypting/decrypting` functions from the `utils` package and using them to show an example. If we run this program, we see the following output:

```
> go run main.go

Original message: I am A Message
Encrypted message: 8/+JCfTb+ibIjzQtmCo=
Decrypted message: I am A Message
```

This program illustrates how we can use the AES algorithm to encrypt a message and get it back using the same secret key. This algorithm is also called the **Rijndael** (pronounced as *rain-dahl*) algorithm.

In the next section, we use this encryption knowledge to create a microservice using Go Micro.

Building a microservice with Go Micro

We will use Go Micro and our encryption logic in `utils` to write a microservice. A Go microservice should be built in a step-wise manner. To create a service, we need to design a few entities upfront. They are as follows:

- A protocol buffer file for defining RPC methods of service
- A handler file that has an actual implementation of methods
- A server that exposes RPC methods
- A client that can make RPC requests and get results

We need two system level-tools called `protoc` and `protoc-gen-micro` for compiling protocol buffers to Go packages. Let's see the steps for creating an encryption microservice, as follows:

1. Let's install those compilers using the `go get` command, as follows:

    ```
    > go get -u github.com/golang/protobuf/protoc-gen-go
    > go get github.com/micro/protoc-gen-micro
    ```

2. Let's create our project directories, like this:

    ```
    > mkdir -p $GOPATH/src/github.com/git-user/chapter11/encryptService
    mkdir $GOPATH/src/github.com/git-user/chapter11/encryptService/
    proto
    ```

3. Now, define an `encryption.proto` protocol buffer file in the `proto` directory, like this:

    ```
    syntax = "proto3";

    service Encrypter {
      rpc Encrypt(Request) returns (Response) {}
      rpc Decrypt(Request) returns (Response) {}
    }

    message Request {
    ```

```
        string message = 1;
        string key = 2;
}

message Response {
        string result = 2;
}
```

It should have a service called `Encrypter` and two messages called `Request` and `Response`. These two messages are for requesting encryption and decryption.

The syntax of the preceding file is `"proto3"`. The `Request` message has two fields, called `message` and `key` respectively. The client uses these field to send a `plaintext/ciphertext` message.

The `Response` message has a field called `result`. It is the result of the encryption/decryption process. The `Encrypter` service has two RPC methods called `Encrypt` and `Decrypt`. Both take a `Request` and return a `Response`.

4. Now, we can generate the Go files by compiling a `.proto` file, like this:

```
> protoc -I=. --micro_out=. --go_out=. proto/encryption.proto
```

This is the breakdown of the command:

Option	Meaning
`-I`	The input of project root
`--go_out`	The output of the Go file that has autogenerated methods
`--micro_out`	Similar to `--go_out`, but generates an extra file with Go micro methods
`proto/encryption.proto`	Path to the protocol buffer file to be compiled

It generates two new files in the project's `proto` directory. Their names are as follows:

- `encryption.pb.go`
- `encryption.pb.micro.go`

These code-generated files should not be modified by hand.

5. Let's copy the `utils.go` file we have defined in the `encryptString` example. It can be reused as it is, except for a small change in the package name, as shown here:

```
> cp $GOPATH/src/github.com/git-user/chapter11/encryptString/utils/
utils.go $GOPATH/src/github.com/git-user/chapter11/encryptService/
```

6. After the copy, change the package name in the file from `utils` to `main` (because now, this file is in the new project's root), as follows:

```
package main

import (
    "crypto/aes"
    "crypto/cipher"
    "encoding/base64"
)
...
```

With this, we have the `EncryptString` and `DecryptString` functions available throughout the Go project.

7. Now, add one more file called `handlers.go`, where we define the business logic for our service. It exports an `Encrypter` struct and a few methods that handle RPC requests. The code for this is shown here:

```
> touch $GOPATH/src/github.com/git-user/chapter11/encryptService/
handlers.go
```

8. The `Encrypter` struct should have two methods, `Encrypt` and `Decrypt`. Each method takes a context object, an RPC request object, and an RPC response object. The job each method does is to call the respective utility function and set the response object with a result, like so:

```
package main

import (
    "context"

    proto "github.com/git-user/chapter11/encryptService/proto"
)

// Encrypter holds the information about methods
type Encrypter struct{}

// Encrypt converts a message into cipher and returns response
```

```
func (g *Encrypter) Encrypt(ctx context.Context,
 req *proto.Request, rsp *proto.Response) error {
    rsp.Result = EncryptString(req.Key, req.Message)
    return nil
}

// Decrypt converts a cipher into message and returns response
func (g *Encrypter) Decrypt(ctx context.Context,
 req *proto.Request, rsp *proto.Response) error {
    rsp.Result = DecryptString(req.Key, req.Message)
    return nil
}
```

9. The `Encrypt` and `Decrypt` methods are mapped to these RPC methods in the protocol buffer file, like so:

```
rpc Encrypt(Request) returns (Response) {}
rpc Decrypt(Request) returns (Response) {}
```

10. Now, we have to plug these handlers into our `main` program, like so:

```
> touch $GOPATH/src/github.com/git-user/chapter11/encryptService/
main.go
```

11. The `main` program imports the `proto` and `go-micro` packages and tries to create a new microservice instance. Then, it registers the service to the `Encrypter` handler we exported from the `handlers.go` file. Finally, it runs the service. All this is illustrated in the following block of code:

```
package main

import (
    fmt "fmt"

    proto "github.com/git-user/chapter11/encryptService/proto"
    micro "github.com/micro/go-micro"
)

func main() {
    // Create a new service. Optionally include some options here.
    service := micro.NewService(
        micro.Name("encrypter"),
    )

    // Init will parse the command line flags.
    service.Init()
```

```
    // Register handler
    proto.RegisterEncrypterHandler(service.Server(),
     new(Encrypter))

    // Run the server
    if err := service.Run(); err != nil {
        fmt.Println(err)
    }
}
```

In the preceding program, `micro.NewService` is being used to create a new microservice. It returns a `service` object. We can also collect command-line arguments by running `service.Init()`. In our example, we are not passing any. We can register the service to the handler by using the `RegisterEncrypterHandler` method. This method is dynamically generated by the protocol buffer compiler. Finally, `service.Run` starts the server. Let's run the service.

12. Try to build the project from the project root directory, `encryptService`, as follows:

```
> go build && ./encryptService

2019/12/22 16:16:18 log.go:18: Transport [http] Listening on
[::]:58043
2019/12/22 16:16:18 log.go:18: Broker [http] Connected to
[::]:58044
2019/12/22 16:16:18 log.go:18: Registry [mdns] Registering node:
encrypter-4d68d94a-727d-445b-80a3-24a1db3639dd
```

As you see from the server output, Go Micro starts the microservice with a transport and a message broker. Now, clients can make requests to these ports. The service is not so useful unless there is a client to consume the API. So, in the next section, we'll try to build a Go Micro client and see how to connect to the preceding server.

If you want to run the program without building it, you have to include all the packages that are imported in the `main` file.

For example, `go run main.go handlers.go utils.go` is equivalent to `go build && ./encryptService`.

Building an RPC client with Go Micro

In Chapter 6, *Working with Protocol Buffers and gRPC*, where we discussed protocol buffers, we mentioned that a server and client should agree on the same protocol buffer. In the same way, Go Micro expects the service and client to use the same .proto file—in our case, encryption.proto. A client can be another service that is requesting some information.

We can build clients using Go Micro. It includes all the necessary constructs to connect and make RPC calls to a microservice. Our plan is to create a client and ask the service to encrypt and decrypt messages. Those requests will be RPC calls. Let's see the steps for creating and using a Go Micro client, as follows:

1. Create a new project for the client, like this:

```
> mkdir -p $GOPATH/src/github.com/git-user/chapter11/encryptClient/
> mkdir $GOPATH/src/github.com/git-user/chapter11/encryptClient/
proto
```

2. Now, add an encryption.proto file in the proto directory, which looks exactly similar to that of the service, like this:

```
syntax = "proto3";

service Encrypter {
  rpc Encrypt(Request) returns (Response) {}
  rpc Decrypt(Request) returns (Response) {}
}

message Request {
  string message = 1;
  string key = 2;
}

message Response {
    string result = 2;
}
```

3. If observed carefully, the service name, messages, and their definitions are matching with that of the service. Now, compile the protocol buffer from the encryptClient project root, as follows:

```
> protoc -I=. --micro_out=. --go_out=. proto/encryption.proto
```

4. After this, the client generates two files in the `proto` directory. Those should not be modified. Now, we are ready with our setup. Add a `main.go` file for making RPC calls to the service, as follows:

```
> touch $GOPATH/src/github.com/git-user/chapter11/encryptClient/
main.go
```

5. The `main` program imports the `proto` and `go-micro` packages where we compiled protocol buffers, like so:

```
package main

import (
    "context"
    "fmt"

    proto "github.com/git-user/chapter11/encryptClient/proto"
    micro "github.com/micro/go-micro"
)
```

6. A client should also be created with a function called `micro.NewService`, like this:

```
func main() {
    // Create a new service
    service := micro.NewService(micro.Name("encrypter.client"))
    // Initialise the client and parse command line flags
    service.Init()

    // Create new encrypter service instance
    encrypter := proto.NewEncrypterService("encrypter",
     service.Client())
    ...
}
```

It can be initialized to collect environment variables. The key difference between a client and a service is that for the client, we create an instance of `service` using the `proto.NewEncrypterService` function. We use that instance to make API calls. Remember that the function is auto-generated by the `protoc` command.

7. The `encrypter` is the service instance in the code. Next, we can make RPC calls by calling RPC methods directly on the service instance. Let's pass a text called `"I am a Message"` with the key `"111023043350789514532147"` to encrypt the method, like this:

```
// Call the encrypter
rsp, err := encrypter.Encrypt(context.TODO(), &proto.Request{
    Message: "I am a Message",
    Key:     "111023043350789514532147",
})

if err != nil {
    fmt.Println(err)
}

// Print response
fmt.Println(rsp.Result)
```

The function, as specified in the protocol buffer, returns a response that has a `Result` field. We are printing that value to the console.

8. Next, let's pass this result back as a cipher for the `Decrypt` function. It should return the original message back. We use the same key as we did for encryption, like this:

```
// Call the decrypter
rsp, err = encrypter.Decrypt(context.TODO(), &proto.Request{
    Message: rsp.Result,
    Key:     "111023043350789514532147",
})

if err != nil {
    fmt.Println(err)
}
// Print response
fmt.Println(rsp.Result)
```

9. These two blocks go into the `main` function. Once we are done adding them, let's build and run the client, as follows:

```
> go build && ./encryptClient

8/+JCfT7+ibIjzQtmCo=
I am a Message
```

We passed the plaintext and key, and the original message is returned back as the final result. It confirms that the `encrypt` and `decrypt` RPC calls are working properly. The benefit of Go Micro is, with a few lines of code, we can create microservices and clients.

In the next section, we see how Go Micro supports EDAs where services and clients can communicate via events.

Building event-driven microservices

In `Chapter 9`, *Asynchronous API Design*, we learned about asynchronous programming. An asynchronous API can be achieved by events. The service and client can talk to each other using events. They don't have to wait until one party finishes their job.

An event generator is an entity that generates events. An event consumer consumes the events from other parties. Publish/Subscribe is an architectural pattern that is possible with events. Go Micro supports Publish/Subscribe by using a message broker interface.

See the following diagram to understand the event flow:

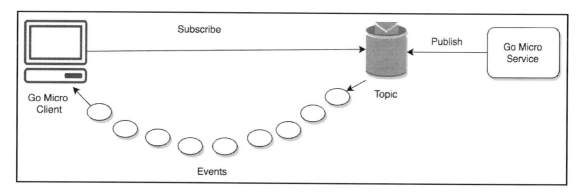

A Go Micro client can **Subscribe** to a topic. A Go microservice can **Publish** messages into that **Topic**. Events flow from right to left in this case.

It comes with an inbuilt HTTP message broker and can be easily replaced with widely used message brokers such as RabbitMQ or Kafka. In our discussion, we stick to the default HTTP broker.

We will illustrate Publish/Subscribe with an example. Let's say a microservice should push weather alerts every 5 seconds. Instead of the client calling the service API, the service can publish those changes to a topic where a client can subscribe. The client consumes those alerts and does the processing.

In all the projects we are working on, we should install Go Micro using the dep tool and running the following code:

```
> dep init
> dep ensure -add "github.com/micro/go-micro"
```

We are going to create an `asyncServer` and an `asyncClient`. The `asyncServer` generates weather events, and the client consumes them. Let's look at the steps for this example here:

1. Create a project directory, like this:

```
> mkdir -p $GOPATH/src/github.com/git-user/chapter11/asyncService
> mkdir $GOPATH/src/github.com/git-user/chapter11/asyncServer/proto

> mkdir -p $GOPATH/src/github.com/git-user/chapter11/asyncClient
> mkdir $GOPATH/src/github.com/git-user/chapter11/asyncClient/proto
```

2. Create a `weather.proto` file in the `proto` directory of both `asyncService` and `asyncClient`. It holds a structure and RPC methods for communication. This file defines an `Event` that is a weather alert, and the code can be seen as follows:

```
syntax = "proto3";

// Example message
message Event {
    // city name
    string city = 1;
    // unix timestamp
    int64 timestamp = 2;
    // temperaure in Celsius
    int64 temperature = 3;
}
```

It has three fields, as follows:

- `city name`
- `unix timestamp`
- `temperature in Celsius`

A service should publish this event to a topic called `alerts`.

3. Now, compile the `.proto` file in both the service and client, and get auto-generated Go files, as follows:

```
> protoc -I=. --micro_out=. --go_out=. proto/weather.proto
```

 For brevity, we are skipping the imports in this example, so please access the chapter repo for the complete code.

4. Coming to the service, the `main.go` file should declare a microservice and a publisher. A publisher is created by the `micro.NewPublisher` method. It takes the topic name `alerts` and a `service.Client()` as its arguments, as follows:

```
func main() {
    // Create a new service. Optionally include some options here.
    service := micro.NewService(
        micro.Name("weather"),
    )
    p := micro.NewPublisher("alerts", service.Client())
    ...
}
```

5. Next, we create a dummy ticker that publishes a weather alert every 15 seconds. We achieve that by using the `time.Tick` built-in Go method. We spawn a `go-routine` that loops forever, listens to a tick, and publishes an event into the topic using the `publisher.Publish` method. The `Publish` method takes a context object and an event with data as arguments, as can be seen in the following code block:

```
go func() {
    for now := range time.Tick(15 * time.Second) {
        log.Println("Publishing weather alert to Topic: alerts")
        p.Publish(context.TODO(), &proto.Event{
            City:        "Munich",
            Timestamp:   now.UTC().Unix(),
            Temperature: 2,
        })
    }
}()
```

6. After this, finally, we have to run the service by calling the `service.Run` method, like this:

```
// Run the server
if err := service.Run(); err != nil {
    log.Println(err)
}
```

7. Both `service` and `go-routine` run in parallel. When you run this service, you see this output:

```
> go build && ./asyncService

2019/12/22 21:31:03 log.go:18: Transport [http] Listening on
[::]:60243
2019/12/22 21:31:03 log.go:18: Broker [http] Connected to
[::]:60244
2019/12/22 21:31:03 log.go:18: Registry [mdns] Registering node:
weather-83982bda-5e9e-445b-9ce2-5439d1560d1f
2019-12-22 21:31:18.379616 I | Publishing event to Topic: alerts
2019-12-22 21:31:33.376924 I | Publishing event to Topic: alerts
```

8. Now, the service is pushing events, but there is no client to consume them. Let's update the `main.go` file `asyncClient` with consuming logic. In the client, we should declare a handler function to process the event. The handler is executed whenever there is an incoming event. It prints out the event in our case, as can be seen here:

```
// ProcessEvent processes a weather alert
func ProcessEvent(ctx context.Context, event *proto.Event) error {
    log.Println("Got alert:", event)
    return nil
}
```

9. After defining the handler function to process events, we can attach the client with the topic. The `micro.RegisterSubscriber` function attaches a `ProcessEvent` handler function to the `alerts` topic, like this:

```
func main() {
    // Create a new service
    service := micro.NewService(micro.Name("weather_client"))
    // Initialise the client and parse command line flags
    service.Init()
    micro.RegisterSubscriber("alerts", service.Server(),
     ProcessEvent)

    if err := service.Run(); err != nil {
```

```
        log.Fatal(err)
    }
}
```

10. If we run this program, it consumes the alerts published by the service we defined previously, as follows:

```
> go build && ./asyncClient

2019/12/22 21:48:07 log.go:18: Transport [http] Listening on
[::]:60445
2019/12/22 21:48:07 log.go:18: Broker [http] Connected to
[::]:60446
2019/12/22 21:48:07 log.go:18: Registry [mdns] Registering node:
weather_client-73496273-31ca-4bed-84dc-60df07a1570d
2019/12/22 21:48:07 log.go:18: Subscribing
weather_client-73496273-31ca-4bed-84dc-60df07a1570d to topic:
alerts
2019-12-22 21:48:18.436189 I | Got event: city:"Munich"
timestamp:1577047698 temperature:2
2019-12-22 21:48:33.431529 I | Got event: city:"Munich"
timestamp:1577047713 temperature:2
```

This is how asynchronous behavior is achieved in microservices. The border between clients and services can blur, as anyone can publish or subscribe. In a distributed system, services are clients to other services. So, Go Micro provides a lightweight and flexible approach to creating microservices.

In the next section, we will discuss the logging and instrumentation of microservices.

Adding logging to microservices

Logging is a crucial aspect of microservices. We can write middleware to capture all requests and responses going into and out of a service. Even for a client, we can capture logs while making RPC calls to a service.

Go Micro is a lean framework and doesn't enforce logging by default. We can easily wrap a service handler with our own custom logger. For example, in the encryptService example, we have a file called handlers.go.

In order to activate logging for each request in a custom format, we have to define a wrapper, and then link it to the service. As an example, if we have to log every incoming encryption request, follow these steps:

1. Create a new `wrapper` function. It takes `Context`, `Request`, and `Response` as arguments. Here, we just print the time of the request arrival, like this:

```
func logWrapper(fn server.HandlerFunc) server.HandlerFunc {
 return func(ctx context.Context, req *proto.Request,
  rsp *proto.Response) error {
 fmt.Printf("encryption request at time: %v", time.Now())
 return fn(ctx, req, rsp)
 }
}
```

2. In `service`, we can attach the wrapper, like this:

```
service := micro.NewService(
micro.Name("encrypter"),
// wrap the client
micro.WrapClient(logWrap),
)
```

Now, the service logs every request in the format defined in the wrapper function, like so:

```
encryption request at time: 2019/12/22 23:07:3
```

 For more information about logging, see the documentation at `https://micro.mu/docs/go-micro.html#wrappers`.

The instrumentation of services is out of the scope of this book, but there is an open standard called **OpenTracing** (`https://opentracing.io/`). It defines a standard for how to metricize API endpoints, number of requests, and so on. Please feel free to explore it.

 The APIs we created in this chapter are RPC-based. To convert them to REST, you just have to use a plugin called **Micro Web**. For more information, see this link for easy conversion to REST (`https://micro.mu/docs/go-web.html`).

Summary

In this chapter, we started with the definition of microservices. The main difference between a monolithic application and a microservice is the way a tightly coupled architecture is broken into a loosely coupled architecture.

Microservices talk to each other using either REST-based JSON or RPC-based protocol buffers. Using microservices, we can break business logic into multiple chunks. Each service does one job pretty well. Go has a lightweight framework called **Go Micro**. Using it, we can create services and clients.

We first created an encryption service using `Micro go`. We then developed a client for consuming the service. Go Micro also allows asynchronous programming by providing a Publish/Subscribe pattern. Any client/service can subscribe or push events to a topic. It uses an HTTP broker by default but can be easily configured to RabbitMQ or Kafka. Go Micro also provides features such as service discovery, and various transport mechanisms such as protocol buffers, JSON, and so on. Small organizations can start with a monolith, but in bigger organizations with huge teams, microservices are better suited.

In the next chapter, we are going to see how to deploy our Go services using nginx. A service needs to be deployed for it to be exposed to the outside world. We also use `docker-compose` and containers for a clean deployment.

12
Containerizing REST Services for Deployment

In this chapter, we will explore how to containerize our Go applications using a few tools such as Docker, Docker Compose, Nginx, and Supervisord. Containerization is required to avoid platform dependency during deployment of an application. To deploy an application properly, we must prepare an ecosystem. That ecosystem consists of a web server, an application server, and a process monitor. This chapter deals with how to take our API server from a standalone application to a production-grade service.

In recent times, most cloud providers tend to host web applications. Some big players such as AWS, Azure, Google Cloud Platform, along with start-ups such as DigitalOcean and Heroku are a few such examples. In the upcoming sections, we will focus on making a platform ready for deploying REST services. In the next chapter, we will look at how to deploy this ecosystem on a famous cloud provider, AWS.

Nginx is a web server that can be a reverse proxy for a web application. It can also act as a load balancer when multiple instances of the server are running. Supervisord makes sure that an application server is up and running in the event of a crash or a system restart. An application server/REST service are both the same, so please consider them in equal context throughout this chapter.

In this chapter, we will cover the following topics:

- Installing the Nginx server
- What is a reverse proxy server?
- Deploying a Go service using Nginx
- Monitoring our Go API server with Supervisord
- `Makefile` and Docker Compose-based deployment

Technical requirements

The following is the software that should be preinstalled for running the code samples:

- OS: Linux (Ubuntu 18.04)/Windows 10/Mac OS X >=10.13
- Go stable version compiler >= 1.13.5
- Dep: A dependency management tool for Go >= 0.5.3
- Docker version >= 18.09.2
- Docker Compose >= 1.23.2

You can download the code for this chapter from `https://github.com/PacktPublishing/Hands-On-Restful-Web-services-with-Go/tree/master/chapter12`. Clone the code and use the code samples in the `chapter12` directory.

Installing the Nginx server

Nginx is a high-performing web server and load balancer. It is well suited for deploying high-traffic websites and API servers. Even though this decision is opinionated, it is a community-driven, industry-strong web server. It is similar to the Apache2 web server.

Nginx can also act as a reverse proxy server that allows us to redirect our HTTP requests to multiple application servers running on the same network. The main contender of Nginx is Apache's `httpd`. Nginx is an excellent static file server that can be used by web clients. Since we are dealing with APIs, we will take a look at how to deal with HTTP requests.

We can access Nginx in two ways:

- Installation on a bare machine
- Using a preinstalled Docker container

Let's understand both in more detail.

Installation on a bare machine

On Ubuntu 18.04, use these commands to install Nginx:

```
> sudo apt-get update
> sudo apt-get install nginx
```

On Mac OS X , you can install it with `brew`:

```
> brew install nginx
```

brew (`https://brew.sh/`) is a very useful software packaging system for Mac OS X users. My recommendation is that you use it for installing software. Once it is successfully installed, you can check it by opening the machine IP in the browser. Open `http://localhost/` on your web browser. You should see this:

Welcome to nginx!

If you see this page, the nginx web server is successfully installed and working. Further configuration is required.

For online documentation and support please refer to nginx.org. Commercial support is available at nginx.com.

Thank you for using nginx.

If you see the preceding message, that means Nginx has been successfully installed. It serves on port `80` and serves the default page. On Mac OS X, the default Nginx listening port will be `80`:

```
> sudo vi /usr/local/etc/nginx/nginx.conf
```

On Ubuntu (Linux), the file will be on this path:

```
> sudo vi /etc/nginx/nginx.conf
```

Open the file and search for a server block. If it is listening on port `80`, everything is fine. However, if it is on some other port, for example `8080`, then change it to `80`:

```
server {
        listen 80; # Nginx listen port
        server_name localhost;
        #charset koi8-r;
        #access_log logs/host.access.log main;
        location / {
            root html;
            index index.html index.htm;
        }
        ...
}
```

Now, everything is ready. The server runs on the 80 HTTP port, which means a client can access it using a URL (http://localhost/). This basic server serves static files from a directory called html. The root parameter can be modified to any directory where we place our web assets. You can check the status of Nginx with the following command:

```
> service nginx status
```

 Nginx for the Windows operating system is quite basic and is not really intended for production-grade deployments. Open source developers usually prefer Debian or Ubuntu servers for deploying the API servers with Nginx.

We can also get a Docker image that has Nginx installed already. In the next section, we will demonstrate how to install it as a Docker container.

Installation via a Docker container

Getting a container that has preinstalled Nginx has two benefits:

- It is easy to ship containers.
- We can destroy and recreate the containers any number of times.

To get the latest Nginx image and start a container, run the following command:

```
> docker run --name nginxServer -d -p 80:80 nginx
```

This pulls the nginx image from Docker Hub (make sure you are connected to the internet). If the image is already pulled, it reuses that. Then, it starts a container with the name of nginxServer and serves it on port 80. Now, visit http://localhost from your browser and you will see the Nginx home page.

However, the preceding command is not useful for configuring Nginx after starting the container. We have to mount a directory from localhost to the container or copy files to the container to make changes to the Nginx configuration file. Let's modify the command:

```
> docker run --name nginxServer -d -p 80:80 --mount
source=/host/path/nginx.conf,destination=/etc/nginx/nginx.conf:readonly
nginx
```

The extra command is `--mount`, which mounts a file/directory from the source (*host*) to the destination (*container*). If you modify a file on the host system in that directory, then it also reflects on the container. The `readonly` option stops users/system processes modifying the Nginx configuration inside the container.

In the preceding command, we are mounting the Nginx configuration file, `nginx.conf`. We use the Docker container-based deployment in the latter part of this chapter, where we use `docker-compose` to deploy our application.

What is a reverse proxy server?

A **reverse proxy server** is a server that holds the information regarding the original servers in it. It acts as the front-facing entity for the client request. Whenever a client makes an HTTP request, it can directly go to the application server. However, if the application server is written in a programming language, then you need a translator that can turn the application response into a response understandable by the clients. **Common Gateway Interface** (**CGI**) does the same thing.

We can run a simple Go HTTP server and it can serve incoming requests (no CGI is required). We should also protect our application server from **Denial of Service** (**DoS**) attacks. So, why are we using another server called Nginx? Well, because it brings a lot of things into the picture.

The benefits of having a reverse proxy server (Nginx) are as follows:

- It can act as a load balancer.
- It can provide access control and rate limiting.
- It can sit in front of a cluster of applications and redirect HTTP requests.
- It can serve a filesystem with a good performance.
- It streams media very well.

If the same machine is running on multiple applications, then we can bring all of those applications under one umbrella. Nginx can also act as the API gateway that can be the starting point for multiple API endpoints. We will explore a dedicated API gateway in the next chapter, but it is good to know that Nginx can also work as one.

Nginx works as a traffic router for incoming requests. It is a protective shield for our application servers.

Take a look at the following diagram:

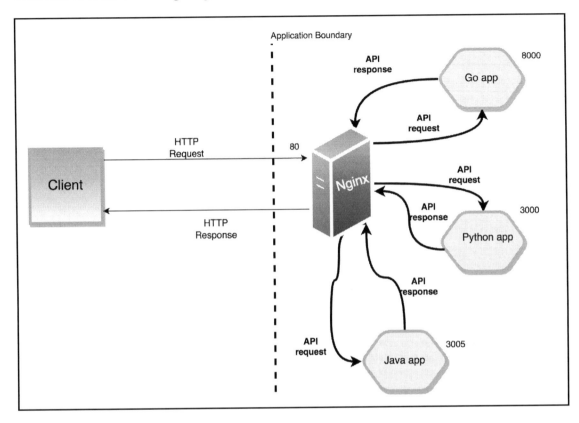

It has three apps running in different programming languages and **Client** only knows a single API endpoint. Let's say that all of the apps run on different ports.

As you can see, the diagram **Client** is talking directly to **Nginx** instead of the ports where other applications are running. In the diagram, Go is running on port 8000 and other applications are running on different ports. This means that the different servers are providing different API endpoints.

Without Nginx, if the client wishes to call an API, it needs to access three different endpoints (ports). Instead, if we have Nginx, it can act as a reverse proxy server for all three and simplifies the client request-response cycle.

Nginx is also an upstream server. An upstream server serves the requests from one server to the other. From the diagram, you can see that a Python app can request an API endpoint from a Go app and Nginx will take care of routing them.

Important Nginx paths

There are a few important Nginx paths that we need to know about in order to work with the proxy server. In Nginx, we can host multiple sites (`www.example1.com`, `www.example2.com`, and so on) at the same time. This means that many API servers can be run under one Nginx instance.

You should be aware of the following paths in the table to configure Nginx properly. An advanced deployment may require bypassing authentication (for example, the Health check API), rate limiting, and a backup of the logs.

Take a look at the following table:

Type	Path	Description
Configuration	/etc/nginx/nginx.conf	This is the base Nginx configuration file. It can be used as the default file.
Configuration	/etc/nginx/sites-available/	If we have multiple sites running within Nginx, we can have a configuration file for each site.
Configuration	/etc/nginx/sites-enabled/	These are the sites currently activated on Nginx.
Log	/var/log/nginx/access.log	This log file records the server activity, such as timestamps and API endpoints.
Log	/var/log/nginx/error.log	This log file logs all proxy server-related errors, such as disk space, filesystem permissions, and more.

These paths are in the Linux operating system. For Mac OS X, use `/usr/local/nginx` as the base path.

In the next section, we will explore server blocks that are mainly used for configuring applications with Nginx.

Using server blocks

Server blocks are the actual configuration pieces that tell the server what to serve and on which port to listen. We can define multiple server blocks in the `sites-available` folder. On Ubuntu, the location will be as follows:

```
/etc/nginx/sites-available
```

On Mac OS X, the location will be as follows:

```
/usr/local/etc/nginx/sites-available
```

Until we create a symlink from the `sites-available` to the `sites-enabled` directory, the configuration has no effect. So, always create a symlink for `sites-available` to `sites-enabled` for every new configuration you create.

Deploying a Go service using Nginx

As we have already discussed, Nginx can be a reverse proxy for a Go application. Let's say that we have a server that provides a REST API to access book data. A client can send a request and get it back in JSON. The server also stores all the logs in an external file. Let's take a look at the steps to create this application:

1. Let's name our project `bookServer`:

   ```
   > mkdir -p $GOPATH/src/github.com/git-user/chapter12/bookServer
   touch $GOPATH/src/github.com/git-user/chapter12/bookServer/main.go
   ```

   This file is a basic Go server to illustrate the functioning of a reverse proxy server. We first run our program on port `8000`. Then, we add a configuration that maps `8000` (Go's running port) to `80` (the Nginx HTTP port).

2. Now, let's write the code. We will use a few packages for our server. We can use Go's built-in `net/http` package for server implementation:

   ```
   package main

   import (
       "encoding/json"
       "fmt"
       "log"
       "net/http"
       "os"
       "time"
   )
   ```

3. Now our server needs a struct to hold the book information. Let's create a struct with fields such as `ID`, `ISBN`, `Author`, and `PublishedYear`:

   ```
   // Book holds data of a book
   type Book struct {
       ID              int
   ```

```
ISBN          string
Author        string
PublishedYear string
}
```

4. Now goes our `main` function. It should open a file for writing logs. We can do that using the `os.Openfile` function. This takes the file and mode as arguments. Let's name the file `app.log`:

```go
func main() {
    // File open for reading, writing and appending
    f, err := os.OpenFile("app.log",
     os.O_RDWR|os.O_CREATE|os.O_APPEND, 0666)
    if err != nil {
        fmt.Printf("error opening file: %v", err)
    }
    defer f.Close()
    // This attaches program logs to file
    log.SetOutput(f)
    // further code goes here...
}
```

The file permission, `os.O_RDWR|os.O_CREATE|os.O_APPEND`, allows the Go program to create, write, and append to the file. `log.SetOutput(f)` redirects app logs to the file.

5. Now, create a function handler and attach it to a route using the `net/http` function. The handler converts a struct into JSON and returns it as an HTTP response. Also, attach that handler to a route called `/api/books`:

```go
// Function handler for handling requests
http.HandleFunc("/api/books", func(w http.ResponseWriter,
r *http.Request) {
    log.Printf("%q", r.UserAgent())
    // Fill the book details
    book := Book{
        ID:            123,
        ISBN:          "0-201-03801-3",
        Author:        "Donald Knuth",
        PublishedYear: "1968",
    }
    // Convert struct to JSON using Marshal
    jsonData, _ := json.Marshal(book)
    w.Header().Set("Content-Type", "application/json")
    w.Write(jsonData)
})
```

The previous code block essentially returns a book whenever a client requests /api/books.

6. Now, start an HTTP server that serves the whole application on port 8000:

```
s := &http.Server{
    Addr:           ":8000",
    ReadTimeout:    10 * time.Second,
    WriteTimeout:   10 * time.Second,
    MaxHeaderBytes: 1 << 20,
}

log.Fatal(s.ListenAndServe())
```

This finishes the main program.

7. We can run our application and see whether it is running correctly:

```
> go run $GOPATH/src/github.com/git-user/chapter12/bookServer/
main.go
```

8. Now, open a shell and make a curl command:

```
> curl -X GET "http://localhost:8000/api/books"
```

It returns the data:

```
{
  "ID":123,
  "ISBN":"0-201-03801-3",
  "Author":"Donald Knuth",
  "PublishedYear":"1968"
}
```

9. However, the client needs to request to port 8000. So, how can we proxy this server using Nginx? As we previously discussed, we need to edit the default sites-available server block, called default:

```
> vi /etc/nginx/sites-available/default
```

10. Edit the preceding file, find the server block, and add proxy_pass to it:

```
server {
        listen 80 default_server;
        listen [::]:80 default_server ipv6only=on;

    location / {
                proxy_pass http://127.0.0.1:8000;
```

```
            }
       }
```

This section of the `config` file is called a `server` block. This controls the setting up of the proxy server where `listen` says where `nginx` should listen. `root` and `index` point to the static files if we need to serve any file. `server_name` is the domain name of yours.

Since we don't have a domain name with us, it is just localhost. `location` is the key section here. In `location`, we can define our `proxy_pass`, which can reverse proxy to a given `URL:PORT`. Since our Go application is running on port `8000`, we mentioned it there. Let's try running our app on a different domain, `example.com`:

```
http://example.com:8000
```

We can give the same name as a parameter to `proxy_pass`. In order to take this configuration into effect, we need to restart the Nginx server. You can do that using the following:

```
> service nginx restart
```

11. Now, make a `curl` request to `http://localhost` and you will see the Go application's output:

```
> curl -X GET "http://localhost"
{
   "ID":123,
   "ISBN":"0-201-03801-3",
   "Author":"Donald Knuth",
   "PublishedYear":"1968"
}
```

12. The `location` is a directive that defines a **Unified Resource Identifier** (URI) that can proxy a given `server:port` combination. This means that, by defining various URI, we can proxy multiple applications running on the same server. It looks like this:

```
server {
    listen ...;
    ...
    location / {
        proxy_pass http://127.0.0.1:8000;
    }
    location /api {
        proxy_pass http://127.0.0.1:8001;
```

```
    }
    location /mail {
        proxy_pass http://127.0.0.1:8002;
    }
    ...
}
```

Here, three applications are running on different ports. These, after being added to our configuration file, can be accessed by the client as follows:

```
http://localhost/
http://localhost/api/
http://localhost/mail/
```

In the next section, we explore how to load balance API requests to multiple instances of applications.

Load balancing with Nginx

In practical cases, multiple servers are deployed instead of one for handling huge sets of incoming requests for APIs. But, who should forward an incoming client request to a server instance? A load balancer does that job. Load balancing is a process where the central server distributes the load to various servers based on certain criteria. Refer to the following diagram:

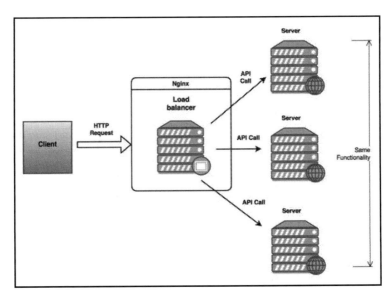

A load balancer employs few strategies such as Round Robin or Least Connection for routing requests to instances. Let's take a look at what each does in a simple table:

Load-balancing method	Description
Round Robin	The incoming requests are uniformly distributed across servers based on the criteria of server weights.
Least Connection	Requests are sent to the server that is currently serving the least number of clients.
IP Hash	This is used to send the requests from a given client's IP to the given server. Only when that server is not available is it given to another server.
Least Time	A request from the client is sent to the machine with the lowest average latency (the time-to-serve client) and the least number of active connections.

We can set which strategy to apply for load balancing in the Nginx configuration.

Let's explore how load balancing is practically achieved in Nginx for our Go API servers. The first step in this process is to create an upstream cluster in the http section of the Nginx configuration file:

```
http {
    upstream cluster {
        server site1.mysite.com weight=5;
        server site2.mysite.com weight=2;
        server backup.mysite.com backup;
    }
}
```

Here, servers are the IP addresses or domain names of the servers running the same code. We are defining an upstream called cluster here. It is a server group that we can refer to in our location directive. Weights should be given in proportion to the resources available. In the preceding code, site1 is given a higher weight because it may be a bigger instance (memory and CPU). Now, in the location directive, we can specify the server group with the proxy_pass command:

```
server {
    location / {
        proxy_pass http://cluster;
    }
}
```

Now, the proxy server that is running will pass requests to the machines in the cluster for all API endpoints hitting the / endpoint. The default request routing algorithm will be Round Robin, which means that all of the server's turns will be repeated one after the other. If we need to change it, we can mention that in the upstream definition. Take a look at the following code snippet:

```
http {
    upstream cluster {
        least_conn;
        server site1.mysite.com weight=5;
        server site2.mysite.com;
        server backup.mysite.com backup;
    }
}

server {
    location / {
        proxy_pass http://cluster;
    }
}
```

The preceding configuration says to *create a cluster of three machines and add load balancing method as least connections*. least_conn is the string we used to mention the load balancing method. The other values could be ip_hash or least_time. You can try this by having a set of machines in the **Local Area Network (LAN)**. Otherwise, we can have Docker installed with multiple virtual containers as different machines to test out load balancing.

 We need to add that http block in the /etc/nginx/nginx.conf file, whereas the server block is in /etc/nginx/sites-enabled/default. It is better to separate these two settings.

Here's a small exercise: try to run three bookServer instances on different ports and enable load balancing on Nginx. In the next section, we'll examine how to rate limit an API in Nginx for certain clients.

Rate limiting our REST API

We can also limit the rate of access to our Nginx proxy server by rate limiting. This provides a directive called limit_conn_zone (http://nginx.org/en/docs/http/ngx_http_limit_conn_module.html#limit_conn_zone). The format of it is this:

```
limit_conn_zone client_type zone=zone_type:size;
```

`client_type` can be one of two types:

- An IP address (limit requests from a given IP address)
- A server name (limit requests from a server)

`zone_type` also changes in correspondence to `client_type`. It takes values as per the following table:

Client type	Zone type
$binary_remote_address	addr
$server_name	servers

Nginx has to save a few things in memory to remember the IP addresses and servers for rate limiting. The `size` parameter is the storage that we allocate for Nginx to perform its memory operations. It takes values such as 8 m (8 MB) or 16 m (16 MB). Now, let's take a look at where to add these settings. The preceding one should be added as a global setting to the `http` directive in the `nginx.conf` file:

```
http {
    limit_conn_zone $server_name zone=servers:10m;
}
```

This allocates the shared memory for Nginx to use. Now, in the server directive of `sites-available/default`, add the following:

```
server {
   limit_conn servers 1000;
}
```

The total number of connections for the given server will not exceed `1000` in the preceding configuration using `limit_conn`. If we try to put the rate limit from a given IP address to the client, then use this:

```
server {
  location /api {
      limit_conn addr 1;
  }
}
```

This setting stops a client (that is, IP address) from opening more than one connection to the server (for example, in an online railway booking session, a user can only use one session per IP address to book tickets). If we have a file that the client downloads and need to set a bandwidth constraint, use `limit_rate`:

```
server {
  location /download {
      limit_conn addr 10;
      limit_rate 50k;
  }
}
```

In this way, we can control the client's interaction with our services that are proxied under Nginx.

Securing our Nginx proxy server

This is the most important piece in the Nginx setup. In this section, we will look at how to restrict access to our server using basic authentication. This is very important for our REST API servers because, suppose we have servers *X*, *Y*, and *Z* that can talk to each other. *X* can serve clients directly, but *X* consults *Y* and *Z* for some information by calling an internal API. We should prevent clients from accessing *Y* and *Z*. We can allow or deny IP addresses using the `nginx` access module. It looks like this:

```
location /api {
    ...
    deny 192.168.1.2;
    allow 192.168.1.1/24;
    allow 127.0.0.1;
    deny all;
}
```

This configuration tells Nginx to allow requests from clients ranging `192.168.1.1/24`, excluding `192.168.1.2`. The next line tells us to allow requests from the same host and block all other requests from any other client. The complete server block looks like this:

```
server {
    listen 80 default_server;
    root /usr/share/nginx/html;

    location /api {

        deny 192.168.1.2;
        allow 192.168.1.1/24;
        allow 127.0.0.1;
```

```
            deny all;
        }
    }
```

For more information regarding this, you can refer to the documentation at `http://nginx.` `org/en/docs/http/ngx_http_access_module.html?_ga=2.117850185.1364707364.` `1504109372-1654310658.1503918562`. We can also add password-secured access to our Nginx serving static files. It is mostly not applicable to the API because there, the application takes care of authenticating the user. The whole idea is to only allow the IP that is approved by us and deny all other requests.

Nginx can only serve requests when the application server's health is good. If the application crashes, we have to restart it manually. A crash can occur from a system shutdown, a problem in the network storage, or various other external factors. In the next section, we will discuss a process monitoring tool called `supervisord` that can automatically restart a crashed application.

Monitoring our Go API server with Supervisord

Sometimes, a web application server may stop due to an operating system restarting or crashing. Whenever a web server is killed, it is someone's job to bring it back to life. It is wonderful if that is automated. Supervisord is a tool that comes to the rescue. To make our API server run all of the time, we need to monitor it and recover it quickly. Supervisord is a generic tool that can monitor running processes (systems) and can restart them when they are terminated.

Installing Supervisord

We can easily install Supervisord using Python's `pip` command.

```
> sudo pip install supervisor
```

On Ubuntu 18.04, you can also use the `apt-get` command:

```
> sudo apt-get install -y supervisor
```

This installs two tools, `supervisor` and `supervisorctl`. `Supervisorctl` is intended to control the supervisor to add tasks, restart tasks, and more.

Let's use the `bookServer.go` program we created for illustrating process monitoring. Install the binary to the `$GOPATH/bin` directory using this command:

```
> go install $GOPATH/src/github.com/git-user/chapter12/bookServer/main.go
```

Always add `$GOPATH/bin` to the system path. Whenever you install the project binary, it is available as a normal executable from the overall system environment. You can add following line to the `~/.profile` or `~/.bashrc` file:
`export PATH=$PATH:$GOPATH/bin`

Now, create a new configuration file for `supervisor`:

/etc/supervisor/conf.d/supervisord.conf

The supervisor reads this file and looks for processes to monitor and rules to apply when they are started/stopped.

You can add any number of configuration files and `supervisord` treats them as separate processes to run.

By default, we have a file called `supervisord.conf` in `/etc/supervisor/`. Look at it for further reference:

- The `[supervisord]` section gives the location of the log file for `supervisord`.
- `[program:myserver]` is the task block that defines a command.

Modify the content of the `supervisord.conf` file to the following:

```
[supervisord]
logfile = /tmp/supervisord.log
[program:myserver]
command=/root/workspace/bin/bookServer
autostart=true
autorestart=true
redirect_stderr=tru
```

The command in the file is the command to launch the application server. `/root/workspace` is `$GOPATH`.

Please use an absolute path while running a command in Supervisord. Relative paths will not work by default.

Now, we can ask our `supervisorctl reread` to reread the configuration and start the task (process). For that, just say the following:

```
> supervisorctl reread
> supervisorctl update
```

Then, launch the controller tool, `supervisorctl`:

```
> supervisorctl
```

You should see something like this:

```
root@ubuntu:~# supervisorctl
myserver                          RUNNING    pid 6886, uptime 0:00:47
supervisor> help

default commands (type help <topic>):
========================================
add     clear  fg         open   quit    remove  restart   start    stop   update
avail   exit   maintail   pid    reload  reread  shutdown  status   tail   version

supervisor>
```

So, here, our book service is getting monitored by `Supervisor`. Let's try to kill the process manually and see what `Supervisor` does:

```
> kill 6886
```

Now, as soon as possible, `Supervisor` starts a new process (using a different pid) by running the binary:

```
root@ubuntu:~# kill 6886
root@ubuntu:~# supervisorctl
myserver                          RUNNING    pid 6903, uptime 0:00:10
supervisor> help

default commands (type help <topic>):
```

This is very useful in a production where a service requires the least downtime. So, how do we start/stop an application service manually? well, you can use the `start` and `stop` commands from `supervisorctl` for those operations:

```
> supervisorctl> stop myserver
> supervisorctl> start myserver
```

For more information about the supervisor, visit `http://supervisord.org/`.

In the next section, we will try to simplify our deployment using containers. We will launch the application and Nginx as separate containers and establish a communication channel between them with the help of `docker-compose`.

Makefile and Docker Compose-based deployment

Until now, we have seen the manual deployment of a reverse proxy server (Nginx). Let's automate that by gluing things together. We are going to use a few tools, as follows:

- `Make`
- `docker-compose`

On Linux-based machines (Ubuntu and Mac OS X), `Make` is available as part of GCC (the C language toolchain). You can install `docker-compose` using the Python `pip` tool:

```
> sudo pip install docker-compose
```

On Windows OS, `docker-compose` is already available as part of Docker Desktop. Our goal is to bundle all deployable entities with one single `Make` command. `Makefile` is used to write control commands for the application. You should define a rule and the `Make` tool will execute it (`https://www.gnu.org/software/make/manual/make.html#Rule-Example`).

Let's create a directory called `deploySetup`. It holds the whole code we are going to show. It has two directories – one for the app and another for Nginx:

```
> mkdir -p $GOPATH/src/github.com/git-user/chapter12/deploySetup
mkdir $GOPATH/src/github.com/git-user/chapter12/deploySetup/nginx-conf
```

Now, let's copy our `bookServer` project into `deploySetup` like this:

```
> cp -r $GOPATH/src/github.com/git-user/chapter12/bookServer
$GOPATH/src/github.com/git-user/chapter12/deploySetup
```

We need this to build an executable and copy it to the container. We should containerize both the Go application and Nginx in order to use them together. So, this is the plan for creating such a workflow:

1. Create a `Dockerfile` for copying Go build into the container.
2. Create an Nginx configuration file called `nginx.conf` to copy into Nginx container.
3. Write a `Makefile` to build binary as well as deploy the containers.

So, first, we should build and run the docker containers for application and Nginx. For that, we can use `docker-compose`. The `docker-compose` tool is very handy for managing multiple containers. It also builds and runs the containers on the fly.

In the `bookServer` directory, we need a Dockerfile that stores a project build binary. Let's say we build our project in `app`. We use Alpine Linux (lightweight) as the base Docker image, so we should target our build to that Linux platform. We should copy the binary on the Docker container and execute it. Let's say we chose the app path as `/go/bin/app`. Create a `Dockerfile` at this location:

```
> touch $GOPATH/src/github.com/git-user/chapter12/deploySetup/
bookServer/Dockerfile
```

The `Dockerfile` looks like this:

```
FROM alpine
WORKDIR /go/bin/
COPY app .
CMD ["./app"]
```

The Dockerfile is basically pulling the Alpine Linux image. It creates and sets the working directory for the application binary. Then, it copies the application binary to the given path, `/go/bin`. After copying, it runs the binary.

Before copying the application binary, someone has to build it. Let's write a `Make` command for building `bookServer` in this `Makefile` here:

```
> touch $GOPATH/src/github.com/git-user/chapter12/deploySetup/Makefile
```

It consists of commands and their respective executions. First, let's add a `build` command:

```
PROJECT_NAME=bookServer
BINARY_NAME=app
GOCMD=go
GOBUILD=$(GOCMD) build
```

```
build:
    $(info Building the book server binary...)
    cd ${PROJECT_NAME} && GOOS=linux GOARCH=arm ${GOBUILD}
    -o "$(BINARY_NAME)" -v
```

The top-level variables in the `Makefile` declare the project root and build (binary) name. It also composes the build commands. The interesting command is `build`, which simply calls the Go build tool with a few `GOOS` and `GOARCH` flags. Those `build` flags are required to target a `binary` for Alpine Linux. Now from the `deploySetup` directory, run this command:

```
> make build
Building the book server binary...
cd bookServer && GOOS=linux GOARCH=arm go build -o "app" -v
```

If you look in the `bookServer` directory, there is an `app` binary newly created. That is our application server. We are launching this binary directly in the container.

Now, let's create a `docker-compose` file that defines two services:

- App Service
- Nginx Service

Each of these services has instructions for where to build the image, which ports to be opened, which network bridge to be used, and more. For more information about `docker-compose`, please refer to (`https://docs.docker.com/compose/`). Let's create a `docker-compose.yml` file in the `deploySetup` directory:

```
# Docker Compose file Reference
(https://docs.docker.com/compose/compose-file/)
version: '3'

services:
 # App Service
 app:
 build:
 context: ./bookServer
 dockerfile: Dockerfile
 expose:
 - 8000
 restart: unless-stopped
 networks:
 - app-network

 # Nginx Service
 nginx:
```

```
image: nginx:alpine
restart: unless-stopped
ports:
- "80:80"
- "443:443"
volumes:
- ./nginx-conf:/etc/nginx/conf.d
depends_on:
- app
networks:
- app-network

networks:
app-network:
driver: bridge
```

In this file, we are defining a network called `app-network` and two services, namely `app` and `nginx`. For the `app` service, we are pointing to `bookServer` to pick `Dockerfile` to build an image.

 We don't need the `supervisord` tool in the Docker deployment because `docker-compose` takes care of restarting crashed containers. It takes a decision from the `restart: unless-stopped` option in the `docker-compose` file.

For the `nginx` service in the Compose file, it pulls a default `nginx:alpine` image from Docker Hub. However, as we have to copy our own configuration file to the Nginx server, we should create a file in the `nginx-conf` directory:

> **touch $GOPATH/src/github.com/git-user/chapter12/deploySetup/nginx-conf/nginx.conf**

We can mount our configuration file in the `nginx-conf` directory to `/etc/nginx/conf.d` in the container using the `volumes` option. Both services use the same network so that they can discover each other. The Nginx service exposes port 80 to host, but `app` only opens up its port internally on `8000`.

Our `nginx.conf` file should have the proxy information like this:

```
upstream service {
  server app:8000;
}

server {
        listen 80 default_server;
        listen [::]:80 default_server;
```

```
        location / {
                proxy_pass http://service;
        }
}
```

The `nginx.conf` file defines an upstream service. It connects to app service in `docker-compose.yml`. This is possible because of the bridging of the network. `docker-compose` takes care of assigning a hostname for the application container. In the last block, we are defining a location that reverses proxy requests to the `upstream service`.

Now, everything is ready. The `docker-compose.yml` file, Supervisord configuration, and Nginx configuration are in place. `docker-compose` has an option to start Docker containers by building images as specified in the `compose` file. We can bring containers up using this command:

```
> docker-compose up --build
```

Let's update the `Makefile` to add two new commands—one to `deploy`, and another one to `build` and `deploy` containers:

```
PROJECT_NAME=bookServer
BINARY_NAME=app
GOCMD=go
GOBUILD=$(GOCMD) build

all:
    make build && make deploy

build:
    $(info Building the book server binary...)
    cd ${PROJECT_NAME} && GOOS=linux GOARCH=arm ${GOBUILD}
     -o "$(BINARY_NAME)" -v

deploy:
    docker-compose rm -f
    docker-compose up --build
```

With the `deploy` command, we are cleaning up the containers first and then launching new ones. We added one more command called `all`.

The `make all` command is a universal command that executes when no command is passed. For example, consider the following:

```
> make all
```

This executes `make all`. Our plan is to build the binary, and start the Docker containers using `docker-compose`.

Now, we have everything we need. From Terminal, run `make` to see the servers up and running:

```
> make

make build && make deploy
Building the book server binary...
cd bookServer && CGO_ENABLED=0 GOOS=linux GOARCH=amd64 go build -o "app" -v
docker-compose rm -f
No stopped containers
docker-compose up --build
Building app
Step 1/4 : FROM alpine
 ---> c85b8f829d1f
Step 2/4 : WORKDIR /go/bin/
 ---> Using cache
 ---> cc95562482f0
Step 3/4 : COPY app .
 ---> Using cache
 ---> 865952cdc77a
Step 4/4 : CMD ["./app"]
 ---> Using cache
 ---> 18d0f4ec074f
Successfully built 18d0f4ec074f
Successfully tagged deploysetup_app:latest
Creating deploysetup_app_1 ... done
Creating deploysetup_nginx_1 ... done
Attaching to deploysetup_app_1, deploysetup_nginx_1
```

You can also confirm that the containers are up and running with the `docker ps` command:

```
> docker ps
CONTAINER ID IMAGE COMMAND CREATED STATUS PORTS NAMES
5f78ea862376 nginx:alpine "nginx -g 'daemon of..." About a minute ago Up
About a minute 0.0.0.0:80->80/tcp, 0.0.0.0:443->443/tcp deploysetup_nginx_1
44973a15783a deploysetup_app "/usr/bin/supervisor..." About a minute ago Up
About a minute 8000/tcp deploysetup_app_1
```

Now, make a `curl` request to see the server output:

```
> curl -X GET "http://localhost/api/books"

{"ID":123,"ISBN":"0-201-03801-3","Author":"Donald
Knuth","PublishedYear":"1968"}
```

Instead of calling the API with the port, now the client is accessing the REST API via Nginx. Nginx routes the request to the application server that is started in the container. With this deployment setup, we can make our code changes and just run the `make` command to update the application service.

This is how Go applications can be containerized using `Makefile` and `docker-compose`. Servers stop gracefully when you hit *Ctrl + C*. If you want them to run in the background, just add a `-d` flag to the `Makefile deploy` command:

```
> docker-compose up --build -d
```

`-d` stands for run containers as daemons. Now, containers silently run in the background, and logs for the `nginx` and `app` containers can be seen with the `docker inspect CONTAINER_ID` command.

 Things may not work properly if the base image (Alpine Linux, in our case) of the container is changed. Always consider the image-specific default configuration path for Nginx (`/etc/nginx/conf.d`) to copy the custom configuration.

Summary

This chapter demonstrated how to prepare API services for deployment in production. We need a web proxy server, application server, and a process monitor for deployment.

Nginx is a web proxy server that can pass requests to multiple servers running on the same host or on a different host.

We learned how to install Nginx and start configuring it. Nginx provides features such as load balancing and rate limiting, which are very important features for APIs to have. Load balancing is the process of distributing loads among similar servers. We explored all the available types of loading mechanisms: Round Robin, IP Hash, Least Connection, and more. Then, we looked at how to add access control to our servers by allowing and denying a few sets of IP addresses. We have to add rules in the Nginx server blocks to achieve that.

Finally, we saw a process monitor named `Supervisord` that brings a crashed application back to life. We saw how to install Supervisord and also launch `supervisorctl`, a command-line application to control running servers. We then tried to automate the deployment process by creating a `Makefile` and `docker-compose` file. We also explored how to containerize a Go application along with Nginx using Docker and Docker Compose. In the real world, containers are the preferable way to deploy software.

In the next chapter, we are going to demonstrate how to make our REST services publicly visible with the help of AWS EC2 and Amazon API Gateway.

Deploying REST Services on Amazon Web Services

13

After preparing a deployable ecosystem, we have to host that ecosystem on a cloud provider to make **application programming interface (API)** endpoints visible to the public internet. We need to leverage cloud services such as **Amazon Web Services (AWS) Elastic Compute Cloud (EC2)** to deploy web services.

The journey doesn't end right after deployment. We have to track our API usage and performance for a better understanding of the clients. Who are the clients that are connecting to an API? How frequent are their requests? How many failed authorizations and so on are important factors for fine-tuning an API? For better security, an API server should not be directly exposed to the public internet.

In this chapter, we will explore AWS. However, sticking to a single cloud provider can be a problem for migration later. So, we will use a tool called Terraform to define and create our resources. Terraform is an **Infrastructure as Code (IaC)** tool that is cloud-agnostic. We provision an EC2 instance and an API Gateway in order to properly deploy our **Representational State Transfer (REST)** services.

In this chapter, we will cover the following topics:

- Basics for working with AWS
- IaC with Terraform
- Why is an API Gateway required?
- Introducing AWS API Gateway
- Other API Gateways

Technical requirements

The following software should be pre-installed for running the code samples:

- Operating system: Linux (Ubuntu 18.04)/Windows 10/Mac OS X>= 10.13
- Go stable version compiler >= 1.13.5
- Dep: A dependency management tool for Go >= 0.5.3
- Docker version >= 18.09.2
- Terraform version >= 0.12.18

You can download the code for this chapter from `https://github.com/PacktPublishing/Hands-On-Restful-Web-services-with-Go/tree/master/chapter13`. Clone the code, and use the code samples in the `chapter13` directory.

Basics for working with AWS

AWS is a cloud provider that manages the infrastructure for cloud applications. The other big players are Microsoft Azure and **Google Cloud Platform** (**GCP**). Each of them is equipped with many diverse solutions for managing a variety of artifacts, such as the following:

- Applications
- Databases
- Message queues
- Network
- Docker image management
- Event buses

There are multiple types of managed services for running applications. We'll discuss a few in the next section.

Managed services for applications from AWS

An application should be hosted on a cloud server to serve an API to the public internet. That server can be an independent machine or a container. AWS provides a standalone server called a **virtual machine** (**VM**), in the form of EC2. AWS EC2 is a managed service that provides easy creation and teardown of VMs.

Elastic Container Service (ECS), another managed service from AWS, allows developers to run their applications in containers. A Go application can be bundled into a Docker image and deployed on AWS ECS.

AWS Lambda is another managed service that can run serverless functions. This is a service that runs Go functions. These functions are short-lived and suitable for use cases such as **Extract-Transform-Load (ETL)** on data. A lambda function definition takes compiled Go code and can run thousands of lambda instances on demand.

Depending on the use case, we should pick the right service for running our application. The Docker container-based ECS is preferable over EC2 for running long-running services as well as short-lived applications because of its simplified build, push, and deploy cycle.

In this chapter, we will try to leverage AWS EC2 to deploy an API server. Next, we secure our server using Amazon API Gateway. The following chart can guide you about picking the right AWS service for managing a Go application:

Type	Where To Use
AWS Lambda	Functions that live less than 15 minutes (as per the time of writing)
AWS ECS	Short-lived and long-running services with AWS-managed containers
AWS EC2	Long-running services with a self-managed VM

In the next section, we'll see how to set up an AWS Free Tier account. We will use that account for all our code examples in this chapter.

Setting up an AWS account

We need an AWS account to work on this chapter. If you don't have one, you can try AWS for 1 year, using the Free Tier program: `https://aws.amazon.com/free/`.

After signing up for the Free Tier, we can get access to our AWS account by setting a password. AWS accounts have a custom URL, where account administrators and other users can log in to the account dashboard: `https://console.aws.amazon.com/billing/home?#/account`.

All the main services are free, but with a few limits. So, always monitor the free-tier usage of AWS services while testing. AWS offers a unique model of roles called **Identity and Access Management** (**IAM**). This enables new users to be created and gives permissions to various services.

After we set up our AWS account, we should create IAM users and roles. But for the sake of simplicity, we will proceed with the account we created previously, where the creator is automatically an admin. We should allow programmatic access to our AWS account in order to deploy applications.

There are three ways we can interact with AWS to provision managed services:

- AWS console
- AWS **Command-Line Interface** (**CLI**) tool
- Third-party **Software Development Kit** (**SDK**)

In the first option, a user logs in to an AWS account and manually configures the AWS resources. In the second one, a user can install the client on their machine and manage resources using a command-line API. The third option is very low-level, where third-party libraries wrap the AWS API and provide a clean interface.

For the second and third options, a security credential has to be generated. A security credential consists of two keys:

- Access Key ID
- Secret access key

This security credential is used to authenticate any third-party applications with AWS. It can be obtained by navigating to **IAM**| **Users**| **User**| **Name**| **Security Credentials** on the AWS account and performing a **Create Access Key** operation.

Creating an `access_key_id` also generates a `secret_access_key`. These should be stored in a safe place. If you lose your secret key, you have to delete it from the IAM security credentials and create a new one.

Once a user obtains an access key ID and a secret access key successfully, they should create two files in the `.aws` directory in the `home` path.

On Linux and Mac OS X, create two files with the names `credentials` and `config`:

- `~/.aws/credentials`:

  ```
  [default]
  aws_access_key_id=YOUR_ACCESS_KEY_ID
  aws_secret_access_key=YOUR_SECRET_KEY
  ```

- `~/.aws/config`:

  ```
  [default]
  region=eu-central-1
  output=json
  ```

The credential file holds information about the access key and the secret access key in order to authenticate with AWS. The configuration file configures settings such as the AWS region in operation and the AWS CLI output format, such as JSON, XML, and so on.

On Windows, files should be created in `C:\> dir "%UserProfile%\.aws"`.

 You have to replace the `YOUR_ACCESS_KEY_ID` and `YOUR_SECRET_KEY` variables with actual security credentials from your AWS account.

The region in the configuration file is the geographical location where the application is hosted. In the preceding configuration, we picked **Frankfurt(eu-central-1)** as the preferred region. You should select the region that's closed to the client.

Our goal is to run an application behind the API Gateway on AWS. Instead of doing that manually from the AWS console, we are going to use a tool called Terraform. Terraform provides IaC, where we can have Terraform scripts record the resource creation on AWS. AWS provides an in-house IaC solution called **CloudFormation**. Terraform is much simpler—as well as less verbose—than AWS CloudFormation. In the next section, we'll explore Terraform and its internals.

IaC with Terraform

Terraform is a software tool for provisioning infrastructure on cloud platforms, including AWS. Using Terraform, we can create, configure, or delete resources. Terraform allows automatic resource provisioning compared to the AWS Console. When compared to low-level REST APIs and SDKs, Terraform has a clean, high-level API. Terraform stores the current state of provisioned infrastructure in a state file.

Let's say the infrastructure provisioned on an account should be replicated on another account as part of disaster recovery. If we do not have IaC, all resources have to be reconfigured manually. However, if the whole infrastructure is modeled in the form of Terraform scripts, then it is easy to replay the infrastructure on any number of accounts. This approach is very readable and maintainable compared to hand-wiring infrastructure on the AWS console.

Terraform provisions almost all AWS managed services on the Cloud. It should be run from a local machine. It generates state files while provisioning. See the following diagram for provisioning direction:

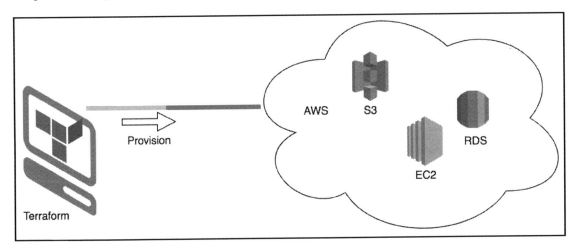

A Terraform installation binary for all platforms can be obtained here: `https://www.terraform.io/downloads.html`.

For Linux and Mac OS X, copy the executable to the respective binary paths so that it is available system-wide. Confirm your installation with this command. It prints out the `version` of the `Terraform` software you've installed:

```
terraform version
Terraform v0.12.18
```

To give a brisk introduction to Terraform, let us provision an EC2 instance for our REST API server using the following steps:

1. Create a project directory called `intro` to hold the script for the provisioning EC2 instance, like this:

```
mkdir -p $GOPATH/src/github.com/git-user/chapter13/intro
```

2. All Terraform files have a `.tf` file extension. So, add a script called `api_server.tf`, like this:

```
touch $GOPATH/src/github.com/git-user/chapter13/intro/api_server.tf
```

3. The language syntax of a Terraform file looks like this:

```
<BLOCK TYPE> "<BLOCK LABEL>" "<BLOCK LABEL>" {
  # Block body
  <IDENTIFIER> = <EXPRESSION> # Argument
}
```

As we can see, a Terraform script is made up of four fundamental building blocks:

- **Block Type**: A set of predefined block types by Terraform—for example, resource and data.
- **Block Label**: The namespace of a block type in a Terraform script.
- **Identifier**: The variable inside a block.
- **Expression**: The value of the variable inside a block.

You can check out all the possible values of these four entities in the Terraform configuration language at `https://www.terraform.io/docs/configuration/index.html`.

4. Now comes the actual script, `api_server.tf`. It should have two blocks, `provider` and `resource` like so:

```
provider "aws" {
  profile    = "default"
  region     = "eu-central-1"

}

resource "aws_instance" "api_server" {
  ami           = "ami-03818140b4ac9ae2b"
  instance_type = "t2.micro"
}
```

The `provider` block defines the type of cloud provider to use and configures the security credentials and region. The `resource` block is used to define the type of resource to be provisioned and its attributes. Here, we are provisioning an EC2 instance, thus we provided `aws_instance` as the resource type. The `api_server` is the name of the instance that gets created. There are many instance types provided by EC2. Here, we use the smaller-capacity instance called `t2.micro`.

AWS uses an **Amazon Machine Image (AMI)** to create a virtual machine. We picked Ubuntu 18.04 as the `ami-03818140b4ac9ae2b` operating system image in the Terraform file. You can find the AMI image closest to your region here: `https://cloud-images.ubuntu.com/locator/ec2/`.

The attributes can change according to the resource type. So, if we pick a different resource, we have to check the Terraform documentation for appropriate attributes. In the preceding resource block, we only defined two attributes: `ami` and `instance_type`. Those two attributes are mandatory for the AWS EC2 API. All other attributes—such as network, security groups, and CPU—default to reasonable values.

5. Now, run the script from the `intro` directory, as follows:

```
terraform apply
```

6. The script outputs the following message, and also asks for confirmation of the `apply` process:

```
Do you want to perform these actions?
  Terraform will perform the actions described above.
  Only 'yes' will be accepted to approve.

  Enter a value: yes

aws_instance.api_server: Creating...
aws_instance.api_server: Still creating... [10s elapsed]
aws_instance.api_server: Still creating... [20s elapsed]
aws_instance.api_server: Creation complete after 24s
[id=i-07a023fc92b73fc06]
```

It successfully created the **EC2 instance**. We can navigate to the **EC2 section** on the **AWS** console to see our instance up and running, as shown in the following screenshot:

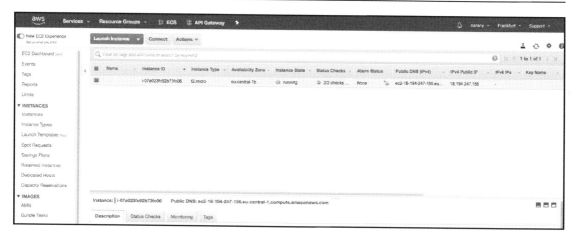

Details such as **Availability Zone**, **Public IP**, and so on are automatically assigned because we didn't specify them as attributes in the Terraform file. AWS creates a default **Virtual Private Cloud** (VPC), subnets, and a public **Domain Name System** (DNS).

If you observe carefully, `terraform apply` generates the following additional files in the directory:

- `terraform.tfstate`: This holds the JSON plan that is executed with AWS.
- `.terraform`: This is a directory that holds plugins, depending on the provider. In our case, the provider type is AWS.

Terraform installs a provider-related executable in the project's `.terraform` directory. This is to reduce the file size of the Terraform binary, which excludes the packages for compiling scripts to other cloud providers.

The plugin version in `.terraform/plugins` also has a version. You should have the latest plugin to benefit from up-to-date Terraform syntax. Otherwise, the syntax for referencing one resource in another may raise errors. To be safe, please upgrade the plugin to the latest version using this command: `terraform 0.12upgrade`.

We have successfully provisioned an EC2 instance, but it is useless until we can SSH into it. For that, we should provide a key pair. Let's look at the steps to do that, as follows:

1. You can generate a public/private key pair on your local machine like this:

   ```
   ssh-keygen -t rsa -b 4096
   ```

   This generates public and private key files in the ~/.ssh directory. A public key is for other parties to encrypt data, and a private key is for the owner to decrypt that data. Your public key file's default name is id_rsa.pub .

2. Create a new resource type called aws_key_pair in the api_server.tf file, like this:

   ```
   resource "aws_key_pair" "api_server_key" {
     key_name   = "api-server-key"
     public_key = "ssh-rsa ABCD...XYZ naren@Narens-MacBook-Air.local"
   }
   ```

   In the preceding block, Terraform creates a new AWS key-pair resource called api_server_key. It takes a key_name and a public_key. This is your newly created public key. AWS adds this key to ~/.ssh/known_hosts on an EC2 instance so that you can log in to the VM once the provision is successful.

3. Next, we should link this newly created resource to our main resource aws_instance, as follows:

   ```
   resource "aws_instance" "api_server" {
     ...
     key_name        = aws_key_pair.api_server_key.key_name
   }
   ```

4. Now, we can see the plan that Terraform executes with the terraform plan command, as follows:

   ```
   terraform plan
   Refreshing Terraform state in-memory prior to plan...
   The refreshed state will be used to calculate this plan,
   but will not be persisted to local or remote state storage.

   aws_instance.api_server: Refreshing state...
   [id=i-07a023fc92b73fc06]


   ------------------------------------------------------------------
   -----

   An execution plan has been generated and is shown below.
   ```

```
Resource actions are indicated with the following symbols:
  + create

Terraform will perform the following actions:

  # aws_instance.api_server must be replaced
-/+ resource "aws_instance" "api_server" {
  ...
  + key_name = "api-server-key" # forces replacement
  ...
}

  # aws_key_pair.api_server_key will be created
```

As it clearly states in the preceding log, Terraform performs the creation of one new resource, `aws_key_pair`, and recreates the server. The Terraform `plan` step is a good way to inspect changes before applying them on AWS.

5. Now, let us actually apply the changes with the `terraform apply` command, as follows:

```
terraform apply
...
aws_key_pair.api_server_key: Creating...
aws_key_pair.api_server_key: Creation complete after 1s [id=api-
server-key]
aws_instance.api_server: Destroying... [id=i-07a023fc92b73fc06]
aws_instance.api_server: Still destroying...
[id=i-07a023fc92b73fc06, 30s elapsed]
aws_instance.api_server: Destruction complete after 30s
aws_instance.api_server: Creating...
aws_instance.api_server: Still creating... [30s elapsed]
aws_instance.api_server: Creation complete after 33s
[id=i-050d7ec98b4d6a814]
```

6. Next, in the **AWS** account console (browser), navigate to the **EC2| NETWORK & SECURITY| Key Pairs** section. You will find the newly added key pair there, as shown in the following screenshot:

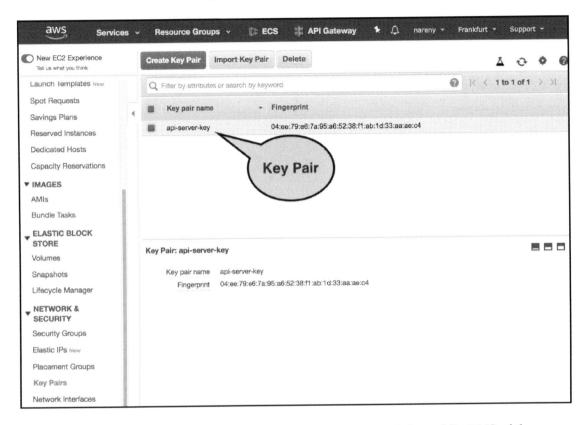

7. Now, in order to SSH into our EC2 instance, we need the public DNS of the instance. We can get the public DNS either from the AWS console or from the `terraform.tfstate` file.

8. The public DNS, in our case, is `ec2-52-59-192-138.eu-central-1.compute.amazonaws.com`. We can now SSH into this system as a Ubuntu user, like this:

```
ssh ubuntu@ec2-52-59-192-138.eu-central-1.compute.amazonaws.com

Welcome to Ubuntu 18.04.3 LTS (GNU/Linux 4.15.0-1052-aws x86_64)

....

52 packages can be updated.
0 updates are security updates.
```

This command picks the ~/.ssh folder and locates the private key. It then does a handshake with the public key we linked with the EC2 instance.

The Ubuntu image comes almost zero configured. Software such as the Go compiler, Docker, and docker-compose is not installed by default on the Ubuntu EC2 instance. We have to install them before deploying our application. Make sure you SSH into the machine.

9. Install the latest version of the Go compiler and Docker, like this:

```
sudo snap install go --classic
sudo snap install docker
```

10. Install docker-compose, as follows:

```
sudo pip install docker-compose
```

As you may have notice, the username we used for SSH is ubuntu. It depends on the AMI used for instance provision. For example, if the image is an Amazon Linux Image, then the SSH username will be ec2-user.

In the next section, we'll walk through the deployment of a REST API on an EC2 instance. We will use the previously provisioned machine in our journey.

Deploying a service on EC2

So far we've provisioned an EC2 instance with a public DNS. Now, we need an API to deploy on the instance. Let us use the bookServer containerized application from *Chapter 12, Containerizing REST Services for Deployment*. There, we developed a Go API server that serves book details on an endpoint. In this section, let us try to deploy that ecosystem on an AWS EC2 instance. Let's look at the steps to deploy bookServer on AWS EC2, as follows:

1. Copy the code from chapter12/deploySetup into the /home/ubuntu directory of the instance. You can do that using the scp command, like this:

```
scp -r $GOPATH/src/github.com/git-user/chapter12/deploySetup
ubuntu@ec2-52-59-192-138.eu-
central-1.compute.amazonaws.com:/home/ubuntu
```

This command copies the source code from Chapter 12, *Containerizing REST Services for Deployment*, to the target instance. We have our application code ready. The code has a Makefile that builds the Go binary and deploys various containers.

2. If you remember building the deploySetup application from Chapter 12, *Containerizing REST Services for Deployment*, then you'll remember that we can launch nginx, the application server, and supervisord using the make command, as follows:

```
sudo make
```

3. This step builds and starts Docker containers in the background, as shown here:

```
Creating deploysetup_app_1 ... done
Creating deploysetup_nginx_1 ... done
```

 We need to use sudo make instead of make because of user permissions. The default ubuntu user doesn't have permissions to the Docker daemon by default.

4. Now, the nginx container and app container are up and running. We can confirm this with the docker ps command, as shown in the following code block:

```
sudo docker ps

CONTAINER ID          IMAGE                 COMMAND
CREATED               STATUS                PORTS
NAMES
a016732f8174          nginx:alpine          "nginx -g 'daemon of..."     2
minutes ago     Up 2 minutes        0.0.0.0:80->80/tcp,
0.0.0.0:443->443/tcp    deploysetup_nginx_1
29b75b09082d          deploysetup_app       "/usr/bin/supervisor..."     2
minutes ago     Up 2 minutes        8000/tcp
deploysetup_app_1
```

This shows that our nginx and app containers are up and running on the EC2 instance, and nginx is serving on port 80.

5. Get the public IP from the AWS console or the terraform.tfstate file.

Always confirm the ports that have been exposed for Docker containers. The format `0.0.0.0:80->80/tcp` means the container TCP port `80` forwards packets to the host port `80`. In our case, the host is an EC2 instance and the container is nginx.

In our case, the instance's public IP is `52.59.192.138`. Refer to the following screenshot to see where we can find out the **public IP** from the **AWS** console **EC2 instances** section:

6. Make a `curl` request to the `http://public-ip/api/books` endpoint from your host machine (not from the EC2 instance). You'll get a JSON response back from the server, as follows:

```
curl http://52.59.192.138/api/books

{"ID":123,"ISBN":"0-201-03801-3","Author":"Donald
Knuth","PublishedYear":"1968"}
```

Hurray! Our API has been published to the web and is accessible worldwide. Here, nginx is acting as an entry point to HTTP requests. The setup we deployed is a minimal way to publish an API on AWS. In a real-world scenario, you have to do a few more things, such as the following, to secure the API:

1. Serve requests on HTTPS (by adding certificates)
2. Configure the VPC, subnets, and security groups properly

Adding the preceding recommendations to our EC2 instance is out of the scope of this book. Please refer to the AWS documentation on these topics for more information.

In the next section, we'll configure our EC2 instance with Amazon API Gateway. As we discussed at the beginning of this chapter, an AWS Gateway is a primary way to secure EC2 instances.

Why is an API Gateway required?

Suppose a company named XYZ developed an API for its internal purposes. There are two ways in which it exposes that API for external use:

- It exposes it using authentication from known clients.
- It exposes it as an API as a service.

In the first case, this API is consumed by the other services inside the company. Since they are internal, we don't restrict access. But in the second case, since the API details are given to the outside world, we need a broker in-between to check and validate the requests. This broker is the API Gateway. An API Gateway is a broker that sits in-between the client and the server and forwards the request to the server, on the passing of specific conditions.

Now, the company XYZ has an API written in Go and also in Java. There are a few common things that apply to any API:

- Authentication
- Logging of requests and responses

Without an API Gateway, we need to write another server that tracks things such as requests and authentication of the API. This can be hectic to implement and maintain when new APIs keep being added to the organization. To take care of these basic things, an API Gateway is a fine piece of middleware.

Basically, an API Gateway does these things:

- Logging
- Security
- Traffic control
- Middleware

Logging is the way in which we track requests and responses. In contrast to application-level logging, which happens in the Go web server, an API Gateway can support organization-level logging across multiple applications.

Authentication is a part of securing applications. It can be basic authentication, token-based authentication, OAuth2.0, and so on. It is essential to restrict access to the API for valid customers/clients.

Traffic control comes into play when an API is a paid service. When an organization sells data as an API, it needs to limit the operations per client. For example, a client can make 10,000 API requests per month. The rate can be set according to the plan the client has opted for. This is a very important feature.

Middleware is for modifying the request before it hits the application server or for modifying the response before it is sent back to the client.

Take a look at the following diagram:

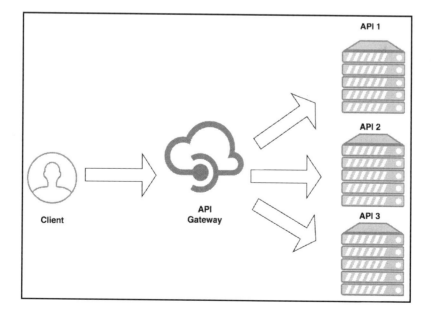

The preceding diagram depicts an **API Gateway** accepting all **client** requests. The API Gateway can forward requests to respective API servers based on HTTP headers, URL path prefix, or IP address. Once the API server finishes its job, the **API Gateway** collects an intermediate response and returns it to the **Client**. In this chapter, we'll try to leverage Amazon API Gateway.

Introducing Amazon API Gateway

Amazon API Gateway has the following features:

- Reverse proxy service
- Rate limiting
- Monitoring
- Authentication

Reverse proxying is the process of passing a REST API request to another endpoint. Amazon API Gateway can register a REST endpoint with a custom path and method. It forwards a matching request to the application server. It can also authenticate using AWS user credentials, as well as security tokens. The user has to be created on AWS IAM in order to access the API.

Monitoring is possible by writing Gateway rules. The logs can be directed to AWS CloudWatch, which is another Amazon-offered service. When there are suspicious incoming requests, the Gateway can also raise a CloudWatch alarm. A CloudWatch alarm is a notification for special situations. These notifications can trigger other actions, such as sending an email or logging an event.

Now, let us provision an API Gateway for our EC2 instance. The architecture diagram looks like this:

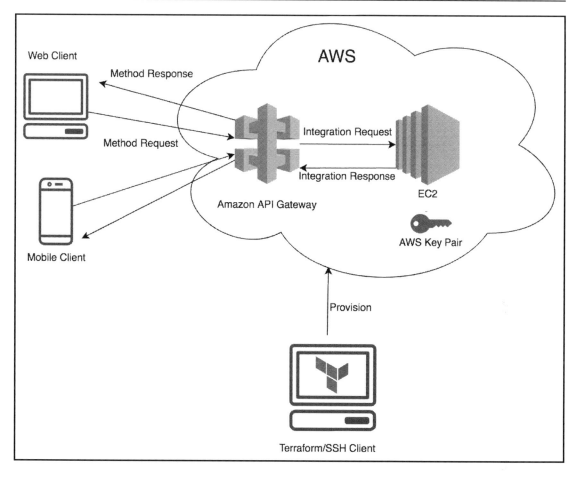

In the preceding diagram, the Amazon API Gateway defines methods and integrations. The target is an EC2 instance where a `books` API is deployed. We should configure six types of components to run API Gateway on AWS. Those are as follows:

- Gateway REST API
- Gateway Method Request
- Gateway Method Response
- Gateway Integration Request
- Gateway Integration Response
- Gateway Deployment

Why do we have to create the preceding components? The Amazon API Gateway architecture defines these components in its design. See the following diagram to see how an API is represented on Amazon API Gateway:

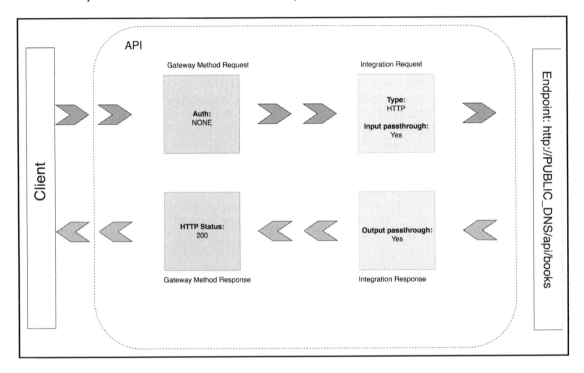

The **Client** request is sent through the **Gateway Method Request** and **Integration Request** stages. The **Integration Request** stage then forwards the request to a configured API endpoint. That endpoint will be /api/books with the GET method and will be running on an EC2 instance. This finishes the request life cycle.

Next, the endpoint returns a response from the EC2 instance. This response is forwarded to the **Integration Response** stage and then to the **Gateway Method Response** stage. This finishes the response life cycle.

Each stage can be configured further to transform responses into different formats. For simplicity, we leave the default settings as they are for each stage. In the next section, we'll try to build the preceding components in Terraform.

 Manually create the API Gateway for our API in the AWS console before writing Terraform scripts. This helps you understand the basic vocabulary of Amazon API Gateway.

Deploying our service behind Amazon API Gateway

Pausing the theory, let us quickly jump into an example. Our goal is to set up the API Gateway for the previously deployed `books` API as a target. Follow these steps:

1. Let us create a new project and write a new Terraform script that creates and deploys an API on Amazon API Gateway, as follows:

   ```
   touch $GOPATH/src/github.com/git-
   user/chapter13/intro/api_gateway.tf
   ```

   It also links our EC2 instance and API endpoints.

2. Let us add the Gateway REST API component to the script:

   ```
   // New API on Amazon API Gateway
   resource "aws_api_gateway_rest_api" "test" {
     name        = "EC2Example"
     description = "Terraform EC2 REST API Example"
     endpoint_configuration {
       types = ["REGIONAL"]
     }
   }
   ```

   It takes a few important attributes, as follows:

   - `name`: Name of the API
   - `description`: Text about the API
   - `endpoint_configuration`: Defines which mode of the API to publish (`REGIONAL` or `EDGE`)

These details are used to identify an API in the Amazon API Gateway. We named our API `EC2Example`. The `aws_api_gateway_rest_api` resource type is a Terraform resource type. Our resource name is `test`. From here on, we will see similar names for all other resource types we create.

When AWS creates the `aws_api_gateway_rest_api` component, it also creates a default Gateway Resource on AWS. A Gateway Resource is a relative path for endpoints we configure as part of the integration.

3. Next, we have to create a gateway method called `test`. It takes the `rest_api_id`, `resource_id`, and `http_method` attributes. These three attributes are common for all components. Let us call these `DEFAULT_ATTRIBUTES`.

4. In addition, we set `Authorization=NONE` on this component. If we set authorization to `AWS_IAM`, then a client has to provide AWS access keys and a token along with the request. We are disabling the gateway authentication for now, as shown in the following code block:

```
// Method request configuration
resource "aws_api_gateway_method" "test" {
    rest_api_id   = aws_api_gateway_rest_api.test.id
    resource_id   = aws_api_gateway_rest_api.test.root_resource_id
    http_method   = "GET"

    authorization = "NONE"
}
```

5. After adding the method request, we should add the method response component. This also takes `DEFAULT_ATTRIBUTES` plus `status_code`. That means whenever a method response receives `200 OK` from an integration response, it passes it to the client as a successful message, as shown in the following code block:

```
// Method response configuration
resource "aws_api_gateway_method_response" "test" {
  rest_api_id = aws_api_gateway_rest_api.test.id
  resource_id = aws_api_gateway_rest_api.test.root_resource_id
  http_method = aws_api_gateway_method.test.http_method

  status_code = "200"
}
```

6. Next, add the integration components. There are two integration components, as we recollect from the API architecture diagram in the previous section. The `integration response` component is similar to the `method_response` component, as shown in the following code block:

```
// Integration response configuration
resource "aws_api_gateway_integration_response"
"MyDemoIntegrationResponse" {
  rest_api_id = aws_api_gateway_rest_api.test.id
  resource_id = aws_api_gateway_rest_api.test.root_resource_id
  http_method = aws_api_gateway_method.test.http_method
```

```
        status_code = aws_api_gateway_method_response.test.status_code
    }
```

The main link between the API Gateway and our API running on an EC2 instance is created in the `integration request` component. It takes `DEFAULT_ATTRIBUTES`, plus three important attributes:

- `integration_http_method`: Decides which HTTP method should be called on the endpoint
- `type`: Denotes which type of endpoint is being used: `HTTP`, `Lambda`, or `AWS_PROXY`
- `uri`: The actual reference of the endpoint

In our case, because we want to link the Gateway and the EC2 instance, we use `HTTP` as our `type`, and the public DNS of our EC2 instance as `uri`. The Terraform block looks like this:

```
// Integration request configuration
resource "aws_api_gateway_integration" "test" {
    rest_api_id = aws_api_gateway_rest_api.test.id
    resource_id = aws_api_gateway_method.test.resource_id
    http_method = aws_api_gateway_method.test.http_method

    integration_http_method = "GET"
    type                    = "HTTP"
    uri                     =
"http://${aws_instance.api_server.public_dns}/api/books"

}
```

We have set `integration_http_method` to `GET` because our `books` API only has an endpoint with the GET method. For the `uri` attribute value, we are referencing `public_dns` from the `aws_instance.api_server` EC2 instance resource. Since both the Terraform scripts— `api_server.tf` and `api_gateway.tf`—are in the same `intro` project directory, we can import the resources from another.

This finishes all five crucial components of the API. We have to deploy the API using a test environment. Terraform provides a resource type called `aws_api_gateway_deployment` to create a deployment. Deployments are useful for testing or publishing Amazon API Gateway endpoints to the web. The deployment takes the following attributes:

```
// Deploy API on Gateway with test environment
resource "aws_api_gateway_deployment" "test" {
  depends_on = [
    aws_api_gateway_integration.test
  ]
```

```
    rest_api_id = aws_api_gateway_rest_api.test.id
    stage_name  = "test"
  }
```

A deployment also depends on an `integration request`, so we added a `depends_on`
attribute. The `stage_name` attribute can take stage, `"test"`, or prod environment types.
This finishes our API Gateway creation. Let us run the script to create and deploy our API
on Amazon API Gateway, as follows:

```
terraform apply -auto-approve

aws_key_pair.api_server_key: Refreshing state... [id=api-server-key]
aws_instance.api_server: Refreshing state... [id=i-050d7ec98b4d6a814]
aws_api_gateway_rest_api.test: Creating...
aws_api_gateway_method.test: Creating...
aws_api_gateway_method.test: Creation complete after 1s [id=agm-kvp9kg9jv6-
hognbzcre0-GET]
aws_api_gateway_method_response.test: Creating...
aws_api_gateway_integration.test: Creating...
aws_api_gateway_method_response.test: Creation complete after 0s [id=agmr-
kvp9kg9jv6-hognbzcre0-GET-200]
aws_api_gateway_integration_response.MyDemoIntegrationResponse: Creating...
aws_api_gateway_integration.test: Creation complete after 0s [id=agi-
kvp9kg9jv6-hognbzcre0-GET]
aws_api_gateway_deployment.test: Creating...
.....
```

Now, where can clients access the new URL of the API Gateway? You can get the
`invoke_url` from the `terraform.tfstate` file, like this:

```
    {
      "mode": "managed",
      "type": "aws_api_gateway_deployment",
      "name": "test",
      "provider": "provider.aws",
      "instances": [
        {
          "schema_version": 0,
          "attributes": {
            ......
            "invoke_url":"https://kvp9kg9jv6.execute-api.eu-central-
            1.amazonaws.com/test",
            ......
          },
            ......
        }
      ]
    }
```

`invoke_url` is the API Gateway endpoint. This endpoint should be attached to a custom domain while publishing an API. If you make a `curl` request to the preceding URL, you should receive books as a JSON response, as follows:

```
curl https://kvp9kg9jv6.execute-api.eu-central-1.amazonaws.com/test

{"ID":123,"ISBN":"0-201-03801-3","Author":"Donald
Knuth","PublishedYear":"1968"}
```

This confirms that all the components are functioning properly and that all requests/responses are routed through API Gateway. You can define many such endpoints and configure components to achieve the desired behavior. Adding authentication is left as an exercise to you.

 Tip for solving this exercise: Try to modify the right component to authenticate and authorize client requests.

In the next section, we'll mention other important API Gateways that are available.

Other API Gateways

There are many other API Gateway providers available in the market. As we mentioned earlier, all gateways provide the same set of features. Similar to AWS API Gateway, Apigee is another well-known API Gateway technology that is a part of Google Cloud. The problem with cloud providers is that they can cause vendor lock (that is, they cannot easily migrate to another platform). There are many open source API Gateways available on the market.

The right way to pick an API Gateway depends on the conditions of the business. If the API server is living on the AWS cloud, AWS API Gateway is a nice choice. For a company that can manage a gateway by itself, it is worth trying the following open source alternatives:

- Kubernetes
- Kong
- Tyk
- KrakenD

There is no best choice, but if workloads are not so big, nginx can also be used as an API Gateway. See `https://www.nginx.com/learn/api-gateway/` for more details.

Kubernetes (`https://kubernetes.io/`) can be a wise choice for those who like to manage the API Gateway by themselves. Also, another good reason to use Kubernetes is that it is getting widely adapted.

Amazon also provides the **Elastic Kubernetes Service** (**EKS**) for running highly available clusters over different regions. With EKS, the API Gateway is included as an installed component.

Summary

In this chapter, we started with the basics of working with AWS. Amazon provides a free-tier to experiment with their cloud. Once we sign up for the free-tier, we should get access to the AWS console and be able to create security credentials. These security credentials are required for applications to access AWS.

We then saw how a tool such as Terraform can provision cloud resources. We picked AWS EC2 as our choice to deploy an API. We wrote a Terraform script to provision an EC2 instance, along with a key pair. This key pair was required to log in to the instance.

Once we were able to log in to the EC2 instance, we installed all the dependencies for our API server. We reused the project code from Chapter 12, *Containerizing REST Services for Deployment*, where we prepared an API ecosystem. We successfully deployed the `books` API from the EC2 instance.

A simple API server has fewer capabilities in terms of rate-limiting to clients, authentication, and authorization. We need a dedicated API Gateway that can pass the requests to the API server. AWS provides a managed gateway solution called `Amazon API Gateway`. We saw the architecture of Amazon API Gateway and provisioned an API on the gateway using Terraform. The architecture has six important components, which discussed in detail.

Finally, we mentioned other gateway solutions available in the market. In the next chapter, we will discuss API authentication patterns, including **JSON Web Token** (**JWT**) authentication, in detail.

14
Handling Authentication for our REST Services

In this chapter, we are going to explore **Representational State Transfer** (**REST**) API authentication patterns. These patterns are session-based authentication, **JSON Web Tokens** (**JWT**), and **Open Authentication 2** (**OAuth 2.0**). We will try to leverage the Gorilla package's `sessions` library to create basic sessions. Then, we will move on to advanced REST API authentication strategies, such as stateless JWT. Finally, we will discuss the OAuth 2.0 authentication pattern and the security aspects of an API. In the previous chapter, the **Amazon Web Services** (**AWS**) API Gateway took care of authentication (using **Identity and Access Management** (**IAM**) roles) for us. If an API Gateway is not present, how do we secure our API? You will find the answer in this chapter.

In this chapter, we will cover the following topics:

- How simple authentication works
- Introducing Postman, a visual client for testing a REST API
- Persisting client sessions with Redis
- Introducing JWT and OAuth 2.0
- JWT in an OAuth 2.0 workflow
- Exercise for the reader
- Security aspects of an API

Technical requirements

The following software should be pre-installed for running the code samples:

- Operating system: Linux (Ubuntu 18.04)/Windows 10/Mac OS X >= 10.13
- Go stable version compiler >= 1.13.5
- Dep: A dependency management tool for Go >= 0.5.3
- Docker version >= 18.09.2

You can download the code for this chapter from `https://github.com/PacktPublishing/ Hands-On-Restful-Web-services-with-Go/tree/master/chapter14`. Clone the code, and use the code samples in the `chapter14` directory.

How simple authentication works

Traditionally, authentication—or simple authentication—works with sessions. The flow starts like this. A client sends an authentication request to the server using user credentials. The server takes those credentials and matches them with the credentials stored on the server. If a match is successful, it writes something called a **cookie** in the response. This cookie is a small piece of information that is transferred by the client for all subsequent requests. Modern websites are being designed to be **single-page applications** (**SPAs**). In those websites, static assets such as HTML and JavaScript files are served from a **Content Delivery Network** (**CDN**) to render the web page initially. After that, the communication between the web page and application server happens only through the REST API/web services.

A **session** is a nice way to record user communication in a given period of time. A session is a concept whereby authentication information is stored in a cookie. The following diagram explains what happens in a basic session-based authentication:

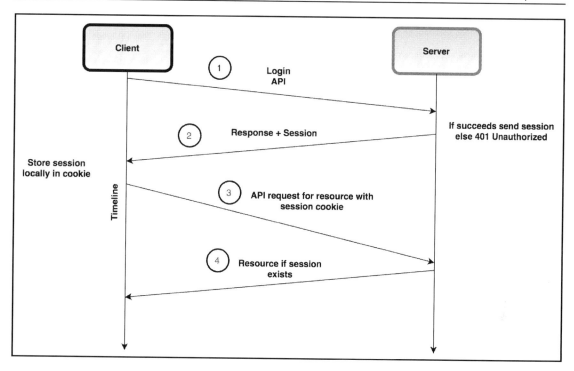

Now, let's look at a practical approach. A **Client** (for example, a browser) sends a request to the **Login API** of the **Server**. The server tries to check those credentials with the database and, if the credentials exist, writes a **cookie** back onto the response saying that this user is authenticated.

A **cookie** is a message consumed by the server at a later point in time. When the client receives the response, it stores that cookie locally. After that, the client can ask for resources from the server by showing the cookie as the key for passage.

When a client decides to terminate the session, it calls the logout API on the server. The server destroys the session in the response. This process is repeated for every login/logout. The server can also place an expiration on cookies so that the authentication window is valid for a certain time if there is no activity. This is how many websites work.

Now, we'll try to implement one such system using the `gorilla/sessions` package. We already learned about gorilla/mux in the initial chapters. We need to install the package first by using the following command:

```
go get github.com/gorilla/mux
go get github.com/gorilla/sessions
```

Alternatively, we could do this by using the Dep tool, as follows:

```
dep init
dep ensure -add github.com/gorilla/mux
dep ensure -add github.com/gorilla/sessions
```

We can create a new session using the `NewCookieStore` method from the `sessions` package, like this:

```
var store = sessions.NewCookieStore([]byte("secret_key"))
```

That `secret_key` should be the key that `gorilla/sessions` uses to encrypt the session cookies. If we add a session as a normal text, anyone can read it. So, the server needs to encrypt a message to a random string. For that, it asks to provide a secret key. This secret key can be any randomly generated string.

Keeping secret keys in code is not a good idea, so we try to store it as an environment variable and read it in code on the fly. In the next section, we'll look at an example of session authentication.

A simple authentication example

Let's build a secure API that gives access to clients only after logging in. In the process, we will define three endpoints:

- `/login`
- `/logout`
- `/healthcheck`

`/healthcheck` is the data API, but it first has to log in using the /login endpoint. Our API should reject all unauthenticated requests. Create a project directory called `simpleAuth`, like this:

```
mkdir -p $GOPATH/src/github.com/git-user/chapter14/simpleAuth
touch $GOPATH/src/github.com/git-user/chapter14/simpleAuth/main.go
```

In the program, we can see how to enable session-based authentication to API endpoints using the gorilla/ sessions package. Follow these steps:

1. We need imports for our program. The main ones are `mux` and `sessions`, as seen in the following code block:

```
package main
import (
    "log"
    "net/http"
    "os"
    "time"
    "github.com/gorilla/mux"
    "github.com/gorilla/sessions"
)
```

2. Now, create a cookie store to store the written cookie information. We can do that using the `sessions.NewCookieStore` method. It takes a byte array of the secret key. The secret key is fetched from the `SESSION_SECRET` environment variable, like this:

```
var store =
sessions.NewCookieStore([]byte(os.Getenv("SESSION_SECRET")))
```

You can set any key you wish to that environment variable.

3. Let us create mock `usernames` and a `password` as we don't have a signup mechanism, as follows:

```
var users = map[string]string{"naren": "passme", "admin":
"password"}
```

These mock username/password combinations are checked against a client request.

4. Now, add a login handler that sets the cookie. The API is a `POST` request with credentials supplied in the **POST** body, as follows:

```
func LoginHandler(w http.ResponseWriter, r *http.Request) {
    ...
}
```

5. In this function, we should first parse the **POST** body, and get the `username` and `password`, like this:

```
err := r.ParseForm()

if err != nil {
http.Error(w, "Please pass the data as URL form encoded",
 http.StatusBadRequest)
    return
}
username := r.PostForm.Get("username")
password := r.PostForm.Get("password")
```

6. Once we have collected the `username` and `password`, our plan is to validate them with the mock data. If the credentials are matching, then set the request session to authenticated. Otherwise, show the error message accordingly, as follows:

```
if originalPassword, ok := users[username]; ok {
    session, _ := store.Get(r, "session.id")
    if password == originalPassword {
        session.Values["authenticated"] = true
        session.Save(r, w)
    } else {
        http.Error(w, "Invalid Credentials",
http.StatusUnauthorized)
        return
    }
} else {
    http.Error(w, "User is not found", http.StatusNotFound)
    return
}
w.Write([]byte("Logged In successfully"))
```

This completes the login handler.

7. In a similar way, let us define the logout handler. The logout handler takes an incoming GET request and sets the session variable authenticated to `false`, like this:

```
// LogoutHandler removes the session
func LogoutHandler(w http.ResponseWriter, r *http.Request) {
    session, _ := store.Get(r, "session.id")
    session.Values["authenticated"] = false
    session.Save(r, w)
    w.Write([]byte(""))
}
```

8. If you see the logout handler implementation, then we have modified the `session` object to invalidate the client session, as follows:

```
session, _ := store.Get(r, "session.id")
session.Values["authenticated"] = false
session.Save(r, w)
```

9. In this way, simple authentication can be implemented using client sessions in any programming language, including Go.

   Don't forget to save the cookie after modifying it. The code for this is `session.Save(r, w)`.

10. Now, let us define our `/healthcheck.` data API. It is an API that sends the system time back. It returns a response if the client session is authenticated. Otherwise, it returns a `403 Forbidden response`. The `session` object from the request can be used for the validity check, as follows:

```
// HealthcheckHandler returns the date and time
func HealthcheckHandler(w http.ResponseWriter, r *http.Request) {
    session, _ := store.Get(r, "session.id")
    if (session.Values["authenticated"] != nil) && session.Values
    ["authenticated"] != false {
        w.Write([]byte(time.Now().String()))
    } else {
        http.Error(w, "Forbidden", http.StatusForbidden)
    }
}
```

11. All the API handlers are ready. We have to write the `main` function, where we map API endpoints (routes) to the preceding handlers. We use the `mux` router for that purpose. Then, we pass this router to an HTTP server that runs on `http://localhost:8000`, as follows:

```
func main() {
    r := mux.NewRouter()
    r.HandleFunc("/login", LoginHandler)
    r.HandleFunc("/healthcheck", HealthcheckHandler)
    r.HandleFunc("/logout", LogoutHandler)
    http.Handle("/", r)

    srv := &http.Server{
        Handler: r,
        Addr:    "127.0.0.1:8000",
        // Good practice: enforce timeouts for servers you create!
        WriteTimeout: 15 * time.Second,
```

```
            ReadTimeout:  15 * time.Second,
        }
        log.Fatal(srv.ListenAndServe())
    }
```

12. This finishes the secured application. We can run the program from the `simpleAuth` root directory by typing the following code:

```
go run main.go
```

This starts the server on `http://localhost:8000`.

The error codes can mean different things. For example, `Forbidden (403)` is issued when the user tries to access a resource without authentication, whereas `Resource Not Found (404)` is issued when the given resource does not exist on the server.

In the next section, we'll introduce a new tool to query an API, called Postman. The Postman tool has a nice **User Interface** (**UI**) and runs on all platforms. We are going to test the `simpleAuth` example with this new tool.

Introducing Postman, a visual client for testing a REST API

Postman is a great UI client that allows Windows, Mac OS X, and Linux users to make HTTP API requests. You can download it from here: `https://www.getpostman.com/ product/api-client`. Instead of making an API request with `curl`, let us use the Postman tool. We will pick the `simpleAuth` example from the previous section. See the following steps:

1. Post-installation, open the Postman tool, then try a `www.example.org` URL in the **Enter request URL** input text. You can select the type of request from the dropdown (**GET**, **POST**, and so on). For each request, you can configure many settings such as **Headers**, **POST** body, and other details as a menu under **URL**. Play with the options and get comfortable with them.

 Please go through the Postman documentation for more details. It comes with various options for replaying API queries. Take some time to explore the features at `https://learning.postman.com/getting-started/`

Take a look at the following screenshot:

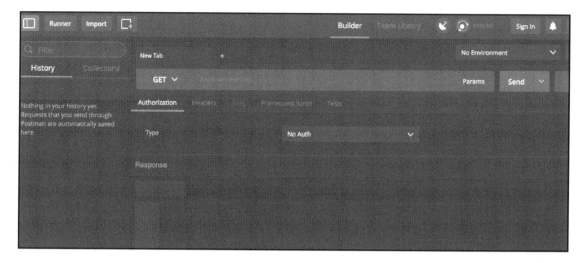

The **Builder** is the top-level menu item, where we can add/edit requests. The preceding screenshot shows the empty builder, where we try to make requests.

2. Next, run the `main.go` file in the preceding `simpleAuth` project and try to call the `/healthcheck` API. Click on the **Send** button. You will see that the response is **403 Forbidden**, as shown in the following screenshot:

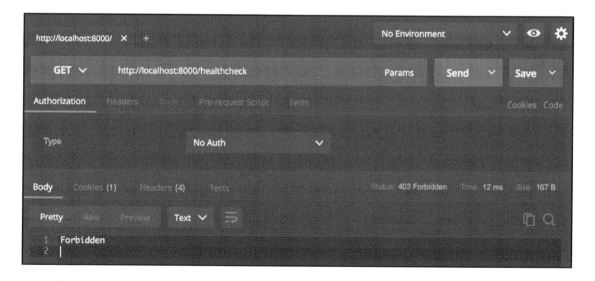

This is because we are not logged in yet. Postman automatically saves the cookie once authentication is successful.

3. Now, call the login API by changing the method type from **GET** to **POST**, and the **URL** to **http://localhost:8000/login**. We should pass the credentials as `multipart/form-data`. We should see the following:

4. Hit the blue **Send** button. This makes a login request to our previously run server. It returns a message, saying **Logged In successfully**. We can inspect the cookies by clicking on the **Cookies** link, just following the **Save** button on the right-hand side.

   It shows the list of cookies saved, and you will find a cookie called `session.id` there for the localhost site. The content will look like this:

   ```
   session.id=MTU3NzI4NTk2NXxEdi1CQkFFQ180SUFBUkFCRUFBQUpmLUNBQVVHYzNS
   eWFXNW5EQThBRFdGMWRHaGxiJwWTJGMFpXUUVabTl2YkFJQ0FBRT18Be0S-
   fIy6T7U-hnASBnPxLU2gFJ0jnAdaKWI6X04GPo=; path=/; domain=localhost;
   Expires=Fri, 24 Jan 2020 14:59:25 GMT;
   ```

5. Try to call the `/healthcheck` API again, which returns the system date and time as a response, like this:

   ```
   2019-12-25 16:00:03.501678 +0100 CET m=+169.811215440
   ```

Let's say a client makes another GET request to the logout API, like this:

```
http://localhost:8000/logout
```

If this happens, the session will be invalidated, and access to the resource will be forbidden until another login request is done.

The admin and password credentials used in our examples are only for illustration purposes and should never be used in a production environment.

Always use randomly generated strong passwords!

Persisting client sessions with Redis

The sessions we've created so far are stored in the program memory. This means if the program crashes or restarts, all the logged sessions will be lost. It needs the client to log in once again to get a new session cookie. This is not helpful for auditing cookies. In order to save sessions somewhere, we can use Redis.

We have discussed running Redis in a Docker container in Chapter 9, *Asynchronous API Design*. To recap, the Redis server stores key-value pairs. It provides basic data types such as strings, lists, hashes, sets, and so on. For more details, visit https://redis.io/topics/data-types.

Now, it is time to put our Redis knowledge into action. We are going to modify our project from simpleAuth to simpleAuthWithRedis. The new project should now use Redis as a session store. Copy the code from the previous example to the new one.

In Chapter 9, *Asynchronous API Design*, we used the go-redis package to interact with the Redis server from a Go program. In this chapter, we'll introduce a new convenient package called redistore.v1 so that we can store sessions in Redis.

Install the package with the following dep command:

```
dep init
dep ensure -add gopkg.in/boj/redistore.v1
```

Create a new program, with a few modifications. Here, instead of using the gorilla/sessions package, we will use the redistore package. redistore has a function called NewRediStore that takes Redis configuration as its arguments, along with the secret key. It returns the same session object as gorilla/sessions.

The rest of the code remains the same. For brevity, these are the only changes we have to make:

```
package main
import (
    ...
    redistore "gopkg.in/boj/redistore.v1"
)

var store, err = redistore.NewRediStore(10, "tcp", ":6379", "",
[]byte(os.Getenv("SESSION_SECRET")))
```

In the logout handler, you will see this code:

```
session.Values["authenticated"] = false
```

Change the preceding code to this:

```
session.Options.MaxAge = -1
```

This step removes the key from the Redis store, which is equivalent to revoking authentication from the client. This improved program works in a very similar way to the previous one, except the session is now saved in Redis.

Run the new program, repeating the API query from the Postman tool. Once login is successful, launch `redis-cli` in the Docker container, like this:

```
docker exec -i -t some-redis redis-cli
```

`some-redis` is the Redis server running the container name. Now, type the `KEYS *` command in the shell to see the newly stored session, as follows:

```
127.0.0.1:6379> KEYS *
1) "session_VPJ54LWRE4DNTYCLEJWAUN5SDLVW6LN6MLB26W2OB4JDT26CR2GA"
127.0.0.1:6379>
```

The lengthy `session_VPJ54LWRE4DNTYCLEJWAUN5SDLVW6LN6MLB26W2OB4JDT26CR2GA` key is the key stored by the `redistore` package. If we delete that key, the client will lose access to the `/healthcheck` API. Now, stop the running program and restart it. You will see that the session is not lost. In this way, we can save the client session.

Redis can serve the purpose of caching for your web applications. It can store temporary data such as sessions, frequently requested user content, and so on. It is usually compared to memcached.

In the next section, we'll explore a new way of authentication, called JWT. It deviates from sessions, and stores no cookies on the client machine.

Introducing JWT and OAuth2

The modern REST API implements token-based authentication. Here, tokens can be any strings generated by the server, which allows the client to access resources by producing a token. The token is computed in such a way that only the client and the server know how to encode/decode the token.

The previous example relates to session-based authentication. This has a limitation of managing sessions by saving them in the program memory, or Redis/SQLite3. JWT takes a different approach and creates tokens that can be passed around for authentication.

Whenever a **Client** passes the authentication details to the **Server**, the server generates a token and passes it back to the **Client**. The client saves that in some kind of storage, such as AWS Secrets Manager, a database, or local storage (in the case of a browser). The **Client** uses that token to ask for resources from any API defined by the server. This process can be seen in the following diagram:

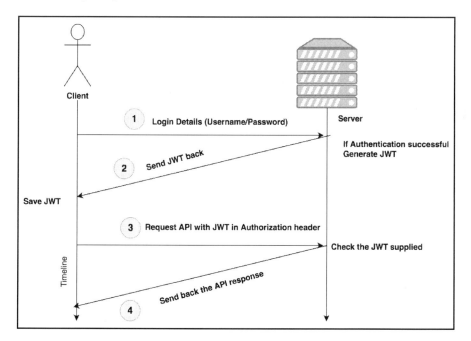

The steps shown in the preceding diagram can be summarized more briefly, as follows:

1. The **Client** passes the **username/password** in a POST request to the login API.
2. The **Server** authenticates the details and, if successful, it generates a **JWT** and returns it instead of creating a cookie. It is the client's responsibility to store this token.
3. Now, the **Client** has the JWT. It needs to add this in the headers section to make subsequent REST API calls.
4. The **Server** checks the JWT from the header and if it is successfully decoded, the server authenticates the client.

JWT ensures that the data is sent from the correct client. The technique for creating a token takes care of that logic. JWT leverages secret key-based encryption.

JWT format

Everything we discussed in the preceding section was about passing a JWT token. In this section, we will see what a JWT looks like, and how it is generated. These are the high-level steps for generating a JWT:

1. Create a JWT header by doing Base64Url encoding on the JSON header.
2. Create a JWT payload by doing Base64Url encoding on the JSON payload.
3. Create a signature by encrypting the appended header and payload using a secret key.
4. A JWT string can be obtained by appending the JWT header, JWT payload, and signature.

A header is a simple JSON object. It looks like the following code snippet in Go:

```
{
  "alg": "HS256",
  "typ": "JWT"
}
```

HS256 is a short form for the algorithm (HMAC with SHA-256) that's used for creating a signature. The message type is JWT. This will be common for all the headers. The algorithm may change, depending on the system.

A payload looks like this:

```
{
  "sub": "1234567890",
  "username": "Indiana Jones",
  "admin": true
}
```

Keys in a payload object are called **claims**. A claim is a key that specifies some special meaning to the server. There are three types of claims:

- Reserved claims
- Private claims (more important)
- Public claims

We'll discuss each of these claims in detail in the upcoming sections.

Reserved claims

Reserved claims are the ones defined by the JWT standard. They are as follows:

- **iat**: Issued at the time
- **iss**: Issuer name
- **sub**: Subject text
- **aud**: Audience name
- **exp**: Expiration time

For example, the server, while generating a token, can set an exp claim in the payload. The client then uses that token to access API resources. The server validates the token each time. When the expiration time is passed, the server will no longer validate the token. The client needs to generate a new token by logging in again.

Private claims

Private claims are used to identify one token from another. They can be used for authorization. **Authorization** is a process of identifying which client made the request. **Multi-tenancy** refers to the situation of multiple clients accessing an API on a system. The server can set a private claim called **username** on the payload of the token. Next time, the server can read this payload back and get the username, and then use that username to authorize and customize the API response. It is similar to a cookie but in a different way.

For example, `username: Indiana Jones` is a private claim in the following payload:

```
{
  "sub": "1234567890",
  "username": "Indiana Jones",
  "admin": true
}
```

Public claims are similar to private claims, but they should be registered with the IANA JWT Registry to make them as a standard. We limit the use of these.

A signature can be created by performing this operation (this is not code, just an illustration):

```
signature = HMACSHA256(
  base64UrlEncode(header) + "." +
  base64UrlEncode(payload),
  secret)
```

This is simply performing an encryption algorithm on the Base64Url-encoded header and payload with a secret. This secret can be any string. It is exactly the same as the secret we used in the previous cookie session. This secret is usually saved in the environment variable and loaded into the program.

Now, we append the encoded header, encoded payload, and signature to get our token string, as follows:

```
tokenString = base64UrlEncode(header) + "." + base64UrlEncode(payload) +
"." + signature
```

This is how a JWT token is generated. There are a few Go packages that can generate and verify a JWT. One such popular package is `jwt-go`. We are going to create a project in the next section that uses `jwt-go` to sign a JWT and also verify it. We can install this package using the following `dep` command:

```
dep ensure -add github.com/dgrijalva/jwt-go
```

This is the official GitHub page for the project: `https://github.com/dgrijalva/jwt-go`.

The package provides a few functions that allow us to create tokens. There are many other packages with different additional features. You can see all the available packages and features that are supported at `https://jwt.io/#libraries-io`.

Creating a JWT in Go

The `jwt-go` package has a function called `NewWithClaims` that takes two arguments:

- A signing method such as `HMAC256`, `RSA`, and so on
- A claims map

For example, it looks like the following code snippet:

```
token := jwt.NewWithClaims(jwt.SigningMethodHS256, jwt.MapClaims{
    "username": "admin",
    "iat":time.Now().Unix(),
})
```

`jwt.SigningMethodHS256` is an encryption algorithm that is available within the package. The second argument is a map with claims such as private (here, username) and reserved (issued iat). Now, we can generate a `tokenString` using the `SignedString` function on a token, as follows:

```
tokenString, err := token.SignedString("my_secret_key")
```

This `tokenString` should then be sent back to the client as part of a successful login response.

Reading a JWT in Go

`jwt-go` also gives us the API to parse a given JWT string. The Parse function takes a string and key function as arguments. The key function is a custom function that validates whether the algorithm is real or not. Let us say this is a sample token string generated by the preceding encoding:

```
tokenString =
"eyJhbGciOiJIUzI1NiIsInR5cCI6IkpXVCJ9.eyJ1c2VybmFtZSI6ImFkbWluIiwiaWF0IjoiM
TUwODc0MTU5MTQ2NiJ9.5m6KkuQFCgyaGS_xcVy4xWakwDgtAG3ILGGTBgYVBmE"
```

We can parse and get back the original JSON using the following code:

```
token, err := jwt.Parse(tokenString, func(token *jwt.Token) (interface{},
error) {
    // key function
    if _, ok := token.Method.(*jwt.SigningMethodHMAC); !ok {
        return nil, fmt.Errorf("Unexpected signing method: %v",
        token.Header["alg"])
    }
    return "my_secret_key", nil
```

```
    })

    if claims, ok := token.Claims.(jwt.MapClaims); ok && token.Valid {
        // Use claims for authorization if token is valid
        fmt.Println(claims["username"], claims["iat"])
    } else {
        fmt.Println(err)
    }
```

`token.Claims` is implemented by a map called **MapClaims**. We can get the original JSON key-value pairs from that map.

In the next section, we'll discuss the OAuth 2.0 workflow and the difference between authentication and authorization.

JWT in an OAuth2.0 workflow

OAuth 2.0 is an authentication framework that is used to create an authentication pattern between different systems. here, the client, instead of making a request to the resource server, makes an initial request to an entity called **resource owner**. This resource owner sends back the authentication grant for the client (if the credentials are authenticated). The client now sends this authentication grant to another entity called an **authentication server**. The authentication server takes the grant and returns an access token. The access token is a

Authentication versus authorization

Authentication is the process of identifying whether a client is genuine or not. When a server authenticates a client, it checks the username/password pair and creates a session `cookie/JWT`.

Authorization is the process of evaluating whether a user has access to a given resource. In cloud services, there should be a mechanism to limit the scope of resource access for certain users/roles, and authorization enables it.

In simple words, authentication decides who is the customer of a service, and authorization determines what are the customer's boundaries for resource access.

OAuth 2.0 is a protocol for authenticating multiple clients to a service, whereas JWT is a token format. We need to encode/decode JWT tokens to implement the second stage (dashed lines in the following diagram) of OAuth 2.0:

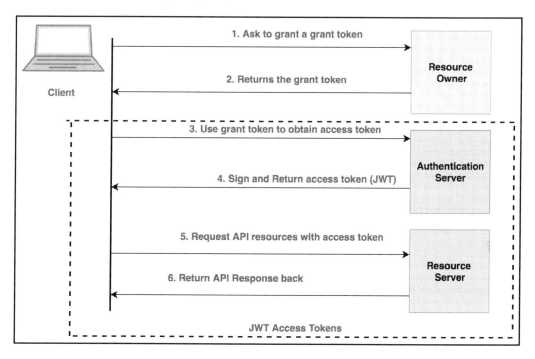

In the preceding diagram, the dotted section is where a **Client** requests an access token from the **Authentication Server**. This is where a JWT life cycle begins.

In the next section, we'll present a development exercise for you to complete. This exercise can be completed by combining all the concepts we have learned about so far.

Exercise

Can you design the following requirements?

Develop a /healthcheck API with token authentication. Its main responsibilities should be as follows:

- Authenticate the client and return a JWT string
- Authorize client API requests by validating the JWT

You should use the knowledge you gained about the `jwt-go` package from the previous section. You have to build two endpoints, as follows:

- `/getToken`
- `/healthcheck`

The first endpoint should successfully log in a client and return a JWT token. The client should then use the second endpoint with the token to receive a successful response.

Post-development, the final API testing scenario should look something similar to this:

1. If you make a GET request to the `/healthcheck` API without any token, you should receive an `Access Denied` message, as shown here:

   ```
   Access Denied; Please check the access token
   ```

2. You should be able to authenticate and get a JWT token from the API server with a POST request, as shown in the following screenshot:

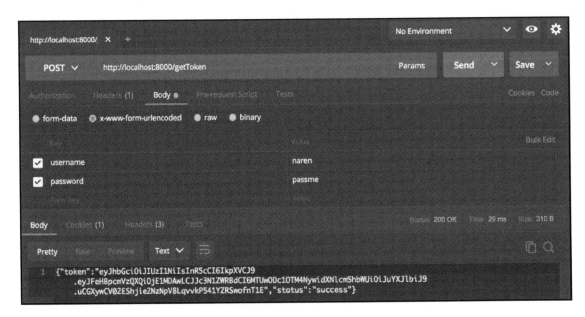

3. With the returned JWT, you can now make a successful GET request to `/healthcheck` with an **access_token** header, as follows:

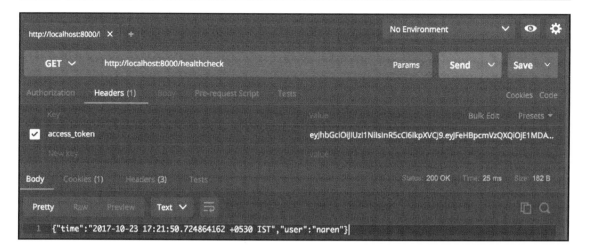

If you can implement the preceding requirements, you have already got a nice understanding of JWT. If not, do not worry. The solution for the challenge is available in the `chapter14/jwtauth` project directory.

Token-based authentication doesn't usually provide a logout API or an API for deleting the tokens that are provided in session-based authentication. The server gives the authorized resources to the client as long as the JWT hasn't expired. Once it expires, the client needs to refresh the token—that is to say, ask the server for a new token.

In the next section, we'll discuss a few tips for securing an API.

Security aspects of an API

Every REST API that is developed can be either open or protected. An open API has no limit regarding the number of clients requesting the resources. But most business APIs are protected. So, what are the important things to keep in mind about security? In the following list, we'll point out all the factors that should be taken care of to secure a REST API:

- Always use HTTPS to deliver the API **Transport Layer Security** (**TLS**).
- Rate limit the API by using user access tokens.
- Design various authentication and authorization roles on the API.
- Use public key/private key encryption to sign a JWT when the client and server are internal.

- Never store user credentials in plain files.
- Sanitize the URL query parameters; use a **POST** body for incoming requests.
- As we mentioned in the previous chapter, use an API Gateway for better performance and protection.
- Use cloud services such as AWS Secrets Manager to store keys/passwords.

Most modern APIs are run as containers/**Virtual Private Servers** (**VPS**) on cloud providers. The security there can be applied at two levels:

- Network level
- Application level

An API developer who develops and deploys their application on the cloud should be aware of the preceding levels. Knowledge of security breach-counteracting measures and patching up the API is a key security skill you will need.

Also, an exposed REST API is the easiest victim for attacks such as **Denial of Service** (**DoS**) attacks. Deploying an API behind a firewall service can increase security from those attacks. In the case of an internal API, where a company's service communicates only with other internal services but from different geographical regions, a VPN is desirable.

Security is a beast of its own domain and needs to be carefully monitored in every aspect of API development.

Summary

In this chapter, we introduced the process of authentication. We saw how authentication usually works. Authentication can be of three types: basic authentication, session-based, or token-based. With basic authentication, every HTTP request supplies a `username` and `password`. Session-based authentication uses a saved session to authenticate a client.

Sessions stored in program memory are lost once a web server crashes/restarts. Redis can be used with a package called `redistore` to help store session cookies.

Next, we learned about JWT, a token-based authentication whereby a client requests a JWT token from the server. Once the client has the JWT token, it can pass that token in the HTTP header while requesting API resources.

We then introduced OAuth 2.0, an authentication framework. There, we saw how the client requests a grant from the resource owner. Once it gets the grant, it requests an access token from the authentication server. After getting the access token from the authentication server, the client can use the token to request an API.

We tested all our APIs with curl and Postman. Postman is a great tool that helps us test our APIs quickly on any machine, whereas curl is limited to Linux and Mac OS X .

We came a long way from the first chapter by learning how to create HTTP routes, middleware, and handlers. We then explored various SQL and NoSQL storage backends for an API. After the basics, we explored performance-tuning aspects such as asynchronous design, the GraphQL API, and microservices. Finally, we learned how to deploy our web services to the cloud and also secure them by enabling authentication.

Other Books You May Enjoy

If you enjoyed this book, you may be interested in these other books by Packt:

Hands-On Software Engineering with Golang
Achilleas Anagnostopoulos

ISBN: 978-1-83855-449-1

- Understand different stages of the software development life cycle and the role of a software engineer
- Create APIs using gRPC and leverage the middleware offered by the gRPC ecosystem
- Discover various approaches to managing package dependencies for your projects
- Build an end-to-end project from scratch and explore different strategies for scaling it
- Develop a graph processing system and extend it to run in a distributed manner
- Deploy Go services on Kubernetes and monitor their health using Prometheus

Go Programming Cookbook - Second Edition
Aaron Torres

ISBN: 978-1-78980-098-2

- Work with third-party Go projects and modify them for your use
- Write Go code using modern best practices
- Manage your dependencies with the new Go module system
- Solve common problems encountered when dealing with backend systems or DevOps
- Explore the Go standard library and its uses
- Test, profile, and fine-tune Go applications

Leave a review - let other readers know what you think

Please share your thoughts on this book with others by leaving a review on the site that you bought it from. If you purchased the book from Amazon, please leave us an honest review on this book's Amazon page. This is vital so that other potential readers can see and use your unbiased opinion to make purchasing decisions, we can understand what our customers think about our products, and our authors can see your feedback on the title that they have worked with Packt to create. It will only take a few minutes of your time, but is valuable to other potential customers, our authors, and Packt. Thank you!

Index

reference link 7

Made in the USA
Middletown, DE
01 June 2022